Percy Bysshe Shelley, Mathilde. oth Blind

A Selection from the Poems of Percy Bysshe Shelley

Percy Bysshe Shelley, Mathilde. oth Blind

A Selection from the Poems of Percy Bysshe Shelley

ISBN/EAN: 9783742836229

Manufactured in Europe, USA, Canada, Australia, Japa

Cover: Foto ©Andreas Hilbeck / pixelio.de

Manufactured and distributed by brebook publishing software (www.brebook.com)

Percy Bysshe Shelley, Mathilde. oth Blind

A Selection from the Poems of Percy Bysshe Shelley

COLLECTION
OF
BRITISH AUTHORS

TAUCHNITZ EDITION.

VOL. 1207.

THE POEMS OF PERCY BYSSHE SHELLEY.

IN ONE VOLUME.

A SELECTION
FROM
THE POEMS
OF
PERCY BYSSHE SHELLEY.

EDITED WITH A MEMOIR

BY

MATHILDE BLIND.

LEIPZIG

BERNHARD TAUCHNITZ

1872.

AUTHORITIES.

1. *Percy Bysshe Shelley*, Letters from Abroad, Translations, and fragments, edited by Mrs. SHELLEY. A new Edition. London, 1854.
2. *Mrs. Shelley*, Notices in her collected edition of the Poems.
3. *Lady Shelley*, Shelley Memorials. London, 1859.
4. *William Michael Rossetti*, The Poetical Works of Percy Bysshe Shelley. A revised Text with Notes and a Memoir. 2 vols. London, 1870. Contains the first methodical narrative of the entire life of the poet.
5. *Thomas Jefferson Hogg*, The Life of Shelley. This reaches only to the beginning of the year 1814. 2 vols. London, 1858.
6. *E. J. Trelawny*, Recollections of the Last Days of Shelley and Byron. London, 1858.
7. *Thomas Medwin*, The Life of Percy Bysshe Shelley. 2 vols. London, 1847. The Shelley Papers and the Conversations with Lord Byron. 1824 and 1833.
8. *Thomas Love Peacock*, 3 articles published in Fraser's Magazine in 1858 and 1860.
9. *Richard Garnett*, Relics of Shelley, London, 1862.
10. *The Autobiography of Leigh Hunt*. A new Edition. London, 1860.

MEMOIR OF SHELLEY.

PERCY BYSSHE SHELLEY, the greatest idealistic poet of England, was born on the 4th of August 1792 at Field Place, near Horsham, Sussex. Is it fanciful to surmise that the tremendous revolutionary storm then, with fierce yet salutary throes, convulsing society touched as with an electric influence this new-born soul? At any rate it is an indisputable fact that the *passion* for a radical reform of the world as regards a juster distribution of human happiness, which was the motive power of that colossal upheaval we term the French Revolution, formed no less the ruling impulse of the divine genius who to quote his own words was in very truth a

"Nerve o'er which did creep
The else unfelt oppressions of the earth."

Meanwhile with the strange discrepancy of events this spiritual child of the Revolution, is by the irony of fate born heir to one Mr. Timothy Shelley, a country gentleman and respectable Whig, able to trace back his pedigree to the times of Edward I. We can hardly wonder that so strange a phenomenon as this wild-eyed poet with his humanitarian enthusiasm startled, perplexed and utterly bewildered the good Sir Timothy, (for such he became on the death of his father) nay doubt if even we should wonder were it clearly proved that the worthy man contemplated sending his son, when ill with brain fever, to a private mad-house. To a beef-eating, port-drinking British Whig and M. P. of that time a passionate fervour for abstract principles probably *did* appear as a most irrefragable symptom of insanity.

The future Anti-christian received in baptism the names of Percy Bysshe. The latter name was that of his grandfather, a man who, to judge from his success in life, possessed considerable practical ability. Originally without means he, through his own exertions and two successive marriages with heiresses, amassed a large fortune and left his son one of the opulent heirs of the kingdom. Of Shelley's mother, who exercised but little influence on her son, nothing further is to be said than that she appears to have been a kind sensible woman. The family besides the poet consisted of four sisters and one brother. As "the child is father to the man" it is of interest to know that Shelley from the days of his infancy delighted in tales of ghosts and fiends, and that at a somewhat later period when at home for the holidays he used to hold his sisters spell-bound by his vivid description of alchemists, wizards, and a "Great Tortoise" with which he peopled the house and garden.

The boy, after having attended a day-school for some years, was sent to Sion House School, Brentford. We can easily conceive that an imaginative delicately reared lad underwent a good deal of acute suffering from a stern Scotch master Dr. Greenlaw, and a set of rude unmannerly boys.

Not much better fared it with Shelley when at the age of fifteen he was sent to Eton. His dauntless championship of the weak against the strong may be said fairly to have commenced there. He rose up in arms against the existing state of things by his violent opposition to the system of fagging then flourishing vigorously at all the public schools. No amount of bullying or persecution proved successful in enforcing his own submission to the obnoxious practice. If he thus put himself in antagonism to his schoolfellows, he was on an equally hostile footing with the ruling powers of the establishment. Dr. Keate the head-master was a strict disciplinarian who did not "spare the rod." The consequence was that Shelley, who by gentle treatment and calm reasoning might have been led as easily as a child was instigated to unflinching resistance. He was on much the same terms with all the other masters: Dr. Lind,[*] a physician,

---

[*] Some interesting particulars about Dr. Lind may be found in Madame D'Arblay's Diary. He died on Oct. 17, 1812.

being the only influential person at Eton to whom he looked up. Between this amiable man and Shelley one of those rare and beautiful intimacies was formed, than which none more sacred exist, that of a wise and gentle old man cherishing the warm enthusiasm of his young friend, and striving to communicate to him the accumulated thought and knowledge of years. What a deep impression this intercourse left on Shelley's mind is shown by the fact that he has twice reproduced the image of this venerable master and friend; once in the *Revolt of Islam*, where he is the prototype of the old sage who liberates Laon, and once in the exquisite fragment of *Prince Athanase*, where he figures as Zonoras.—

Shelley's taste for chemistry was greatly stimulated if not first awakened by Dr. Lind, and this study engrossed a great portion of his time at Eton. The fact of its being forbidden fruit may possibly have added zest to the pursuit. Certain is it that mischief on mischief was brewed by this chemical infatuation. We hear of a tree set on fire on the common by lighting gunpowder with a burning glass; of a tutor violently hurled against a wall by a highly charged electrical machine, and other like exploits productive to this martyr of science of unpleasantly tangible results in the shape of floggings.

Shelley, although neglectful of school attendance, was yet in his own way zealous in his literary studies; he evinced a marked facility in making Latin verses, and translated Pliny's *Natural History*.* It may also be worthy of notice

* According to Medwin, this translation comprised a portion of Pliny's second book. It is very remarkable that one of the chapters included in it should have been that *On God*, in which the germ of much of Shelley's subsequent speculation may be detected, and to which as if led by an irresistible fatality, he involuntarily (for the words are not his own) returns in almost the last of his productions:—

"I am now
Debating with myself upon a passage
Of Plinius, and my mind is racked with doubt
To understand and know who is the God
Of whom he speaks."
Scenes from Calderon, sc. 2.

that even at this early period he went among his schoolfellows by the title of "Shelley the Atheist." This nickname however was used by Etonians not in the common acceptation of the word, but implied that the youth thus styled had distinguished himself by unusual pluck in his defiance of the powers that be, viz. the school authorities.

We will now accompany Shelley to Oxford, where he was entered at University College in the autumn of 1810. Between his transit from Eton to *Alma Mater* some time elapsed, which was spent at Field Place and the occasion was diligently improved by Shelley to sprout forthwith into a lover and an author. The object of his first passion was his cousin Harriet Grove, said to have resembled the poet in features; the first products of the author, two extravagant romances possessed of no merit, are best, even as regards their titles, consigned to oblivion. A volume of poems entitled "Original Poetry by Victor and Cazire" not only deserved the same fate but has actually incurred it, for not a single copy is known to exist.

Settled at Oxford, Shelley, with characteristic vehemence, plunged into the studies most attractive to him. Mr. Jefferson Hogg in his delightfully picturesque although somewhat overcharged "Life of Shelley" has brought before us the warm almost breathing image of the poet whose inseparable companion he became. It is clear from this narrative that in those days Shelley possessed a glow and buoyancy of spirits quenched by the tragic events of his later life.

Not uninstructive for a full comprehension of the poet's individuality will it be to follow him into privacy as it were and note those tricks of manner and trifling habits which are often surer indications of character than long descriptions or important actions would be. Let us then watch him, as on a frosty winter's afternoon, he sallies forth with his friend to enjoy his favourite recreation, a long country ramble. See how he strides across country, the tall active frame somewhat lessened by a slight stoop, the hands ever and anon rapidly passed through the eccentric quantity of dark brown curly hair, the wide eyes with a fixed far-away look, as if they saw over and beyond all visible objects. Thus impetuously pushing on, he yet all the while with half-reverted head argues with his friend,—(for to argue on all questions was his dominant passion) expatiating probably in glowing terms on the Platonic theory of knowledge being but a reminiscence of an antenatal state. In the course of their walk he swings to and fro a pair of duelling pistols, and his companion assures us he had perpetual reason to apprehend that, as a trifling episode in the grand and heroic work of drilling a hole through the back of a card, he would shoot himself or me, or both of us."--But a new object now serves to attract his attention. They have sighted a pond. Shelley, riveted to its side, hastily seizes on any letter or paper he has about him, dexterously fashions tiny paper boats then with rapt attention, as though his fate depended thereon, he watches the fortune of the fairy fleet as it battles with miniature waves and mimic storms. The hungry Hogg, who does not share his friend's childlike tastes, stamps impatiently up and down the frozen soil, and at last by sheer force drags oblivious Shelley out of the icy night-air in to fireside and supper. The eager disputant has on a sudden become unaccountably silent. What has become of him? When lo and behold the marvellous boy stretched on the rug in a dead sleep, his little round head exposed to the blazing fire; but seemingly as impervious to its heat as a cat. The awaking process is accomplished with as startling a rapidity as the going to sleep; and to dash instantaneously into a vehement argument or launch into the recital of verses protracted with inexhaustible enthusiasm till late into the night was the frequent practice of the student.

These were the pleasures of our poet. As regards study we have it on the authority of Hogg that he was a whole University in himself in respect of the stimulus and incitement which his example afforded. Sixteen hours out of the twenty-four were frequently spent in reading. Locke, Hume, the French Encyclopædists,* together with Plato, as yet chiefly known from Dacier's translation, formed some of the works most eagerly perused. Absorbed by speculations on religious and philosophical subjects, and under the impression that by honest argument many sound conclusions might be arrived at, he was in the habit of writing anonymously to various persons of literary celebrity. He likewise drew up a little syllabus entitled *The Necessity of Atheism*, which he circulated enclosed in letters and wherein he professed to have come across the pamphlet and to be unable to refute its arguments. This pamphlet became known to the authorities, who, suspecting Shelley to be the author, summoned him to admit or deny the charge, and on his refusing to do either instantly expelled him (March 25, 1811.). Hogg who ventured to protest shared the same fate. It is doubtful whether Shelley was, even at this period, a confirmed materialist. To judge from *Queen Mab*, which embodies the poet's thought at this time, a strong admixture of Platonic idealism tinctured his views even then, nevertheless to all practical intents and purposes he was an Atheist.

We may still add that Shelley's residence at the University had been marked throughout by the singular purity of his morals, the gentleness of his manners, and an abstemiousness in diet that verged on the ascetic. He already inclined to vegetarianism, which from March 1812 he resolutely adopted.

In a certain sense it may be said that Shelley now found himself cast adrift on the Metropolis. His father refused to receive him, and his mother and sister she could only see by stealth; neither was any allowance made him at that time,

---

* A French author who seems to have influenced Shelley a good deal was Volney, whose famous *Ruines* appear to have produced a great effect upon him. The celebrated lines in Queen Mab,
"From an eternity of idleness
I, God, awoke,"
are almost a literal translation of "Dieu après avoir passé une éternité sans rien faire, prit enfin le dessin de produire le monde." Les Ruines. Chapitre XXI. p. 123.

and he subsisted mainly on the pocket-money supplied him by the latter. To one exquisitely sensitive as Shelley, although buoyed up by the proud consciousness of martyrdom, the situation was painful enough. He was separated from his best friend Hogg, and the courtship which had been carried on for some time with the lady already mentioned was now finally broken off. To judge from expressions in letters the poet suffered severely from this defection of the girl he loved. In this frame of mind it was but natural that any new object which could rouse an affectionate interest would possess double attraction for the desolate young heart. This was not long in making its appearance on the scene of action in the shape of a beautiful girl "with a complexion brilliant in pink and white—hair quite like a poet's dream and Bysshe's peculiar admiration." This was Harriet Westbrook, daughter of a retired hotel-keeper in easy circumstances, and who, placed in the same boarding-school as Shelley's sisters, used to be despatched by them with pecuniary help to their brother. Thus an intimacy commenced, and Shelley as was his wont carried on a correspondence with her, in which he dilated on his moral and religious convictions. During a sojourn in Wales he received a letter from the girl in which she complained of her father's petty tyranny and expressed herself as ready to "throw herself on his protection." The result of all this was that Shelley eloped with her in September 1811 to Edinburgh, where they were speedily married.

This was unquestionably an unfortunate step, the result of which might easily be foreseen. But we will not anticipate. Shelley and his wife for the next three years led a very nomadic existence. We find the young couple at York, where they were joined by Harriet's elder sister Eliza and intended to spend the winter with Hogg who pursued his law studies in that city;—at the Lakes, where Shelley made the acquaintance of Southey;—at Dublin (1812) where he was engrossed by efforts to further Catholic Emancipation;—at Lynmouth in Devonshire circulating printed bills for the enlightenment of the people, which contained a Declaration of Rights similar to those of the French Revolution;—at Tanyrallt in Carnarvonshire whence he precipitately retreated hurried off by an actual or imaginary attempt at assassination. As the would be murderer was never traced, and no adequate reason appears to exist for the attempt having been made, it seems probable that the incident was a hallucination produced by the unstrung condition of Shelley's nerves and the effects of laudanum which to mitigate acute spasmodic pains he was then in the habit of taking. After another erratic flitting to Ireland the wanderers at last settled in London, where Shelley's daughter Ianthe was born in 1813.

Shelley now printed but did not publish *Queen Mab;* and the audacious poem created a certain sensation; it was considered by Byron, to whom the author sent a copy, as a work of great power. We share in this opinion. The principal charm lies doubtless in the exuberance of its boundless hope, in its strong vital sympathy with the past sufferings and faith in a happier future of Humanity; it is the first irrepressible burst of a "High spirit winged Heart" through its chrysalis; and as such its fresh spontaneity would redeem verse more manifestly imperfect than that of Queen Mab.

A domestic crisis was now approaching. Shelley's theory, as may be gathered from notes to *Queen Mab*, was that "From the abolition of marriage, the fit and natural arrangement of sexual connexion would result. I by no means assert," he writes, "that the intercourse would be promiscuous: on the contrary it appears from the relation of parent to child, that this union is generally of long duration, and marked above all others with generosity and self-devotion." If in spite of these tenets he married first Harriet and afterwards Mary Godwin it was chiefly on account as he writes of "the disproportionate sacrifice which the female is called upon to make." We may easily surmise that such being the theoretical conclusion, in the event of radical incompatibility of nature such as that existing between Shelley and his first wife, there would be no inherent obstacle to prevent the severing of the tie. According to this view if Harriet acceded to the separation there was not the slightest dereliction of duty. The question then is whether Harriet was equally willing with himself to dissolve their connection, and as to this we possess no positive evidence. At the same time it must be admitted that whatever the outward causes of dissension may have been, under no circumstances whatever is it probable that the union could have been productive, to Shelley at least, of anything but intolerable anguish. There is reason for inferring that he struggled for a time with the growing misery of his lot and this stanza written only in thought, as he says in a heart-rending letter addressed to his friend Hogg, will give some insight into the state of his feelings:

> "Thy dewy looks sink in my breast
> Thy gentle words stir poison there;
> Thou hast disturbed the only rest
> That was the portion of despair!
> Subdued to Duty's hard control,
> I could have borne my wayward lot:
> The chains that bind this ruined soul
> Had cankered then—but crushed it not."

This state of things however could not last. Shelley left Harriet in May 1814, and afterwards came to some sort of understanding with her. His relations with her seem to have continued on a certain friendly footing, but it is impos-

---

* A glimpse of Shelley's own feelings on this subject is afforded by the original reading of stanza VI, l. 6, 7. of the Dedication to the Revolt of Islam. He had written,

> "One whom I found (Harriet Grove)
> was dear but false to me,
> The other's (Harriet Westbrook)
> heart was like a heart of stone."

He perceived, however, that the allusions were too direct and personal, and with his usual delicacy softened the passage down to its present form. For this interesting detail not hitherto made public as well as other particulars contained in the foot-notes I am indebted to the kindness of Mr. Garnett.

sible to decide whether on Harriet's part this was owing to meek acquiescence in the inevitable, or whether she was herself not averse to the step. However this may be, she returned to her father, and soon gave birth to a son, Charles Bysshe; Shelley making such arrangements for her comfort as his circumstances allowed.

"Fair and fair-haired, pale indeed, and with a piercing look" such was the impression Mary Godwin at the age of sixteen, made on Hogg. She was the daughter of the author of *Political Justice* and of Mary Wollstonecraft, whose powerfully written *Rights of Woman* had won for her a wide celebrity. The child of such "glorious parents" had imbibed from their united teachings many opinions, which, while directly at variance with those held by the world at large, closely resembled Shelley's. To her the poet violently in love declared his passion, as they met one day in St. Pancras Churchyard, by her mother's grave. Mary, who had learned to regard marriage as a ceremony, which could in no wise sanctify the union of two beings truly loving each other, unhesitatingly joined her fate to that of her lover's, and the two, accompanied by Miss Clairmont (a daughter of the second Mrs. Godwin by her previous marriage) started on the 28th of July 1814 in an open boat for Calais. The three fugitives (for such they were in a sense as the wrathful Mrs. Godwin went after them, in pursuit of *her* daughter be it remarked) after tossing about on the Channel all night sighted land and the rising sun at the same time.

They then, after some days' stay at Paris, chiefly in order to procure the necessary funds to proceed on their travels, set off with the intention of walking through France. Whether haunted by shadowy recollections of the travels of "The Holy family in Egypt" or not, they likewise procured for themselves the services of one of the mild and long-eared species and another Mary graced the back of another ass. But it was soon alas! discovered that the poor little donkey instead of carrying stood more in need of being carried itself, and had in time to be exchanged for a mule, which not acquitting itself with much more credit, was in its turn replaced by a *voiture*. In the course of their wanderings they passed through the country which had been the immediate seat of war, and the sight of the burnt villages, the impoverished inhabitants, the devastated fields, left an indelible impression on Shelley's mind, which gave double force to his description of such scenes in the *Revolt of Islam*. Impressions of a more inspiring kind awaited them in Switzerland, whence however, they were quickly driven by pecuniary difficulties. They returned to England by way of the Reuss and the Rhine, the river-navigation enchanting Shelley, who has reproduced its magical effects in *Alastor* and the *Witch of Atlas*.

The pecuniary embarrassments already adverted to had about this time reached their climax. The poet had never been free from something of this kind since his expulsion from Oxford, although shortly afterwards, his father had been induced to make him an allowance of £200 per annum; he was so lavishly generous, however, that he continually gave away the better part of his income before he was even possessed of it. To give only one instance of his disposition in this respect, Shelley, a few years later than the time of which we are now writing, made his friend Leigh Hunt, with money raised by an effort, a present of fourteen hundred pounds, to extricate him from debt. The above mentioned allowance had been discontinued on Shelley's leaving England with Mary, and the bare means of subsistence were often raised with difficulty. It should also be mentioned that at one time he had rejected with indignation £2000 a year offered him by his father on the sole condition of the estate being entailed on his eldest son, or in default on his younger brother.

The death of Sir Bysshe in January 1815 materially improved the poet's prospects; his father finding it prudent to make him, as he was next heir to the estate and might have encumbered it with debts, an allowance of £1000 a year. Shelley and Mary now settled at Bishopgate, where the former diligently pursued his Greek studies. Here, in comparative tranquillity, the magnificent woodland of Windsor Great Park serving as study, *Alastor* was written. This beautiful poem, pervaded by a

> "deep autumnal tone
> Sweet though in sadness"

is evidently the product of a revulsion the feelings of Shelley had undergone since their first fiery outburst had fallen so flat on an unresponsive world. Notwithstanding its exquisite charm and greater perfection of form it must be admitted that this poem partakes less of the essential *Shelleyan* quality than *Queen Mab*.

In the summer of 1816 Shelley with Mary and Miss Clairmont settled at Mont Alègre on the lake of Geneva: Byron, who occupied the Villa Diodati being their next neighbour. In these scenes hallowed by the genius of another "world-worn heart" that of the author of the *Nouvelle Héloise*, (which Shelley now read for the first time with enthusiastic admiration) the two poets felt strongly attracted towards each other, and the greater part of each day they spent together in boating on the Lake. On one of these excursions they were overtaken by a sudden squall, which placed their lives in imminent peril. Shelley, who could never learn to swim, writes in allusion to this: "I felt in this near prospect of death a mixture of sensations, among which terror entered but subordinately. My feelings would have been less painful, had I been alone; but I knew that my companion would have attempted to save me, and I was overcome with humiliation, when I thought that his life might have been risked to save mine."

In the evenings the whole party, consisting besides the above mentioned of Dr. Polidori, Byron's secretary and at one time of Lewis a then well-known author, frequently assembled, when the recital of wild unearthly tales would form the chief topic of interest. "After tea 12 o'clock, really began to talk ghostly" writes Dr. Polidori. On one of these occasions Shelley worked himself up to such a pitch of excitement that he rushed out of the room and was found by those who followed him in a trance of horror. The remarkable production of *Frankenstein* then begun by Mary owed its origin to these weird story-tellings at the witching hour of night.

The uninterrupted intercourse with so transcendent a mind as that of Shelley's left its mark on Byron. We can trace the spiritualizing influence of the author of *Adonais* and *Epipsychidion* in much that is loftiest in the speculations of the third Canto of *Childe Harold* and *Manfred;* speculations we do not find in any of the noble poet's earlier works. What was the latter's opinion of our poet may be gathered amongst others from the following expressions: "You should have known Shelley to feel how much I must regret him. He was the most gentle, the most amiable and least worldly-minded person I ever met; full of delicacy, disinterested beyond all other men, and possessing a degree of genius joined to simplicity as rare as it is admirable. He had formed to himself a *beau idéal* of all that is fine, high-minded and noble, and he acted up to this ideal even to the very letter."

By September 1816 we find the Shelleys again in England and on the point of settling at Marlow in Buckinghamshire, when they were struck with grief and horror by the news of Harriet's suicide. There is good cause for believing that this tragic occurence had no direct connection with any act of Shelley's; but was brought about by new relations into which the unfortunate Harriet had entered. Still we believe it can hardly be denied, that indirectly, if only in the disintegrating influence he had exercised on her views of life in general, he must in a certain sense have conduced to this lamentable result. This, this it is which constitutes the tragic pathos of Shelley's short life, that one whose every heart-beat from earliest youth had vibrated with an unquenchable love of his kind, a burning zeal for promoting the general happiness, should in his impetuous course carry along with him and shatter the life of a fellow-creature; preparing so sad a fate for himself and another by reaching out after a nobler morality than that in common practice. Truly may Leigh Hunt remark: "Let the conventional sowers of their wild oats, with myriads of unhappy women behind them, rise up in judgment against him!"

Another affliction with crushing force soon befel the poet. He was deprived of his children. On the death of Harriet, Shelley naturally claimed Ianthe and Bysshe, and, marvellous to relate, the law intervened. The facts were as follows: Mr. Westbrook refused to give up the children, and instituted against Shelley a suit in Chancery, to prevent his obtaining possession of them. It was stated in the bill then filed, "that the father, *since* his marriage had written and published a work, in which he blasphemously denied the truth of the Christian religion, and denied the existence of a God . . . . . . and that he intended, if he could get hold of the persons of his children to educate them as he thought proper." The suit was not long protracted, being decided against Shelley on the 17th of March 1817 Lord Eldon giving his judgment to the effect that as "the father's conduct, which I cannot but consider as highly immoral, has been established in proof, and established as the *effect* of those principles" he could not think himself therefore justified in delivering his children to their father's care. In consequence of this decision the infants were placed under the guardianship of Mr. and Miss Westbrook and their education entrusted, oh irony of circumstances! to a clergyman of the Church of England, £200 being deducted from Shelley's allowance by his father for their maintenance.

"No words can express the anguish he felt when his elder children were torn from him," says Mrs. Shelley, and again later when the "two gentle babes" he had by her lay buried in Italian cemeteries, she adds his words, "I envy death the body far less than the oppressors the minds of those whom they have torn from me."

Let us however turn from the contemplation of these sorrowful subjects, which affected Shelley for life, and follow him to his retreat at Marlow, where, with Mary, whom he married in December 1816, for a beloved companion, and his two children, he now passed his days divided between the composition of the *Revolt of Islam* and active exertions for the relief of the poor in the neighbourhood. He was deeply shocked at the sufferings of the lace-makers and bestirred himself to ameliorate their condition. He had walked an hospital in London in 1815 chiefly in the hope of being useful to the destitute and now carried out these benevolent intentions. He caught a serious attack of ophthalmia while thus visiting the sick.

About the same time the acquaintance with Leigh Hunt ripened into a warm friendship, and he would often pass several days under his roof at Hampstead. At his house he likewise made the acquaintance of Horatio Smith and Keats. Shelley's daily life at Marlow is thus described by Leigh Hunt: "He rose early in the morning, walked and read before breakfast, took that meal sparingly, wrote and studied the greater part of the morning, walked and read again, dined on vegetables (for he took neither meat nor wine), conversed with his friends to whom his house was ever open, again walked out, and usually finished with reading to his wife till ten o'clock, when he went to bed. This was his daily existence. His book was generally Plato, or Homer, or one of the Greek tragedians, or the Bible, in which last he took a great though peculiar, and often admiring interest."

The *Revolt of Islam* being now finished he thus addresses Mary in the dedication:

"So now my summer-task is ended, Mary,
    And I return to thee, mine own heart's home;
As to his Queen some victor Knight of Faëry,
    Earning bright spoils for her enchanted dome.
Nor thou disdain that, ere my fame become
A star among the stars of mortal night
    (If it indeed may cleave its natal gloom),
Its doubtful promise thus I would unite
With thy belovèd name, thou child of love and light."

This first great poem with its magical charm of inwoven rhythm was made by Shelley the vehicle of the loftiest conceptions of self-devotion, endurance and heroism. But the most witching spell of his genius he cast round the loves of Laon and Cythna. Nothing more divinely sweet probably exists in the whole range of poetry than the description in Canto VI. of their meeting after years of struggles, endeavours and unimaginable woes. It is as if from the very inmost sources of emotion welled forth an inexhaustible stream of love, so pure, intense and delicately subtle that these wonderful verses may fitly be termed the very incarnation of passion in words. Nothing is more characteristic of Shelley than his constant endeavour to exalt the relations subsisting between man and woman, and in none of his poems is this endeavour so manifest, as in the one we are now discussing.

Through the whole of this mighty liberative chaunt of *The Revolt* there runs like a golden thread the yearning sympathy with that half of human kind, which although the weaker, is yet burdened with a double weight of oppression, and he cries:

"Can man be free if woman be a slave?"

Cythna herself is a unique creation. She embodies the poet's idea of pure and lofty womanhood; of a female redeemer walking forth through a great city rousing women "from their cold, careless, willing slavery;" of a creature self-contained, not as a satellite moving around man as the centre of her thoughts and actions, but rather in unison with him revolving round the nucleus of a common aim. Yet withal there is nothing cold, hard or abstract about her, she steals on the imagination with the soft glory of sunset and dwells there for ever as a "form more real than living man."

With these few inadequate words we must take leave of the Revolt of Islam or Laon and Cythna as the title originally stood, and without pausing to analyse its brilliant qualities of sound and description return to the facts of the poet's actual existence.

He was again on the point of becoming a wanderer. For, partly impelled by the distressing events above mentioned, partly by ill-health and an inborn restlessness, he once again on the 11th of March 1818, quitted England with his family, and was destined never to return. This time the goal was Italy, where they stayed in succession at Milan, Pisa, Leghorn, the Baths of Lucca, Venice, Este, Rome, Naples, and back again to Rome whither they returned in March 1819.

The sad and terrible vicissitudes which we have recorded as chequering Shelley's life had now in a great measure come to an end. His remaining years flowed on with a smoother current, their progress being chiefly marked by the series of astonishing poems, which with rapidity bordering on the miraculous, were now in succession the products of his pen. To take a brief survey of these therefore, glancing at the same time at the surroundings which constantly shifting exercised an influence quasi atmospheric on his imagination, must now form the leading object of these pages.

Rosalind and Helen, a narrative poem, does not strictly speaking belong to this period, having already been commenced in England and being now at the instance of Mrs. Shelley completed. A good deal of the author's personal experience, such as Rosalind's deprivation of her children, the obloquy cast on Helen on account of her connection with Lionel, has been introduced into this poem, which is of a more domestic character than is usually to be met with in Shelley.

Shelley's sojourn in Venice, where he met Lord Byron, who was delighted at seeing him again, was productive of *Julian and Maddalo*, one of the most captivating and intrinsically original of our poet's productions. With marvellous success the tone of the familiar conversation of persons of genius and refinement is here given back, in fact the conversation of Byron and Shelley. Of this poem it may also be said that with the exception of the closing act of the *Cenci* it is the only instance of true human pathos to be found in Shelley, this being an affection of the mind only to be produced by dwelling on the simplest and most generic of emotions, and therefore apt to be a plant of rare growth where the imaginative reason prevailed as was the case here.

Prometheus Unbound was begun at the same place as *Julian and Maddalo, I Cappucini*, Lord Byron's villa, at Este placed by him at the disposal of the Shelleys. The bulk of the poem, however, was written at Rome and that chiefly during the delicious spring of 1819 amid the mountainous ruins of the Baths of Caracalla. In letters addressed to friends in England is a minute description of this characteristic study, and on account of its suavity as well as for being a specimen of Shelley's epistolary style we quote it.

"The Thermæ of Caracalla consist of six enormous chambers, above 200 feet in height, and each enclosing a vast space like that of a field. There are in addition, a number of towers and labyrinthine recesses, hidden and woven over by the wild growth of weeds and ivy. Never was any desolation more sublime and lovely. The perpendicular wall of ruin is cloven into steep ravines filled up with flowering shrubs, whose thick twisted roots are knotted in the rifts of the stones. At every step the aërial pinnacles of shattered stone grow into new combinations of effect, and tower above the lofty yet level walls, as the distant mountains change their aspect to one travelling rapidly along the plain.... The blue sky canopies it, and is as the everlasting roof of these enormous halls.

"But the most interesting effect remains. In one of the buttresses, that supports an immense and lofty arch, "which bridges the very winds of heaven," are the crumbling remains of an antique winding staircase, whose sides are open in many places to the precipice. This you ascend, and arrive on the summit of these piles. There grow on every side thick entangled wildernesses of myrtle, and the myrletus, and bay, and the flowering laurustinus, whose white blossoms are just developed, the white fig, and a thousand nameless plants sown by the wandering winds. These woods are intersected on every side by paths, like sheep-tracks through the copse-wood of steep mountains, which wind to every part of the immense labyrinth. From the midst rise those pinnacles and masses, themselves like mountains, which have been seen from below. In one place you wind along a narrow strip of weed-grown ruin: on one side is the immensity of earth and sky, on the other a narrow chasm, which is bounded by an arch of enormous size, fringed by the many-coloured foliage and blossoms, and supporting a lofty and irregular pyramid, overgrown like itself with the all-prevailing vegetation. Around rise other crags and other peaks, all arrayed, and the deformity of their vast desolation softened down, by the undecaying investiture of nature. Come to Rome. It is a scene by which expression is overpowered; which words cannot convey."

Sublime as these environments were so sublime even was that stupendous effort of human genius, that astonishing lyrical drama now produced by Shelley, *Prometheus Unbound*. Nothing less is here aimed at than the pourtrayal of indomitable Resistance to omnipotent Force. Three types of vastest significance lay ready to the poet's hand; Satan, Ahasuerus, Prometheus. The first two, awful forms of power though they be, yet are representative of a purely negative resistance. Their defiance, being prompted not by sympathy with mankind but by pride and will respectively, remains in consequence either barren to it or productive of evil. In Prometheus alone a Titanic Sufferer dares oppose himself for the love of a world in bondage to the dominion of an arbitrary but illimitable power. These were the appropriate conditions for the working out of the idea of man's ultimate deliverance from subjection to Creeds and Crowns, as embodied in the dread shape of Jupiter, through the agency of the patient but deathless struggle of Prometheus, the impersonation of that ideal towards which the supremely human tends to approximate. To say that the artistic handling of this poem is on the whole adequate to the infinite scope of its subject-matter, is to give it the highest possible praise; it can hardly however be averred that the requirements, of so tremendous a design have been completely fulfilled on all sides. Compared to the majesty of the first act, where the Titan's pity of the Furies as they torture him reaches the utmost limit of moral elevation, the second act partakes too much of the character of purely poetic beauty, whose very excess of loveliness militates in some degree against the awful character of the action. Nor is the description in the third act of the liberation of the world and the marvellous change coming over it in consequence, wrought up to the intensest possible pitch of excellence: but on the other hand the choral songs of the conclusion, expressive of the same idea from a still more comprehensive point of view, as including in the transformation not only all animated nature but the planetary orbs themselves, are of so transcendent a quality that they well-nigh appear as a rendering in language of the fabled music of the spheres.

In the summer of this same year 1819 Shelley with the rapidity characteristic of his genius wrote the *Cenci*, a work which conclusively proves that over and above his inimitable lyrical faculty he was possessed of a creative dramatic power second to it alone. Shrinking as a rule from the delineation in concrete forms of the dark and malignant passions of men, he here faces them under their most horrible aspect, and in the characters of Count Cenci and Beatrice has in a masterly way contrasted the moral deformity and hideous guilt of the one with the other's light-like beauty and lofty gentleness; while the fearless energy belonging to both indicates their blood-relationship. The action throughout is of deep and vivid interest, the tragic passion and pathos culminating in such scenes as that of the banquet where Cenci offers a thanksgiving to God for the sudden death of his sons, or that heartrending one in the prison when the unfortunate victims of the hoary criminal after being convicted of his murder are informed of their doom, and the ensuing noble resignation of Beatrice casts over the lurid tumult of guilt and woe the ray as of final reconciliation.

Shelley, naturally desirous of procuring the representation of his drama on the stage, exerted himself to that effect chiefly with a hope that the excellent actress Miss O'Neil might undertake to appear in the part of Beatrice. But the manager of Covent Garden not only declined it, but on account of the abnormal horror of its subject even refused to submit the character to her consideration, declaring himself ready at the same time to accept a drama by the author on a less revolting theme.

We must now retrace our steps in order to follow up the events of actual life which had occurred in the meanwhile. The sojourn in Rome had been embittered to the Shelleys by the loss of William their eldest now remaining child, a little girl Clara having died the year before. This misfortune was intensely felt by both parents, and Mary only began to be somewhat consoled when five months afterwards in November 1819 she gave birth at Florence to a son, the present baronet Sir Percy Shelley.

They resided for some months near Leghorn enjoying the intimacy of Mr. and Mrs. Gisborne. With the latter, an accomplished woman, the intimate friend of William Godwin in her youth, the poet studied Spanish, he subsequently translated the dramas of Calderon whose "Magico Prodigioso" revealed a new source of poetic delight. About the same time he was also much interested in the project of building a steamboat, the first that should have plied between Marseilles, Genoa and Leghorn. This was undertaken by Mrs. Gisborne's son, an engineer, but after considerable sums had been embarked by Shelley in this enterprise it fell to the ground by reason of the Gisbornes' abrupt departure for England, Shelley in the most amiable way making light of the loss thus incurred.

The latter part of the year 1819 was spent at Florence, where Shelley assiduously studied the works of art, recording in his own pellucid style his impressions of the statues that struck him most forcibly.

It was found however that the climate of Florence disagreed particularly with· the poet's health and the Shelleys therefore removed on the 26th of January 1820 to Pisa, which henceforth became their headquarters. This quiet old city with its half-deserted streets, its river, its near mountains and not distant sea seemed to possess a peculiar charm for Shelley, while the mildness of its climate and the quality of the water suited him physically better than any spot he had yet visited. It possessed another advantage in the shape of Vaccà the celebrated physician, whose advice to Shelley was to abstain from all medicine. Another reason doubtless for becoming more stationary was the fear for their child's health; for the benefit of which they moved in the spring to the Bagni di Pisa.

Shelley from thence during the hottest days of August undertook a solitary journey on foot to the summit of Monte San Pellegrino. On the three days immediately following this excursion he wrote the *Witch of Atlas*. This is of all Shelley's poems the most purely fanciful; it might indeed be called the Midsummer Night's Dream of his imagination. Nowhere else does he give so unfettered a scope to the fantastic qualities of his genius, and the result is a rare piece of work whose accumulated treasures of remote and exquisite imagery are embalmed in verse no less exquisitely delicate.

In the autumn of this year we find the Shelleys again at Pisa, and a circle of friends now gradually gathering round them; this on the whole appears to have exercised a beneficial influence on the poet's health and spirits. Captain Medwin, his second cousin, old schoolfellow and ultimate biographer, had returned from India and settling at Pisa now saw a good deal of Shelley. It is to him that we owe a detailed account of Emilia Viviani, with whom the latter now became acquainted. This unfortunate girl was the daughter of an Italian count, who having married again late in life, was induced by his wife, jealous of the remarkable beauty of her step-daughter, to immure her in the gloomy convent of St. Anne, until such time as he should have fitted her with a husband. These facts, which Shelley learnt from the confessor of her family, roused his keenest sympathies and accompanied by the latter and Medwin, he went to see the poor captive; but his sympathy was heightened to rapturous admiration when he saw the Contessina herself, who with transcendent personal attractions and fine powers of mind was thus, in the flower of her youth, condemned to languish in dismal solitude. He as well as Mrs. Shelley henceforth visited her repeatedly, and obtained permission for her to return these visits during the carnival. They also corresponded and Shelley made unavailing efforts to obtain her liberation. She was afterwards married by her father to a man utterly unsuited for her, and after enduring six years of a miserable wedded life in the marshy solitudes of the Maremma, left her husband with her father's consent, and died of consumption, brought on through broken-heartedness according to Medwin, in a tumble-down old Campagne at Florence. Such was the short sad career of her who inspired Shelley with *Epipsychidion*, that Apotheosis of Love inasmuch as that passion has become the last efflorescence of a few divinely aspiring natures. What the Song of Solomon is in the sphere of sensuous love, that is its most intense and exhaustive expression, Epipsychidion is to the most spiritual phase of this Protean passion, which perpetually changes its character according to the nature it informs. In Epipsychidion the channel it had passed through was the highly subtilised medium of Shelley's divine heart kindled to a white heat of ecstatic melody: the result is a matchless marvel of impassioned song, the emotions of which have become so rarefied that like the air of the High Alps it is found difficult to absorb so distilled an atmosphere.

Along with Epipsychidion we may mention *Adonais* written in commemoration of the death of Keats, which had taken place on the 23rd of February 1821 at Rome, as it was then erroneously believed in consequence of a savage attack on him in the Quarterly Review. Shelley always prone to generous admiration of contemporary genius, always ready to resent injustice and cruelty to others, was eager to testify to the world what he thought of the author of Hyperion, and of his vile detractors, and that magnificent and most musical of Elegies Adonais was the result. In it he also finds occasion to render a splendid tribute to the genius of Byron, to whom he paid a visit at Ravenna in August 1821. Writing from thence to his wife he says of one of the unpublished cantos of Don Juan, "It sets him not only above but far above all the poets of the day—every word is stamped with immortality;" and in allusion to a delicate task entrusted to him by Lord Byron he remarks, "It seems that I am always to have an active share in everybody's affairs whom I approach." As Byron finally determined to settle at Pisa he asked Shelley to look out for a palace for him, and in the autumn of that year he settled at the Casa Lanfranchi, while Shelley and his wife occupied a floor in the Tre Palazzi on the opposite side of the Lungarno.

The Shelleys had now plenty of society. They were on especially intimate terms with Captain and Mrs. Williams, who, according to the Italian fashion occupied a flat in the same house. Williams is described by Mrs. Shelley as gentle, generous and fearless, he shared with Shelley the passion for boating, and seems to have possessed some aptitude for poetry, for under the former's auspices he was in time delivered of parts of a drama, to the delight of the poet, who compared himself to the sparrow educating the cuckoo's young. Mrs. Williams was considered by Shelley, to realise his conception of the Lady of the *Sensitive Plant* which at once stamps her image on the mind's eye as one of exceeding grace. A bond of the tenderest friendship subsisted between the poet and this lady to whom are addressed many of the loveliest of his shorter lyrics, amongst others that aërially delicate piece, "the Lines to a Lady with a Guitar." Another intimate associate at that time was Prince Alexander Mavrocordato, a Greek, full of ardent enthusiasm in the cause of his country, who on the 1st of April 1821 brought Shelley the proclamation issued by his cousin Prince Ypsilanti which declared that Greece should again be free. With what intense sympathy news of this kind was received by the poet may be imagined. He had already in 1820 celebrated the uprising of Spain and Naples in two Odes of consummate power and beauty. They are more especially remarkable for the impress they bear as of a soul possessed by a demonic rush and frenzy of inspiration, grappling therewith in breathless energy till exhausted with the spiritual stress and strain it droops under its melodious burden, seeming literally to suffocate with song. If the cause of liberty in any land could thus awaken in Shelley the highest chords of his genius, how did he kindle when the modern Greek "the descendant of those glorious beings whom the imagination almost refuses to figure to itself as belonging to our kind" shook off the stagnation of the Turkish rule in a noble endeavour after political independence! The lyrical drama, *Hellas*, Shelley's last finished production of any considerable length, was founded on the events of the moment, and is by him called a "mere improvise." An astonishing improvise to say the least of it, whose choruses, ranging from the softest sweetest notes of the lullaby to the trancelike harmonies of prophetic rapture, exhibit as in vision the struggle and triumph of the Greek cause, which represents to Shelley the vaster cause of the general progress of mankind. He was not himself destined to witness the realisation of a portion of his prophecy which took place a few years later, and in the attempt at attaining which his friend Lord Byron lost his life.

We now touch on the last fateful year of Shelley's existence, the year 1822. It opened auspiciously enough. Byron's daily companionship was no doubt pleasurable, and his more serious conversation according to Shelley a sort of intoxication. The Williamses were friends after his own heart, and Leigh Hunt, to whom he was warmly attached, was expected to arrive with his family in the summer. This journey to Italy was chiefly undertaken by Leigh Hunt in consequence of a project suggested by Byron to Shelley during the latter's stay at Ravenna, the pith of which was that they should establish a periodical paper in which Byron and his friends might publish all their original compositions and share the profits. Leigh Hunt, who had been the editor of the Examiner, a widely read paper of the time, seemed a fit person to join in such an undertaking, and Shelley strongly urged him, both in regard of the pecuniary advantages and literary lustre to enter into such a partnership. For himself he deprecated taking any essential share in the concern both on account of the odium attached to his name, and because he neither wished to shackle the free expression of his opinions nor to injure the reputation and success of his friends by refraining from so doing.

A most welcome addition to this circle was formed by the arrival in Pisa of Captain Trelawny in January 1822. Of all those who from personal knowledge wrote about Shelley, he is the one who had most sympathetic insight and genuine appreciation of the poet's lofty qualities. His manly straightforward description of the last months of Shelley's life is simply invaluable, and while the picture it enables us to form tallies in many respects with the youthful outlines drawn by Mr. Jefferson Hogg, yet it commends itself at once to the judgment as possessing what the other fails in, a severe truthfulness and dignity in dealing with his subject. No other narrative brings us more directly in contact with Shelley than Trelawny's picturesque sketch of his first introduction to the poet, and it is with the utmost reluctance that from want of space we refrain from quoting the entire passage. Trelawny on his arrival hastened to the Williamses', when in the midst of animated conversation he saw a pair of glittering eyes steadily fixed on his, and Mrs. Williams observing the direction of Trelawny's called out;—"Come in Shelley, it's only our friend Tre just arrived."

"Swiftly gliding in," to quote Trelawny, "blushing like a girl, a tall thin stripling held out both his hands; and although I could hardly believe as I looked at his flushed feminine and artless face that it could be the Poet, I returned his warm pressure. After the ordinary greetings he sat down and listened, I was silent from astonishment: was it possible this mild-looking beardless boy could be the veritable monster at war with all the world?—excommunicated by the Fathers of the Church, deprived of his civil rights by the fiat of a grim Lord Chancellor, discarded by every member of his family, and denounced by the rival sages of our literature as the founder of a Satanic school? I could not believe it; it must be a hoax. He was habited like a boy in a black jacket and trowsers, which he seemed to have outgrown, or his tailor as is the custom had most shamefully stinted him in his "sizings." All possible doubt, however, was removed when at the instance of Mrs. Williams the poet read passages from his translation of Calderon's Magico Prodigioso he was just then engaged upon, and which at once gave Trelawny a true touch of his quality. Suddenly as he had appeared he vanished and to Trelawny's "Where is he?" Mrs. Williams said, "Who? Shelley? Oh, he comes and goes like a spirit, no one knows when or where."

Two favourite pastimes of his youth were now resumed. We have already adverted to his practice of pistol shooting. This became now his daily relaxation in company with Byron, Medwin, Williams, Trelawny and some others. They usually assembled at Byron's residence and conversed till about three o'clock, when horses were brought to the door and the party after some hours "slow riding and lively talk" stopped at a small *podere* on the roadside. They then dismounted, had their pistols brought, and began firing. It was on such an occasion, as the usual riding party returned from their shooting, that a sergeant-major of dragoons dashing insolently through their midst, gave rise to a fray, in which several of the party were wounded, Shelley being knocked off his horse in the act of interposing his body between the assailant and Trelawny. This affair, much noised abroad, became the ostensible reason for sending Byron's best Italian friends, the Gambas, out of Tuscany, and resulted in his own removal to Leghorn.

Shelley's other favourite pastime, passion would be the more appropriate expression, was boating. Water of whatsoever kind be it rivulet, stream, lake, but the sea above all, seemed to draw him to it as with a magnetic influence. He now, therefore, chose for his summer residence a lonely sea-washed house near Lerici on the gulf of Spezzia. This place was as wild as could be; the half-savage inhabitants sometimes on moonlit nights dancing among the waves and howling in chorus; provisions only to be procured from a distance; the accommodation of the villa of the scantiest; all this however, so far from deterring, was an additional incitement to the poet for settling amid the soft and sublime scenery of this enchanting bay, and on the 26th of April 1822 the Shelleys and Williamses moved in consequence to the Villa Magni. Here, rambling about the country and seashore, or afloat on the tideless sea, Shelley in the society of congenial friends probably passed the most unclouded days of his life.

He was now engaged on the composition of the *Triumph of Life*, written in terza rima and deeply tinged by the splendours of land and sea by the glow and glare which alternating from gorgeous sunshine to gloom and storm especially marked that season. Fragment though it is, it ranks among the most quintessentially Shelleyan productions, possessing in the highest degree that power he had of clothing the most remote spiritual conceptions in forms of beauty or horror equally transcendent. In this marvellous effort to sound the depths of human existence the hand stopped midway—the painted veil was riven asunder—and to the question "Then what is life?" with which the poem abruptly closes, death responded. Other forebodings as of the approach of destiny were not wanting at this time. Williams tells us that walking by moonlight on the terrace Shelley suddenly grasped his arm, and staring on the white surf on the beach, cried horror-struck "There it is again—there!" On becoming calmer he explained that he had seen a naked child (Byron's daughter Allegra lately dead) rise from the sea, and clap its hands as in joy smiling at him. Another time he terrified the entire household by his screams at midnight. He had seen a figure veiled and shrouded, which coming to his bedside beckoned him to follow. He did so; and on entering another room the phantom lifted the hood of its cloak revealed Shelley's own features and saying "Siete soddisfatto?" vanished.* This was a fortnight before his death.

The ill-fated boat, the Don Juan, which Shelley had ordered to be built for him by Captain Roberts at Genoa arrived in May, and the Hunts (eagerly expected) landing at Leghorn in June, Shelley and Williams started in their much admired boat to meet them. Besides themselves they had only a sailor boy, Charles Vivian, to man her. For in spite of Trelawny's verdict that Shelley would be of no use, till his books and papers were hurled overboard, his wisps of hair shorn off, and his arms plunged in a tar-bucket up to the elbows, and his suggestion consequent thereon of adding an experienced Genoese sailor to their crew, the two friends, in almost boyish glee at their nautical performances, scouted the idea of additional help.

Shelley, inexpressibly delighted at meeting again with Leigh Hunt, accompanied him to Pisa, where he was installed in the ground-floor of Lord Byron's palace. The latter, now fearful of the enterprise, was trying to edge out of it thus jeopardising Hunt's prospects. He seemed, to Shelley's infinite disgust, inclined to take his departure without coming to any definite arrangement with Hunt as to the share to be

---

* Shelley was himself the subject of supernatural legend. Lord Byron asserted, and seems to have actually believed, that a few days before his shipwreck, his phantom had been seen to enter a wood near Pisa.

taken by him in the proposed magazine, which appeared under the title of the Liberal. In this review some fragments from Faust translated by Shelley with exquisite felicity, appeared.

Thus much dispirited, Shelley, after a few days' delay in Hunt's affairs, started from Leghorn in the Don Juan on Monday the 8th of July 1822. It was past one P. M. when he and Williams went on board, Trelawny, who was unfortunately prevented from accompanying them, watching them with a ship's glass. Soon after starting the Don Juan was shrouded in a sea fog, the atmosphere became unusually sultry, and towards evening a short but violent storm convulsed the lead-like sea, drove the vessels in shoals to the harbour, and Trelawny, startled from an oppressive slumber, long and anxiously watched for the re-appearance of the Don Juan, but in vain. Two days of anxious suspense had elapsed when he rode to Pisa to communicate with Hunt and Byron. He remarks that when he told the latter "his lips quivered and his voice faltered" while questioning him.*

A search was immediately instituted and Byron's yacht the Bolivar was dispatched to cruise along the shore; but it was not till the 22nd of July that the corpses of Shelley and Williams were discovered. The sorrowful task of acquainting the two wives of their terrible bereavement fell to Captain Trelawny. "As I stood on the threshold," he writes, "my memory reverted to our joyous parting a few days before. The two families then had all been in the verandah, overhanging a sea so clear and calm that every star was reflected on the water, as if it had been a mirror; the young

* Mrs. Shelley and Mrs. Williams passed days of intolerable suspense. Mrs. Shelley unable to endure it longer hurried to Pisa, and rushing into Lord Byron's room with a face of marble asked passionately, "Where is my husband?" Lord Byron afterwards said he had never seen anything in dramatic tragedy to equal the terror of Mrs. Shelley's appearance on that day. *Mr. Peacock*, in *Fraser's Magazine*, Jan. 1860. Shelley's death by drowning is foreshadowed in the most startling manner in Mrs. Shelley's novel, *Valperga*, written some time previously.

mothers singing some merry tune, with the accompaniment of a guitar. Shelley's shrill laugh—I heard it still—rang in my ears, with Williams's friendly hail, the general *buona notte* of all the joyous party, and the earnest entreaty to me to return as soon as possible." And now he crossed their doorway once more the bearer of news that would overshadow two lives for ever. The misery of the days and nights which followed he declares himself unable either to describe or forget, over sorrows so irremediable the veil of silence is best drawn.

Shelley's body had been found in a deplorable condition near Via Reggio. It seemed as if he had been reading up to the last moment, for a volume of Keats was found in his pocket doubled back at the Eve of St. Agnes as if hastily thrust aside; he had also upon him a volume of his favourite Aeschylus.* The body, hastily interred, had however according to Tuscan law to be burned as a safeguard against plague from objects cast ashore. This it was determined to carry out in the Greek fashion. Permission having been obtained from the Tuscan government Captain Trelawny procured all necessaries for the funeral ceremony, and at the appointed time Byron and Leigh Hunt arrived. The waste and solitary place bounded by the Apennines and the sea, the sun blazing down, the flames leaping up, thus the perishable part of an immortal genius ceased in fiery annihilation. Astonishing fact, the heart remained unconsumed! This Trelawny snatched from the blazing furnace, his hand being much burned in consequence. The ashes were then conveyed to the Protestant cemetery in Rome of which he had written on the occasion of his Elegy on Keats, now in its deeply prophetic strain far more applicable to himself, that it might make one in love with death to think that one should be buried in so sweet a place. They laid him near his "lost William" and Keats and the inscription on his grave runs as follows

* Generally said to have been one of Sophocles, but erroneously.

Percy Bysshe Shelley
Cor Cordium
Natus IV AUG MDCCXCII
Obiit VIII IUL MDCCCXXII

To which Trelawny added the lines from the "Tempest"

> "Nothing of him that doth fade
> But doth suffer a sea-change
> Into something rich and strange."

Mary Shelley returned to England in 1823 and survived her husband 29 years. Their son Percy Florence succeeded to the baronetcy on the death of Sir Timothy in April 1844.

Thus in his thirtieth year, still a youth in appearance, but with world-worn heart the author of the Westwind, the Skylark Epipsychidion and Adonais was snatched away; snatched away by that element he had loved so passionately, praying he might hear

> "The sea
> Breathe o'er my dying brain its last monotony."

However sad and tragic this end, yet how softly and solemnly is the short agitated life rounded by it! How has it secured for him beyond all other poets the dewy halo of perpetual youth! Truly while Shelley was writing his poems he was unconsciously acting a poem as transcendent. If his lyrics are divinely beautiful so is his life. And this to our thinking makes a study of him so fruitful. Others there may be possibly greater as pure artists. But he is a singer whose acts sang no less sublimely than his lips, whose every day existence moved as well as his thoughts and words to the sound of celestial music. If we would in an embodiment of flesh and blood seek for that haunting aspiration which lurks more or less dimly in the minds of all of us; if we would seek for a being in whom the spiritual tendencies completely triumphed over the more material parts of nature; in one word if we would seek the purely human stripped of all its grosser adjuncts and see as in a mirror how little less than angelic it is given to man to be, let us turn with glad eyes and adoring hearts to Percy Bysshe Shelley.

No doubt a carping criticism may take exception at much in his productions; may complain of a "certain want of reality in the characters with which he peoples his glorious scenes;" of his "mystifying metaphysics;" of his failing or never attempting to attain to "completeness of form." But all such cavillers would only prove that they never had penetrated into the inmost spirit of Shelley's poetry, the characteristic excellences of which necessarily excluded certain others, the attributes of minds fundamentally opposed to his. In our opinion the true mental attitude towards such an one as Shelley should be a deep and devout gratitude. He lavished his marvellous gifts so prodigally on a world that heeded him not that the least one can do is to pay to his memory some portion of that enormous debt accumulating to him from his own to the present and future generations. For it should never be forgotten that poetry when it becomes the highest expression of the highest truths possesses a power for setting the soul in motion which at a time when traditional religion has lost its vivid *actual* hold on men's minds, is simply the most sovereign promoter of the inner life. The mighty harmony of its inspiration enables thousands and succeeding thousands to soar to spiritual heights and kindle with spiritual fires unattainable, unimaginable save for such aid. What higher glory of the beneficent triumph of genius is possible on earth? and what poet has achieved such triumph more gloriously than Shelley?

CONTENTS.

	Page
EARTH, OCEAN, AIR, BELOVED BROTHERHOOD!	1
MISCELLANEOUS POEMS.	
Ode to the West Wind	3
To a Skylark	5
Ode to Liberty	9
Ode to Naples	18
Liberty	23
Lines written on hearing the News of the Death of Napoleon	24
Sonnet.—Ozymandias	25
Time	26
Ode to Heaven	26
The two Spirits	28
The Cloud	29
Arethusa	32
Hymn of Apollo	35
Hymn of Pan	36
Songs from Prometheus Unbound	37
To Constantia, singing	39
Music	40
To Night	41
The Question	42
Stanzas written in Dejection near Naples	43
Delight	45
Misery	46
Lines written among the Euganean Hills	48
Letter to Maria Gisborne	59
To ——	68
The Aziola	70
Lines to a Critic	70
An Exhortation	71
To ——	72
The Sensitive Plant	72
Dirge for the Year	82

CONTENTS.

MISCELLANEOUS POEMS—(*Continued*).

	Page
The Invitation	83
The Recollection	85
To a Lady with a Guitar	88
Lines written in the Bay of Lerici	90
To ——	92
The Indian Serenade	92
Love's Philosophy	93
From the Arabic, an Imitation	94
To Emilia Viviani	94
The Dirge	95
Sonnet	96
Time Long Past	96
To-morrow	97
A Bridal Song	97
To ——	97
Lines	98
A Lament	99
To the Moon	100
The Waning Moon	100
The World's Wanderers	100
A Dirge	101
Song	101
A Lament	101
To ——	102

SELECTIONS FROM THE REVOLT OF ISLAM.

Canto II.	103
Canto V.	107
Canto VI.	112
Canto IX.	122
Canto X.	126
Canto XI.	130

1st AND 4th ACTS OF PROMETHEUS UNBOUND	132
THE CENCI	177
JULIAN AND MADDALO	253
THE WITCH OF ATLAS	272
EPIPSYCHIDION	294
ADONAIS	313
CHORUSES FROM HELLAS	330

Earth, Ocean, Air, beloved brotherhood!
If our great Mother has imbued my soul
With aught of natural piety to feel
Your love, and recompense the boon with mine;
If dewy morn, and odorous noon, and even,
With sunset and its gorgeous ministers,
And solemn midnight's tingling silentness;
If Autumn's hollow sighs in the sere wood,
And Winter robing with pure snow and crowns
Of starry ice the grey grass and bare boughs—
If Spring's voluptuous pantings when she breathes
Her first sweet kisses—have been dear to me;
If no bright bird, insect, or gentle beast,
I consciously have injured, but still loved
And cherished these my kindred;—then forgive
This boast, beloved brethren, and withdraw
No portion of your wonted favour now!

Mother of this unfathomable world,
Favour my solemn song! for I have loved
Thee ever, and thee only; I have watched
Thy shadow, and the darkness of thy steps,
And my heart ever gazes on the depth
Of thy deep mysteries. I have made my bed
In charnels and on coffins, where black Death
Keeps record of the trophies won from thee;
Hoping to still these obstinate questionings
Of thee and thine by forcing some lone ghost,
Thy messenger, to render up the tale
Of what we are. In lone and silent hours,

When night makes a weird sound of its own stillness,
Like an inspired and desperate alchemist
Staking his very life on some dark hope,
Have I mixed awful talk and asking looks
With my most innocent love; until strange tears,
Uniting with those breathless kisses, made
Such magic as compels the charmèd night
To render up thy charge. And, though ne'er yet
Thou hast unveiled thy inmost sanctuary,
Enough from incommunicable dream,
And twilight phantasms, and deep noonday thought,
Has shone within me, that serenely now
And moveless as a long-forgotten lyre
Suspended in the solitary dome
Of some mysterious and deserted fane
I wait thy breath, Great Parent; that my strain
May modulate with murmurs of the air,
And motions of the forests and the sea,
And voice of living beings, and woven hymns
Of night and day, and the deep heart of man.

MISCELLANEOUS POEMS.

ODE TO THE WEST WIND.

I.

O WILD West Wind, thou breath of Autumn's being,
   Thou, from whose unseen presence the leaves dead
Are driven, like ghosts from an enchanter fleeing,

   Yellow, and black, and pale, and hectic red,
Pestilence-stricken multitudes! O thou
   Who chariotest to their dark wintry bed

The wingèd seeds, where they lie cold and low,
   Each like a corpse within its grave, until
Thine azure sister of the spring shall blow

   Her clarion o'er the dreaming earth, and fill
(Driving sweet buds like flocks to feed in air)
   With living hues and odours plain and hill;

Wild Spirit which art moving everywhere;
Destroyer and preserver; hear, oh hear!

II.

Thou on whose stream, 'mid the steep sky's commotion,
   Loose clouds like earth's decaying leaves are shed,
Shook from the tangled boughs of Heaven and Ocean,

   Angels of rain and lightning! there are spread
On the blue surface of thine airy surge,
   Like the bright hair uplifted from the head

Of some fierce Mænad, even from the dim verge
   Of the horizon to the zenith's height,
The locks of the approaching storm. Thou dirge

   Of the dying year, to which this closing night
Will be the dome of a vast sepulchre,
   Vaulted with all thy congregated might

Of vapours, from whose solid atmosphere
Black rain and fire and hail will burst: Oh hear!

III.

Thou who didst waken from his summer dreams
   The blue Mediterranean, where he lay,
Lulled by the coil of his crystalline streams,

   Beside a pumice isle in Baiæ's bay,
And saw in sleep old palaces and towers
   Quivering within the wave's intenser day,

All overgrown with azure moss, and flowers
   So sweet, the sense faints picturing them! Thou
For whose path the Atlantic's level powers

   Cleave themselves into chasms, while far below
The sea-blooms and the oozy woods which wear
   The sapless foliage of the ocean, know

Thy voice, and suddenly grow grey with fear,
And tremble and despoil themselves: Oh hear!

IV.

If I were a dead leaf thou mightest bear;
   If I were a swift cloud to fly with thee;
A wave to pant beneath thy power, and share

   The impulse of thy strength, only less free
Than thou, O uncontrollable! if even
   I were as in my boyhood, and could be

The comrade of thy wanderings over heaven,
   As then, when to outstrip thy skiey speed
Scarce seemed a vision, I would ne'er have striven

As thus with thee in prayer in my sore need.
Oh! lift me as a wave, a leaf, a cloud!
  I fall upon the thorns of life! I bleed!
A heavy weight of hours has chained and bowed
One too like thee: tameless, and swift, and proud.

V.

Make me thy lyre, even as the forest is:
  What if my leaves are falling like its own!
The tumult of thy mighty harmonies

  Will take from both a deep autumnal tone,
Sweet though in sadness. Be thou, Spirit fierce,
  My spirit! Be thou me, impetuous one!

Drive my dead thoughts over the universe
  Like withered leaves to quicken a new birth;
And, by the incantation of this verse,

  Scatter, as from an unextinguished hearth
Ashes and sparks, my words among mankind!
  Be through my lips to unawakened earth

The trumpet of a prophecy! O Wind,
If Winter comes, can Spring be far behind!

TO A SKYLARK.

I.

Hail to thee, blithe spirit!
Bird thou never wert,
That from heaven, or near it,
Pourest thy full heart
In profuse strains of unpremeditated art.

II.

Higher still and higher,
From the earth thou springest

Like a cloud of fire;
    The blue deep thou wingest,
And singing still dost soar, and soaring ever singest.

III.

In the golden lightning
    Of the sunken sun
O'er which clouds are brightening,
    Thou dost float and run;
Like an unbodied joy whose race is just begun.

IV.

The pale purple even
    Melts around thy flight;
Like a star of heaven
    In the broad daylight
Thou art unseen, but yet I hear thy shrill delight:

V.

Keen as are the arrows
    Of that silver sphere
Whose intense lamp narrows
    In the white dawn clear,
Until we hardly see, we feel that it is there.

VI.

All the earth and air
    With thy voice is loud,
As, when night is bare,
    From one lonely cloud
The moon rains out her beams, and heaven is overflowed.

VII.

What thou art we know not;
    What is most like thee?
From rainbow clouds there flow not
    Drops so bright to see
As from thy presence showers a rain of melody:—

VIII.

Like a poet hidden
  In the light of thought,
Singing hymns unbidden,
  Till the world is wrought
To sympathy with hopes and fears it heeded not:

IX.

Like a high-born maiden
  In a palace tower,
Soothing her love-laden
  Soul in secret hour
With music sweet as love which overflows her bower:

X.

Like a glow-worm golden
  In a dell of dew,
Scattering unbeholden
  Its aërial hue
Among the flowers and grass which screen it from the view:

XI.

Like a rose embowered
  In its own green leaves,
By warm winds deflowered,
  Till the scent it gives
Makes faint with too much sweet these heavy-wingèd thieves.

XII.

Sound of vernal showers
  On the twinkling grass,
Rain-awakened flowers,
  All that ever was
Joyous, and clear, and fresh, thy music doth surpass.

XIII.

Teach us, sprite or bird,
  What sweet thoughts are thine:

I have never heard
    Praise of love or wine
That panted forth a flood of rapture so divine.

XIV.

Chorus hymeneal
    Or triumphal chaunt,
Matched with thine, would be all
    But an empty vaunt—
A thing wherein we feel there is some hidden want.

XV.

What objects are the fountains
    Of thy happy strain?
What fields, or waves, or mountains?
    What shapes of sky or plain?
What love of thine own kind? what ignorance of pain?

XVI.

With thy clear keen joyance
    Languor cannot be:
Shadow of annoyance
    Never came near thee:
Thou lovest, but ne'er knew love's sad satiety.

XVII.

Waking or asleep,
    Thou of death must deem
Things more true and deep
    Than we mortals dream,
Or how could thy notes flow in such a crystal stream?

XVIII.

We look before and after,
    And pine for what is not:
Our sincerest laughter
    With some pain is fraught
Our sweetest songs are those that tell of saddest thought.

XIX.

Yet, if we could scorn
   Hate, and pride, and fear;
If we were things born
   Not to shed a tear,
I know not how thy joy we ever should come near.

XX.

Better than all measures
   Of delightful sound,
Better than all treasures
   That in books are found,
Thy skill to poet were, thou scorner of the ground!

XXI.

Teach me half the gladness
   That thy brain must know,
Such harmonious madness
   From my lips would flow
The world should listen then, as I am listening now.

ODE TO LIBERTY.

Yet, Freedom, yet, thy banner, torn but flying,
Streams like a thunder-storm against the wind.—BYRON.

I.

A GLORIOUS people vibrated again
   The lightning of the nations: Liberty,
From heart to heart, from tower to tower, o'er Spain,
   Scattering contagious fire into the sky,
Gleamed. My soul spurned the chains of its dismay,
     And in the rapid plumes of song
     Clothed itself, sublime and strong;
As a young eagle soars the morning clouds among;
   Hovering in verse o'er its accustomed prey,
     Till from its station in the heaven of Fame
   The Spirit's whirlwind rapt it; and the ray
     Of the remotest sphere of living flame

ODE TO LIBERTY.

...ch paves the void was from behind it flung,
　...s foam from a ship's swiftness, when there came
　...ce out of the deep: I will record the same.

II.

"The Sun and the serenest Moon sprang forth:
　The burning stars of the abyss were hurled
Into the depths of heaven. The dædal earth,
　That island in the ocean of the world,
Hung in its cloud of all-sustaining air:
　　But this divinest universe
　　Was yet a chaos and a curse,
For Thou wert not: but, Power from worst producing worse,
　The spirit of the beasts was kindled there,
　　And of the birds, and of the watery forms,—
And there was war among them, and despair
　Within them, raging without truce or terms:
The bosom of their violated nurse
　Groaned, for beasts warred on beasts, and worms on worms,
And men on men; each heart was as a hell of storms.

III.

"Man, the imperial shape, then multiplied
　His generations under the pavilion
Of the sun's throne: palace and pyramid,
　Temple and prison, to many a swarming million
Were as to mountain-wolves their ragged caves.
　　This human living multitude
　　Was savage, cunning, blind, and rude,—
For Thou wert not; but o'er the populous solitude,
　Like one fierce cloud over a waste of waves,
　　Hung tyranny; beneath sate deified
The sister-pest, congregator of slaves
　Into the shadow of her pinions wide.
Anarchs and priests, who feed on gold and blood
　Till with the stain their inmost souls are dyed
Drove the astonished herds of men from every side.

IV.

"The nodding promontories and blue isles
  And cloud-like mountains and dividuous waves
Of Greece, basked glorious in the open smiles
  Of favouring heaven: from their enchanted caves
Prophetic echoes flung dim melody
    On the unapprehensive wild.
    The vine, the corn, the olive mild,
Grew, savage yet, to human use unreconciled;
  And, like unfolded flowers beneath the sea,
    Like the man's thought dark in the infant's brain,
  Like aught that is which wraps what is to be,
    Art's deathless dreams lay veiled by many a vein
Of Parian stone: and, yet a speechless child,
    Verse murmured, and Philosophy did strain
Her lidless eyes for Thee;—when o'er the Ægean main

V.

"Athens arose: a city such as vision
  Builds from the purple crags and silver towers
Of battlemented cloud, as in derision
  Of kingliest masonry: the ocean floors
Pave it; the evening sky pavilions it;
    Its portals are inhabited
    By thunder-zonèd winds, each head
Within its cloudy wings with sun-fire garlanded,
  A divine work! Athens diviner yet
    Gleamed with its crest of columns, on the will
  Of man, as on a mount of diamond set;
    For Thou wert, and thine all-creative skill
Peopled, with forms that mock the eternal dead
    In marble immortality, that hill
Which was thine earliest throne and latest oracle.

VI.

"Within the surface of Time's fleeting river
  Its wrinkled image lies, as then it lay,

Immovably unquiet, and for ever
    It trembles, but it cannot pass away.
The voices of thy bards and sages thunder
    With an earth-awakening blast
    Through the caverns of the past;
Religion veils her eyes, Oppression shrinks aghast:
    A wingèd sound of joy and love and wonder,
    Which soars where Expectation never flew,
Rending the veil of space and time asunder.
    One ocean feeds the clouds and streams and dew,
    One sun illumines heaven; one Spirit vast
    With life and love makes chaos ever new;—
As Athens doth the world with thy delight renew.

VII.

"Then Rome was, and from thy deep bosom fairest,
    Like a wolf-cub from a Cadmean Mænad,
She drew the milk of greatness, though thy dearest
    From that Elysian food was yet unweanèd;
And many a deed of terrible uprightness
    By thy sweet love was sanctified;
    And in thy smile, and by thy side,
Saintly Camillus lived, and firm Attilius died.
    But, when tears stained thy robe of vestal whiteness,
    And gold profaned thy capitolian throne,
Thou didst desert, with spirit-wingèd lightness,
    The senate of the tyrants: they sunk prone,
    Slaves of one tyrant. Palatinus sighed
    Faint echoes of Ionian song; that tone
Thou didst delay to hear, lamenting to disown.

VIII.

"From what Hyrcanian glen or frozen hill,
    Or piny promontory of the Arctic main,
Or utmost islet inaccessible,
    Didst thou lament the ruin of thy reign,
Teaching the woods and waves, and desert rocks,

And every Naiad's ice-cold urn,
   To talk in echoes sad and stern
Of that sublimest lore which man had dared unlearn?
   For neither didst thou watch the wizard flocks
     Of the Scald's dreams, nor haunt the Druid's sleep.
   What if the tears rained through thy shattered locks
     Were quickly dried? for thou didst groan, not weep,
When from its sea of death, to kill and burn,
     The Galilean serpent forth did creep,
And made thy world an undistinguishable heap.

IX.

"A thousand years the Earth cried 'Where art thou?'
   And then the shadow of thy coming fell
On Saxon Alfred's olive-cinctured brow:
   And many a warrior-peopled citadel,
Like rocks which fire lifts out of the flat deep,
     Arose in sacred Italy,
     Frowning o'er the tempestuous sea
Of kings and priests and slaves, in tower-crowned majesty.
   That multitudinous anarchy did sweep
     And burst around their walls, like idle foam,
   Whilst from the human spirit's deepest deep
     Strange melody with love and awe struck dumb
Dissonant arms; and Art, which cannot die,
     With divine wand traced on our earthly home
Fit imagery to pave heaven's everlasting dome.

X.

"Thou Huntress swifter than the Moon! thou terror
   Of the world's wolves! thou bearer of the quiver
Whose sunlike shafts pierce tempest-wingèd Error,
   As light may pierce the clouds when they dissever
In the calm regions of the orient day!
     Luther caught thy wakening glance:
     Like lightning from his leaden lance
Reflected, it dissolved the visions of the trance

In which, as in a tomb, the nations lay;
   And England's prophets hailed thee as their queen,
In songs whose music cannot pass away
   Though it must flow for ever.   Not unseen,
Before the spirit-sighted countenance
   Of Milton, didst thou pass from the sad scene
Beyond whose night he saw, with a dejected mien.

XI.

"The eager Hours and unreluctant Years
   As on a dawn-illumined mountain stood,
Trampling to silence their loud hopes and fears,
   Darkening each other with their multitude,—
And cried aloud Liberty! Indignation
      Answered Pity from her cave;
      Death grew pale within the grave,
And Desolation howled to the destroyer: Save!
   When, like heaven's sun, girt by the exhalation
      Of its own glorious light, thou didst arise,
   Chasing thy foes from nation unto nation
      Like shadows: as if day had cloven the skies
At dreaming midnight o'er the western wave,
   Men started, staggering with a glad surprise,
Under the lightnings of thine unfamiliar eyes.

XII.

"Thou heaven of earth! what spells could pall thee then
   In ominous eclipse?   A thousand years
Bred from the slime of deep oppression's den
   Dyed all thy liquid light with blood and tears,
Till thy sweet stars could weep the stain away.
      How, like Bacchanals of blood,
      Round France, the ghastly vintage, stood
Destruction's sceptred slaves, and Folly's mitred brood!
   When one, like them, but mightier far than they,
      The Anarch of thine own bewildered powers,
   Rose: armies mingled in obscure array,
      Like clouds with clouds darkening the sacred bowers

Of serene heaven. He, by the past pursued,
  Rests with those dead but unforgotten hours
Whose ghosts scare victor kings in their ancestral towers.

XIII.

"England yet sleeps: was she not called of old?
  Spain calls her now, as with its thrilling thunder
Vesuvius wakens Ætna, and the cold
  Snow-crags by its reply are cloven in sunder:
O'er the lit waves every Æolian isle
    From Pithecusa to Pelorus
    Howls and leaps and glares in chorus:
They cry, Be dim, ye lamps of heaven suspended o'er us!
Her chains are threads of gold, she need but smile,
  And they dissolve; but Spain's were links of steel,
Till bit to dust by virtue's keenest file.
  Twins of a single destiny! appeal
To the eternal years enthroned before us
  In the dim West! Impress us from a seal,
All ye have thought and done, time cannot dare conceal.

XIV.

"Tomb of Arminius! render up thy dead,
  Till, like a standard from a watch-tower's staff,
His soul may stream over the tyrant's head!
  Thy victory shall be his epitaph!
Wild Bacchanal of truth's mysterious wine,
    King-deluded Germany,
    His dead spirit lives in thee!
Why do we fear or hope? Thou art already free!
And thou, lost paradise of this divine
  And glorious world! thou flowery wilderness!
Thou island of eternity! thou shrine
  Where Desolation, clothed with loveliness,
Worships the thing thou wert! O Italy,
  Gather thy blood into thy heart; repress
The beasts who make their dens thy sacred palaces.

XV.

"O that the free would stamp the impious name
 Of *King* into the dust; or write it there,
So that this blot upon the page of fame
 Were as a serpent's path which the light air
Erases, and the flat sands close behind!
 Ye the oracle have heard:
 Lift the victory-flashing sword,
And cut the snaky knots of this foul gordian word,
 Which, weak itself as stubble, yet can bind
 Into a mass irrefragably firm
The axes and the rods which awe mankind;
 The sound has poison in it, 'tis the sperm
Of what makes life foul, cankerous, and abhorred.
 Disdain not Thou, at thine appointed term,
To set thine armèd heel on this reluctant worm.

XVI.

"O that the wise from their bright minds would kindle
 Such lamps within the dome of this dim world
That the pale name of *Priest* might shrink and dwindle
 Into the hell from which it first was hurled,
A scoff of impious pride from fiends impure!
 Till human thoughts might kneel alone,
 Each before the judgment-throne
Of its own aweless soul, or of the Power unknown.
O that the words which make the thoughts obscure
 From which they spring, as clouds of glimmering dew
From a white lake blot heaven's blue portraiture,
 Were stripped of their thin masks and various hue,
And frowns and smiles and splendours not their own,
 Till in the nakedness of false and true
They stand before their Lord, each to receive its due.

XVII.

"He who taught man to vanquish whatsoever
 Can be between the cradle and the grave

Crowned him the King of Life. O vain endeavour!
If on his own high will, a willing slave,
He has enthroned the oppression and the oppressor!
    What if earth can clothe and feed
    Amplest millions at their need,
And power in thought be as the tree within the seed,—
  Or what if Art, an ardent intercessor,
    Diving on fiery wings to Nature's throne,
  Checks the great Mother stooping to caress her,
    And cries, 'Give me, thy child, dominion
  Over all height and depth'—if Life can breed
    New wants, and Wealth, from those who toil and groan,
Rend, of thy gifts and hers, a thousandfold for one?

XVIII.

"Come Thou! But lead out of the inmost cave
  Of man's deep spirit, as the morning star
Beckons the Sun from the Eoan wave,
    Wisdom. I hear the pennons of her car
Self-moving, like cloud charioted by flame;
    Comes she not! And come ye not,
    Rulers of eternal thought,
To judge with solemn truth life's ill-apportioned lot:
  Blind Love, and equal Justice, and the Fame
    Of what has been, the Hope of what will be?
O Liberty! if such could be thy name
    Wert thou disjoined from these, or they from thee—
If thine or theirs were treasures to be bought
    By blood or tears, have not the wise and free
Wept tears, and blood like tears?"—The solemn harmony

XIX.

Paused, and the Spirit of that mighty singing
  To its abyss was suddenly withdrawn.
Then, as a wild swan, when sublimely winging
  Its path athwart the thunder-smoke of dawn,
Sinks headlong through the aërial golden light

On the heavy-sounding plain,
When the bolt has pierced its brain;
As summer clouds dissolve unburthened of their rain,
As a far taper fades with fading night;
As a brief insect dies with dying day;
My song, its pinions disarrayed of might,
Drooped: o'er it closed the echoes far away
Of the great voice which did its flight sustain,—
As waves which lately paved his watery way
Hiss round a drowner's head in their tempestuous play.

ODE TO NAPLES.

Epode I. *a.*

I stood within the city disinterred;
And heard the autumnal leaves like light footfalls
Of spirits passing through the streets; and heard
The Mountain's slumberous voice at intervals
Thrill through those roofless halls.
The oracular thunder penetrating shook
The listening soul in my suspended blood;
I felt that Earth out of her deep heart spoke—
I felt, but heard not:—through white columns glowed
The isle-sustaining ocean-flood,
A plane of light between two heavens of azure:
Around me gleamed many a bright sepulchre,
Of whose pure beauty Time, as if his pleasure
Were to spare Death, had never made erasure;
But every living lineament was clear
As in the sculptor's thought; and there
The wreaths of stony myrtle, ivy, and pine,
Like winter leaves o'ergrown by moulded snow,
Seemed only not to move and grow
Because the crystal silence of the air
Weighed on their life, even as the Power divine
Which then lulled all things brooded upon mine.

EPODE II. a.

Then gentle winds arose,
With many a mingled close
Of wild Æolian sound and mountain odour keen.
And where the Baian ocean
Welters with air-like motion
Within, above, around its bowers of starry green,
 Moving the sea-flowers in those purple caves,
 Even as the ever stormless atmosphere
  Floats o'er the Elysian realm,
It bore me: like an Angel, o'er the waves
Of sunlight, whose swift pinnace of dewy air
  No storm can overwhelm.
  I sailed where ever flows
  Under the calm serene
  A spirit of deep emotion
  From the unknown graves
  Of the dead kings of Melody.
Shadowy Aornos darkened o'er the helm
The horizontal æther; heaven stripped bare
Its depths over Elysium, where the prow
Made the invisible water white as snow;
From that Typhæan mount, Inarime,
There streamed a sunlit vapour, like the standard
  Of some ethereal host;
  Whilst from all the coast,
Louder and louder, gathering round, there wandered
Over the oracular woods and divine sea
Prophesyings which grew articulate—
They seize me—I must speak them;—be they fate!

STROPHE I. a.

NAPLES! thou Heart of men which ever pantest
 Naked beneath the lidless eye of heaven!
Elysian City, which to calm enchantest
 The mutinous air and sea,—they round thee, even
 As Sleep round Love, are driven!

Metropolis of a ruined Paradise
　Long lost, late won, and yet but half regained!
Bright altar of the bloodless sacrifice
　Which armèd Victory offers up unstained
　　To Love the flower-enchained!
Thou which wert once, and then didst cease to be,
Now art, and henceforth ever shalt be, free,
If Hope and Truth and Justice can avail,—
　　　Hail, hail, all hail!

Strophe II. *β*.

　　Thou youngest giant birth
　　Which from the groaning earth
Leap'st, clothed in armour of impenetrable scale!
　　Last of the intercessors
　　Who 'gainst the crowned transgressors
Pleadest before God's love! arrayed in wisdom's mail,
　　Wave thy lightning lance in mirth;
　　Nor let thy high heart fail,
Though from their hundred gates the leagued oppressors
With hurried legions move! Hail, hail, all hail!

Antistrophe I. *α*.

What though Cimmerian Anarchs dare blaspheme
　Freedom and thee? Thy shield is as a mirror
To make their blind slaves see, and with fierce gleam
　To turn his hungry sword upon the wearer;
　　A new Actæon's error
Shall theirs have been—devoured by their own hounds!
　Be thou like the imperial basilisk,
Killing thy foe with unapparent wounds!
　Gaze on Oppression, till, at that dread risk
　　Aghast, she pass from the earth's disk;
Fear not, but gaze—for freemen mightier grow,
And slaves more feeble, gazing on their foe.
If Hope and Truth and Justice may avail,
　　Thou shalt be great.—All hail!

ANTISTROPHE II. β.

From Freedom's form divine,
From Nature's inmost shrine,
Strip every impious gawd, rend error veil by veil:
    O'er Ruin desolate,
    O'er Falsehood's fallen state,
Sit thou sublime, unawed; be the Destroyer pale!
    And equal laws be thine,
    And wingèd words let sail,
Freighted with truth even from the throne of God!
That wealth, surviving fate, be thine.—All hail!

STROPHE III. γ.

Didst thou not start to hear Spain's thrilling pæan
    From land to land re-echoed solemnly,
Till silence became music? From the Ææan
    To the cold Alps, eternal Italy
        Starts to hear thine! The sea
Which paves the desert streets of Venice laughs
    In light and music; widowed Genoa wan,
By moonlight, spells ancestral epitaphs,
    Murmuring "Where is Doria?" fair Milan,
        Within whose veins long ran
The viper's palsying venom, lifts her heel
To bruise his head. The signal and the seal
(If Hope and Truth and Justice can avail)
    Art thou of all these hopes.—Oh hail!

STROPHE IV. δ.

Florence, beneath the sun,
Of cities fairest one,
Blushes within her bower for Freedom's expectation:
    From eyès of quenchless hope
    Rome tears the priestly cope,
As ruling once by power, so now by admiration,—
    An athlete stripped to run
    From a remoter station

For the high prize lost on Philippi's shore:—
As then Hope, Truth, and Justice, did avail,
    So now may Fraud and Wrong! Oh hail!

Epode I. β.

Hear ye the march as of the Earth-born Forms
  Arrayed against the ever-living Gods?
The crash and darkness of a thousand storms
  Bursting their inaccessible abodes
    Of crags and thunder-clouds?
See ye the banners blazoned to the day,
  Inwrought with emblems of barbaric pride?
Dissonant threats kill silence far away;
  The serene heaven which wraps our Eden wide
    With iron light is dyed.
The Anarchs of the North lead forth their legions,
  Like chaos o'er creation, uncreating;
An hundred tribes nourished on strange religions
And lawless slaveries. Down the aërial regions
    Of the white Alps, desolating,
    Famished wolves that bide no waiting,
Blotting the glowing footsteps of old glory,
    Trampling our columned cities into dust,
    Their dull and savage lust
  On Beauty's corse to sickness satiating—
They come! The fields they tread look black and hoary
With fire—from their red feet the streams run gory!

Epode II. β.

  Great Spirit, deepest Love,
    Which rulest and dost move
All things which live and are within the Italian shore;
    Who spreadest heaven around it;
    Whose woods, rocks, waves, surround it;
Who sittest in thy star, o'er ocean's western floor!—
  Spirit of Beauty, at whose soft command
    The sunbeams and the showers distil its foison

From the earth's bosom chill!—
O bid those beams be each a blinding brand
Of lightning! bid those showers be dews of poison!
Bid the earth's plenty kill!
Bid thy bright heaven above,
Whilst light and darkness bound it,
Be their tomb who planned
To make it ours and thine!
Or with thine harmonizing ardours fill
And raise thy sons, as o'er the prone horizon
Thy lamp feeds every twilight wave with fire!
Be man's high hope and unextinct desire
The instrument to work thy will divine!
Then clouds from sunbeams, antelopes from leopards,
And frowns and fears from Thee,
Would not more swiftly flee
Than Celtic wolves from the Ausonian shepherds.—
Whatever, Spirit, from thy starry shrine
Thou yieldest or withholdest, oh let be
This City of thy worship ever free!

LIBERTY.

The fiery mountains answer each other,
　Their thunderings are echoed from zone to zone;
The tempestuous oceans awake one another,
　And the ice-rocks are shaken round Winter's throne,
　When the clarion of the Typhoon is blown.
From a single cloud the lightning flashes,
　Whilst a thousand isles are illumined around;
Earthquake is trampling one city to ashes,
　An hundred are shuddering and tottering,—the sound
　　Is bellowing underground.
But keener thy gaze than the lightning's glare,
　And swifter thy step than the earthquake's tramp;

Thou deafenest the rage of the ocean; thy stare
  Makes blind the volcanoes; the sun's bright lamp
    To thine is a fen-fire damp.

From billow and mountain and exhalation
  The sunlight is darted through vapour and blast;
From spirit to spirit, from nation to nation,
  From city to hamlet, thy dawning is cast,—
  And tyrants and slaves are like shadows of night
    In the van of the morning light.

LINES

WRITTEN ON HEARING THE NEWS OF THE DEATH OF NAPOLEON.

I.

WHAT! alive and so bold, O Earth?
  Art thou not over-bold?
  What! leapest thou forth as of old
In the light of thy morning mirth
The last of the flock of the starry fold?
  Ha! leapest thou forth as of old?
Are not the limbs still when the ghost is fled,
And canst thou move, Napoleon being dead?

II.

How! is not thy quick heart cold?
  What spark is alive on thy hearth?
How! is not *his* death-knell knolled,
  And livest *thou* still, Mother Earth?
Thou wert warming thy fingers old
O'er the embers covered and cold
Of that most fiery spirit, when it fled—
What, Mother, dost thou laugh now he is dead?

III.

"Who has known me of old," replied Earth,
  "Or who has my story told?
  It is thou who art over-bold."

And the lightning of scorn laughed forth
  As she sung, "To my bosom I fold
  All my sons when their knell is knolled;
And so with living motion all are fed,
And the quick spring like weeds out of the dead.

IV.

"Still alive and still bold," shouted Earth,
  "I grow bolder and still more bold.
  The dead fill me ten thousand fold
Fuller of speed and splendour and mirth.
  I was cloudy and sullen and cold,
  Like a frozen chaos uprolled,
Till by the spirit of the mighty dead
My heart grew warm: I feed on whom I fed.

V.

"Ay, alive and still bold," muttered Earth.
  "Napoleon's fierce spirit rolled
  In terror and blood and gold,
A torrent of ruin to death from his birth.
  Leave the millions who follow to mould
  The metal before it be cold;
And weave into his shame, which, like the dead
Shrouds me, the hopes that from his glory fled."

SONNET.—OZYMANDIAS.

I MET a traveller from an antique land
  Who said: Two vast and trunkless legs of stone
Stand in the desert. Near them on the sand
  Half sunk, a shattered visage lies, whose frown
And wrinkled lip and sneer of cold command
Tell that its sculptor well those passions read
  Which yet survive, stamped on these lifeless things,
The hand that mocked them and the heart that fed;
And on the pedestal these words appear:
  'My name is Ozymandias, King of Kings:

Look on my works, ye Mighty, and despair!'
　Nothing beside remains.　Round the decay
Of that colossal wreck, boundless and bare,
　The lone and level sands stretch far away.

TIME.

UNFATHOMABLE Sea, whose waves are years!
　Ocean of Time, whose waters of deep woe
Are brackish with the salt of human tears!
　Thou shoreless flood which in thy ebb and flow
Claspest the limits of mortality,
And, sick of prey yet howling on for more,
Vomitest thy wrecks on its inhospitable shore!
Treacherous in calm, and terrible in storm,
　　Who shall put forth on thee,
　　Unfathomable Sea?

ODE TO HEAVEN.

CHORUS OF SPIRITS.

FIRST SPIRIT.

PALACE-ROOF of cloudless nights!
Paradise of golden lights!
Deep, immeasurable, vast,
　Which art now, and which wert then!
Of the present and the past,
　Of the eternal where and when,
Presence-chamber, temple, home!
Ever-canopying dome
Of acts and ages yet to come!

Glorious shapes have life in thee:—
Earth, and all earth's company;
Living globes which ever throng
　Thy deep chasms and wildernesses;

ODE TO HEAVEN.

And green worlds that glide along;
  And swift stars with flashing tresses
And icy moons most cold and bright;
And mighty suns beyond the night,
Atoms of intensest light.

Even thy name is as a god,
Heaven! for thou art the abode
Of that Power which is the glass
  Wherein man his nature sees.
Generations as they pass
  Worship thee with bended knees.
Their unremaining gods and they
Like a river roll away;
Thou remainest such alway.

Second Spirit.

Thou art but the mind's first chamber,
Round which its young fancies clamber,
Like weak insects in a cave
  Lighted up by stalactites;
But the portal of the grave,—
  Where a world of new delights
Will make thy best glories seem
But a dim and noonday gleam
From the shadow of a dream!

Third Spirit.

Peace! the abyss is wreathed with scorn
At your presumption, atom-born!
What is heaven? and what are ye
  Who its brief expanse inherit?
What are suns and spheres which flee
  With the instinct of that Spirit
Of which ye are but a part?
Drops which Nature's mighty heart
Drives through thinnest veins. Depart!

What is heaven? A globe of dew,
Filling in the morning new

Some eyed flower whose young leaves waken
  On an unimagined world:—
Constellated suns unshaken,
  Orbits measureless, are furled
In that frail and fading sphere,
With ten millions gathered there,
To tremble, gleam, and disappear.

THE TWO SPIRITS.
AN ALLEGORY.

FIRST SPIRIT.

O THOU who plumed with strong desire
  Wouldst float above the earth, beware!
A shadow tracks thy flight of fire—
  Night is coming!
Bright are the regions of the air,
And among the winds and beams
  It were delight to wander there—
  Night is coming!

SECOND SPIRIT.

The deathless stars are bright above:
  If I would cross the shade of night,
Within my heart is the lamp of love,
  And that is day;
And the moon will shine with gentle light
On my golden plumes where'er they move;
The meteors will linger round my flight
  And make night day.

FIRST SPIRIT.

But if the whirlwinds of darkness waken
  Hail and lightning and stormy rain?
See, the bounds of the air are shaken—
  Night is coming!
The red swift clouds of the hurricane

Yon declining sun have overtaken,
  The clash of the hail sweeps over the plain—
    Night is coming!

   SECOND SPIRIT.
I see the light, and I hear the sound.
I'll sail on the flood of the tempest dark,
With the calm within and the light around
  Which makes night day:
And thou, when the gloom is deep and stark,
Look from thy dull earth, slumber-bound;
  My moonlike flight thou then mayst mark
    On high, far away.

———

Some say there is a precipice
  Where one vast pine is frozen to ruin
O'er piles of snow and chasms of ice
    'Mid Alpine mountains;
  And that the languid storm, pursuing
That wingèd shape, for ever flies
  Round those hoar branches, aye renewing
    Its aëry fountains.

Some say, when nights are dry and clear,
  And the death-dews sleep on the morass,
Sweet whispers are heard by the traveller,
    Which make night day:
And a silver shape like his early love doth pass,
  Upborne by her wild and glittering hair;
    And, when he awakes on the fragrant grass,
      He finds night day.

———

THE CLOUD.

I.

I BRING fresh showers for the thirsting flowers
  From the seas and the streams;

I bear light shade for the leaves when laid
    In their noonday dreams.
From my wings are shaken the dews that waken
    The sweet buds every one,
When rocked to rest on their Mother's breast,
    As she dances about the sun.
I wield the flail of the lashing hail,
    And whiten the green plains under;
And then again I dissolve it in rain,
    And laugh as I pass in thunder.

II.

I sift the snow on the mountains below,
    And their great pines groan aghast;
And all the night 'tis my pillow white,
    While I sleep in the arms of the blast.
Sublime on the towers of my skiey bowers
    Lightning my pilot sits;
In a cavern under is fettered the thunder,
    It struggles and howls at fits.
Over earth and ocean with gentle motion
    This pilot is guiding me,
Lured by the love of the Genii that move
    In the depths of the purple sea;
Over the rills and the crags and the hills,
    Over the lakes and the plains,
Wherever he dream under mountain or stream
    The Spirit he loves remains;
And I all the while bask in heaven's blue smile,
    Whilst he is dissolving in rains.

III.

The sanguine Sunrise, with his meteor eyes,
    And his burning plumes outspread,
Leaps on the back of my sailing rack,
    When the morning star shines dead:
As on the jag of a mountain crag
    Which an earthquake rocks and swings

An eagle alit one moment may sit
    In the light of its golden wings.
And, when Sunset may breathe, from the lit sea beneath,
    Its ardours of rest and of love,
And the crimson pall of eve may fall
    From the depth of heaven above,
With wings folded I rest on mine airy nest,
    As still as a brooding dove.

IV.

That orbèd maiden with white fire laden
    Whom mortals call the Moon
Glides glimmering o'er my fleece-like floor
    By the midnight breezes strewn;
And wherever the beat of her unseen feet,
    Which only the angels hear,
May have broken the woof of my tent's thin roof,
    The Stars peep behind her and peer.
And I laugh to see them whirl and flee
    Like a swarm of golden bees,
When I widen the rent in my wind-built tent,—
    Till the calm rivers, lakes, and seas,
Like strips of the sky fallen through me on high,
    Are each paved with the moon and these.

V.

I bind the Sun's throne with a burning zone,
    And the Moon's with a girdle of pearl;
The volcanoes are dim, and the stars reel and swim,
    When the whirlwinds my banner unfurl.
From cape to cape, with a bridge-like shape,
    Over a torrent sea,
Sunbeam-proof, I hang like a roof;
    The mountains its columns be.
The triumphal arch through which I march,
    With hurricane, fire, and snow,
When the Powers of the air are chained to my chair,
    Is the million-coloured bow;

The sphere-fire above its soft colours wove,
    While the moist earth was laughing below.

VI.

I am the daughter of earth and water,
    And the nursling of the sky:
I pass through the pores of the ocean and shores;
    I change, but I cannot die.
For after the rain, when with never a stain
    The pavilion of heaven is bare,
And the winds and sunbeams with their convex gleams
    Build up the blue dome of air,
I silently laugh at my own cenotaph,—
    And out of the caverns of rain,
Like a child from the womb, like a ghost from the tomb,
    I arise, and unbuild it again.

ARETHUSA.

    ARETHUSA arose
    From her couch of snows
In the Acroceraunian mountains,—
    From cloud and from crag
    With many a jag
Shepherding her bright fountains.
    She leapt down the rocks
    With her rainbow locks
Streaming among the streams;
    Her steps paved with green
    The downward ravine
Which slopes to the western gleams:
    And gliding and springing,
    She went ever singing,
In murmurs as soft as sleep;
    The Earth seemed to love her,
    And Heaven smiled above her,
As she lingered towards the deep.

ARETHUSA.

      Then Alpheus bold,
      On his glacier cold,
With his trident the mountain strook;
      And opened a chasm
      In the rocks:—with the spasm
All Erymanthus shook.
      And the black south wind
      It concealed behind
The urns of the silent snow,
      And earthquake and thunder
      Did rend in sunder
The bars of the springs below:
      The beard and the hair
      Of the river God were
Seen through the torrent's sweep,
      As he followed the light
      Of the fleet nymph's flight
To the brink of the Dorian deep.

      "Oh save me! Oh guide me!
      And bid the deep hide me!
For he grasps me now by the hair!"
      The loud Ocean heard,
      To its blue depth stirred,
And divided at her prayer;
      And under the water
      The Earth's white daughter
Fled like a sunny beam;
      Behind her descended
      Her billows, unblended
With the brackish Dorian stream:
      Like a gloomy stain
      On the emerald main
Alpheus rushed behind,—
      As an eagle pursuing
      A dove to its ruin
Down the streams of the cloudy wind.

        Under the bowers
        Where the Ocean Powers
Sit on their pearlèd thrones:
        Through the coral woods
        Of the weltering floods,
Over heaps of unvalued stones;
        Through the dim beams
        Which amid the streams
Weave a network of coloured light;
        And under the caves,
        Where the shadowy waves
Are as green as the forest's night:—
        Outspeeding the shark,
        And the sword-fish dark,
Under the ocean foam,
        And up through the rifts
        Of the mountain clifts
They passed to their Dorian home.

        And now from their fountains
        In Enna's mountains,
Down one vale where the morning basks
        Like friends once parted
        Grown single-hearted,
They ply their watery tasks.
        At sunrise they leap
        From their cradles steep
In the cave of the shelving hill;
        At noon-tide they flow
        Through the woods below
And the meadows of Asphodel;
        And at night they sleep
        In the rocking deep
Beneath the Ortygian shore;—
        Like spirits that lie
        In the azure sky
When they love but live no more.

HYMN OF APOLLO.

THE sleepless Hours who watch me as I lie,
  Curtained with star-inwoven tapestries
    From the broad moonlight of the sky,
  Fanning the busy dreams from my dim eyes,
Waken me when their Mother, the grey Dawn,
Tells them that dreams and that the moon is gone.

Then I arise, and, climbing heaven's blue dome,
  I walk over the mountains and the waves,
Leaving my robe upon the ocean foam;—
  My footsteps pave the clouds with fire; the caves
Are filled with my bright presence; and the air
Leaves the green Earth to my embraces bare.

The sunbeams are my shafts, with which I kill
  Deceit, that loves the night and fears the day;
All men who do or even imagine ill
  Fly me, and from the glory of my ray
Good minds and open actions take new might,
Until diminished by the reign of Night.

I feed the clouds, the rainbows, and the flowers,
  With their ethereal colours; the moon's globe,
And the pure stars in their eternal bowers,
  Are cinctured with my power as with a robe;
Whatever lamps on earth or heaven may shine
Are portions of one power, which is mine.

I stand at noon upon the peak of Heaven;
  Then with unwilling steps I wander down
Into the clouds of the Atlantic even;
  For grief that I depart they weep and frown.
What look is more delightful than the smile
With which I soothe them from the western isle?

I am the eye with which the Universe
  Beholds itself, and knows itself divine;

All harmony of instrument or verse,
   All prophecy, all medicine, are mine,
All light of art or nature;—to my song
Victory and praise in its own right belong.

HYMN OF PAN.

From the forests and highlands
   We come, we come;
From the river-girt islands,
   Where loud waves are dumb
Listening to my sweet pipings.
   The wind in the reeds and the rushes,
      The bees on the bells of thyme,
   The birds on the myrtle bushes,
      The cicale above in the lime,
   And the lizards below in the grass,
Were as silent as ever old Tmolus was,
   Listening to my sweet pipings.

Liquid Peneus was flowing,
   And all dark Tempe lay
In Pelion's shadow, outgrowing
   The light of the dying day,
Speeded by my sweet pipings.
   The Sileni and Sylvans and Fauns,
      And the Nymphs of the woods and waves,
   To the edge of the moist river-lawns,
      And the brink of the dewy caves,
And all that did then attend and follow,
Were silent with love,—as you now, Apollo,
   With envy of my sweet pipings.

I sang of the dancing stars,
   I sang of the dædal earth,
And of heaven, and the Giant wars,
   And love, and death, and birth.

And then I changed my pipings,—
Singing how down the vale of Mænalus
   I pursued a maiden, and clasped a reed:
Gods and men, we are all deluded thus;
   It breaks in our bosom, and then we bleed.
All wept—as I think both ye now would,
If envy or age had not frozen your blood—
   At the sorrow of my sweet pipings.

SONGS FROM PROMETHEUS UNBOUND.

I.

A SPIRIT.

Life of Life! thy lips enkindle
   With their love the breath between them;
And thy smiles, before they dwindle
   Make the cold air fire; then screen them
In those looks where whoso gazes
Faints, entangled in their mazes.

Child of Light! thy limbs are burning
   Through the vest which seems to hide them,
As the radiant lines of morning
   Through the clouds, ere they divide them;
And this atmosphere divinest
Shrouds thee wheresoe'er thou shinest.

Fair are others; none beholds thee,
   But thy voice sounds low and tender,
Like the fairest, for it folds thee
   From the sight, that liquid splendour,
And all feel yet see thee never,
As I feel now, lost for ever!

Lamp of Earth! where'er thou movest,
   Its dim shapes are clad with brightness,

And the souls of whom thou lovest
   Walk upon the winds with lightness,
Till they fail, as I am failing,
Dizzy, lost, yet unbewailing!

II.

ASIA.

My soul is an enchanted boat,
   Which, like a sleeping swan, doth float
Upon the silver waves of thy sweet singing;
   And thine doth like an angel sit
   Beside the helm conducting it,
Whilst all the winds with melody are ringing
   It seems to float ever, for ever,
   Upon that many-winding river,
   Between mountains, woods, abysses,
   A paradise of wildernesses!
   Till, like one in slumber bound
Borne to the ocean, I float down, around,
Into a sea profound of ever-spreading sound.

   Meanwhile thy spirit lifts its pinions
   In music's most serene dominions,
Catching the winds that fan that happy heaven
   And we sail on, away, afar,
   Without a course, without a star,
But by the instinct of sweet music driven
   Till through Elysian garden islets,
   By thee, most beautiful of pilots,
   Where never mortal pinnace glided,
   The boat of my desire is guided:
   Realms where the air we breathe is love,
Which in the winds and on the waves doth move,
Harmonizing this earth with what we feel above.

   We have passed Age's icy caves,
   And Manhood's dark and tossing waves,

And Youth's smooth ocean, smiling to betray:
  Beyond the glassy gulfs we flee
  Of shadow-peopled Infancy,
Through Death and Birth, to a diviner day:
  A paradise of vaulted bowers
  Lit by downward-gazing flowers,
  And watery paths that wind between
  Wildernesses calm and green,
  Peopled by shapes too bright to see,
  And rest, having beheld,—somewhat like thee,—
Which walk upon the sea, and chant melodiously!

TO CONSTANTIA, SINGING.

THUS to be lost and thus to sink and die
  Perchance were death indeed!—Constantia, turn!
In thy dark eyes a power like light doth lie,
  Even though the sounds which were thy voice, which burn
    Between thy lips, are laid to sleep;
Within thy breath, and on thy hair, like odour, it is yet,
    And from thy touch like fire doth leap.
Even while I write, my burning cheeks are wet;
Alas, that the torn heart can bleed, but not forget!

  A breathless awe, like the swift change
    Unseen but felt in youthful slumbers,
Wild, sweet, but uncommunicably strange,
Thou breathest now in fast-ascending numbers.
  The cope of heaven seems rent and cloven
    By the enchantment of thy strain,
  And on my shoulders wings are woven,
    To follow its sublime career
    Beyond the mighty moons that wane
Upon the verge of nature's utmost sphere,
Till the world's shadowy walls are past and disappear.

Her voice is hovering o'er my soul—it lingers
  O'ershadowing it with soft and lulling wings;
The blood and life within those snowy fingers
  Teach witchcraft to the instrumental strings.
    My brain is wild, my breath comes quick—
      The blood is listening in my frame,
    And thronging shadows, fast and thick,
      Fall on my overflowing eyes;
    My heart is quivering like a flame;
As morning dew that in the sunbeam dies,
I am dissolved in these consuming ecstasies.

I have no life, Constantia, now, but thee,
  Whilst, like the world-surrounding air, thy song
Flows on, and fills all things with melody.—
  Now is thy voice a tempest swift and strong,
    On which, like one in trance upborne,
      Secure o'er rocks and waves I sweep,
    Rejoicing like a cloud of morn:
    Now 'tis the breath of summer night,
      Which, when the starry waters sleep,
Round western isles, with incense-blossoms bright,
Lingering, suspends my soul in its voluptuous flight.

MUSIC.

I PANT for the music which is divine,
  My heart in its thirst is a dying flower;
Pour forth the sound like enchanted wine,
  Loosen the notes in a silver shower;
Like a herbless plain for the gentle rain,
I gasp, I faint, till they wake again.

Let me drink of the spirit of that sweet sound
  More, O more!—I am thirsting yet!
It loosens the serpent which care has bound
  Upon my heart, to stifle it;

The dissolving strain, through every vein,
Passes into my heart and brain.

As the scent of a violet withered up,
   Which grew by the brink of a silver lake,
When the hot noon has drained its dewy cup,
   And mist there was none its thirst to slake—
And the violet lay dead while the odour flew
On the wings of the wind o'er the waters blue:

As one who drinks from a charmèd cup
   Of foaming, and sparkling, and murmuring wine,
Whom a mighty enchantress, filling up,
   Invites to love with her kiss divine.

TO NIGHT.

SWIFTLY walk over the western wave,
      Spirit of Night!
Out of the misty eastern cave
Where, all the long and lone daylight,
Thou wovest dreams of joy and fear
Which make thee terrible and dear,—
      Swift be thy flight!

Wrap thy form in a mantle grey,
      Star-inwrought!
Blind with thine hair the eyes of day,
Kiss her until she be wearied out,
Then wander o'er city, and sea, and land
Touching all with thine opiate wand—
      Come, long-sought!

When I arose and saw the dawn,
      I sighed for thee;
When light rode high, and the dew was gone,
And noon lay heavy on flower and tree,

And the weary Day turned to her rest,
Lingering like an unloved guest,
    I sighed for thee.

Thy brother Death came, and cried,
    Wouldst thou me?
Thy sweet child Sleep, the filmy-eyed,
    Murmured like a noontide bee,
Shall I nestle near thy side?
Wouldst thou me?—And I replied,
    No, not thee.

Death will come when thou art dead,
    Soon, too soon—
Sleep will come when thou art fled;
Of neither would I ask the boon
I ask of thee, belovèd Night—
Swift be thine approaching flight,
    Come soon, soon!

THE QUESTION.

I DREAMED that, as I wandered by the way,
  Bare winter suddenly was changed to spring,
And gentle odours led my steps astray,
  Mixed with a sound of waters murmuring
Along a shelving bank of turf, which lay
  Under a copse, and hardly dared to fling
Its green arms round the bosom of the stream,
But kissed it and then fled, as thou mightest in dream.

There grew pied wind-flowers and violets,
  Daisies, those pearled Arcturi of the earth,
The constellated flower that never sets;
  Faint oxlips; tender bluebells, at whose birth
The sod scarce heaved; and that tall flower that wets,
  Like a child, half in tenderness and mirth,

Its mother's face with heaven-collected tears,
When the low wind, its playmate's voice, it hears.

And in the warm hedge grew lush eglantine,
  Green cow-bind and the moonlight-coloured may,
And cherry-blossoms, and white cups, whose wine
  Was the bright dew yet drained not by the day;
And wild roses, and ivy serpentine
  With its dark buds and leaves wandering astray;
And flowers azure, black, and streaked with gold,
Fairer than any wakened eyes behold.

And nearer to the river's trembling edge
  There grew broad flag-flowers, purple prankt with white,
And starry river-buds among the sedge,
  And floating water-lilies, broad and bright,
Which lit the oak that overhung the hedge
  With moonlight beams of their own watery light;
And bulrushes, and reeds of such deep green
As soothed the dazzled eye with sober sheen.

Methought that of these visionary flowers
  I made a nosegay, bound in such a way
That the same hues which in their natural bowers
  Were mingled or opposed, the like array
Kept these imprisoned children of the Hours
  Within my hand,—and then, elate and gay,
I hastened to the spot whence I had come,
That I might there present it—Oh! to whom?

STANZAS

WRITTEN IN DEJECTION NEAR NAPLES.

THE sun is warm, the sky is clear,
  The waves are dancing fast and bright;
Blue isles and snowy mountains wear
  The purple noon's transparent light:
  The breath of the moist earth is light

Around its unexpanded buds;
  Like many a voice of one delight
The winds', the birds', the ocean floods';
  The city's voice itself is soft like Solitude's.

  I see the Deep's untrampled floor
    With green and purple sea-weeds strown;
  I see the waves upon the shore
    Like light dissolved in star-showers thrown:
    I sit upon the sands alone;
  The lightning of the noontide ocean
    Is flashing round me, and a tone
  Arises from its measured motion,—
How sweet, did any heart now share in my emotion.

  Alas! I have nor hope nor health,
    Nor peace within nor calm around,
  Nor that content, surpassing wealth,
    The sage in meditation found,
    And walked with inward glory crowned—
  Nor fame, nor power, nor love, nor leisure.
    Others I see whom these surround—
  Smiling they live, and call life pleasure;
To me that cup has been dealt in another measure.

  Yet now despair itself is mild,
    Even as the winds and waters are;
  I could lie down like a tired child,
    And weep away the life of care
    Which I have borne and yet must bear,
  Till death like sleep might steal on me,
    And I might feel in the warm air
  My cheek grow cold, and hear the sea
Breathe o'er my dying brain its last monotony.

  Some might lament that I were cold,
    As I when this sweet day is gone,
  Which my lost heart, too soon grown old,
    Insults with this untimely moan;
    They might lament—for I am one

Whom men love not, and yet regret;
  Unlike this day, which, when the sun
Shall on its stainless glory set,
Will linger, though enjoyed, like joy in memory yet.

DELIGHT.

RARELY, rarely, comest thou,
  Spirit of Delight!
Wherefore hast thou left me now
  Many a day and night?
Many a weary night and day
'Tis since thou art fled away.

How shall ever one like me
  Win thee back again?
With the joyous and the free,
  Thou wilt scoff at pain.
Spirit false! thou hast forgot
All but those who need thee not.

As a lizard with the shade
  Of a trembling leaf,
Thou with sorrow art dismayed;
  Even the sighs of grief
Reproach thee that thou art not near,
And reproach thou wilt not hear.

Let me set my mournful ditty
  To a merry measure;—
Thou wilt never come for pity,
  Thou wilt come for pleasure;
Pity then will cut away
Those cruel wings, and thou wilt stay.

I love all that thou lovest,
  Spirit of Delight!
The fresh Earth in new leaves dressed,
  And the starry night;

Autumn evening, and the morn
When the golden mists are born.

I love snow, and all the forms
   Of the radiant frost;
I love waves, and winds, and storms,
   Everything almost
Which is Nature's, and may be
Untainted by man's misery.

I love tranquil solitude,
   And such society
As is quiet, wise, and good;
   Between thee and me
What difference? but thou dost possess
The things I seek, not love them less.

I love Love—though he has wings,
   And like light can flee,
But above all other things,
   Spirit, I love thee—
Thou art love and life! Oh come!
Make once more my heart thy home!

MISERY.

Come, be happy,—sit near me,
Shadow-vested Misery:
Coy, unwilling, silent bride,
Mourning in thy robe of pride,
Desolation deified!

Come, be happy,—sit near me:
Sad as I may seem to thee,
I am happier far than thou,
Lady, whose imperial brow
Is endiademed with woe.

MISERY.

Misery! we have known each other,
Like a sister and a brother
Living in the same lone home,
Many years—we must live some
Hours or ages yet to come.

'Tis an evil lot, and yet
Let us make the best of it;
If love can live when pleasure dies,
We two will love, till in our eyes
This heart's Hell seem Paradise.

Come, be happy,—lie thee down
On the fresh grass newly mown,
Where the grasshopper doth sing
Merrily—one joyous thing
In a world of sorrowing.

There our tent shall be the willow,
And mine arm shall be thy pillow;
Sounds and odours, sorrowful
Because they once were sweet, shall lull
Us to slumber deep and dull.

Ha! thy frozen pulses flutter
With a love thou dar'st not utter.
Thou art murmuring—thou art weeping—
Is thine icy bosom leaping,
While my burning heart lies sleeping?

Kiss me—oh! thy lips are cold!
Round my neck thine arms enfold—
They are soft, but chill and dead;
And thy tears upon my head
Burn like points of frozen lead.

Hasten to the bridal bed—
Underneath the grave 'tis spread:
In darkness may our love be hid,
Oblivion be our coverlid—
We may rest, and none forbid.

Clasp me, till our hearts be grown
Like two lovers into one;
Till this dreadful transport may
Like a vapour fade away
In the sleep that lasts alway.

We may dream in that long sleep
That we are not those who weep;
Even as Pleasure dreams of thee,
Life-deserting Misery,
Thou may'st dream of her with me.

Let us laugh and make our mirth
At the shadows of the earth;
As dogs bay the moonlight clouds
Which, like spectres wrapped in shrouds,
Pass o'er night in multitudes.

All the wide world, beside us,
Show like multitudinous
Puppets passing from a scene;
What but mockery can they mean
Where I am—where thou hast been?

LINES WRITTEN AMONG THE EUGANEAN HILLS.

MANY a green isle needs must be
In the deep wide sea of Misery,
Or the mariner, worn and wan,
Never thus could voyage on
Day and night, and night and day,
Drifting on his dreary way,
With the solid darkness black
Closing round his vessel's track;
Whilst above the sunless sky,
Big with clouds, hangs heavily,
And behind the tempest fleet
Hurries on with lightning feet,

Riving sail, and cord, and plank,
Till the ship has almost drank
Death from the o'er-brimming deep,
And sinks down, down, like that sleep
When the dreamer seems to be
Weltering through eternity;
And the dim low line before
Of a dark and distant shore
Still recedes, as ever still
Longing with divided will;
But no power to seek or shun,
He is ever drifted on
O'er the unreposing wave
To the haven of the grave.
What if there no friends will greet;
What if there no heart will meet
His with love's impatient beat;
Wander wheresoe'er he may,
Can he dream before that day
To find refuge from distress
In friendship's smile, in love's caress?
Then 'twill wreak him little woe
Whether such there be or no.
Senseless is the breast, and cold,
Which relenting love would fold;
Bloodless are the veins, and chill,
Which the pulse of pain did fill;
Every little living nerve
That from bitter words did swerve
Round the tortured lips and brow,
Is like a sapless leaflet now
Frozen upon December's bough.

On the beach of a northern sea
Which tempests shake eternally
As once the wretch there lay to sleep,
Lies a solitary heap,

One white skull and seven dry bones,
On the margin of the stones,
Where a few grey rushes stand,
Boundaries of the sea and land.
Nor is heard one voice of wail
But the sea-mews' as they sail
O'er the billows of the gale,
Or the whirlwind up and down
Howling, like a slaughtered town,
When a king in glory rides
Through the pomp of fratricides:
Those unburied bones around
There is many a mournful sound;
There is no lament for him,
Like a sunless vapour, dim,
Who once clothed with life and thought
What now moves nor murmurs not.

Ay, many flowering islands lie
In the waters of wide Agony:
To such a one this morn was led
My bark, by soft winds piloted.
'Mid the mountains Euganean,
I stood listening to the pæan
With which the legioned rooks did hail
The sun's uprise majestical;
Gathering round with wings all hoar,
Through the dewy mist they soar
Like grey shades, till the eastern heaven
Bursts, and then, as clouds of even
Flecked with fire and azure lie
In the unfathomable sky,
So their plumes of purple grain,
Starred with drops of golden rain,
Gleam above the sunlight woods,
As in silent multitudes
On the morning's fitful gale

Through the broken mist they sail,
And the vapours cloven and gleaming
Follow, down the dark steep streaming,
Till all is bright, and clear, and still,
Round the solitary hill.

Beneath is spread like a green sea
The waveless plain of Lombardy,
Bounded by the vaporous air,
Islanded by cities fair;
Underneath day's azure eyes,
Ocean's nursling, Venice lies,—
A peopled labyrinth of walls,
Amphitrite's destined halls,
Which her hoary sire now paves
With his blue and beaming waves.
Lo! the sun upsprings behind,
Broad, red, radiant, half-reclined
On the level quivering line
Of the waters crystalline;
And before that chasm of light,
As within a furnace bright,
Column, tower, and dome, and spire,
Shine like obelisks of fire,
Pointing with inconstant motion
From the altar of dark ocean
To the sapphire-tinted skies;
As the flames of sacrifice
From the marble shrines did rise,
As to pierce the dome of gold
Where Apollo spoke of old.

Sun-girt City! thou hast been
Ocean's child, and then his queen;
Now is come a darker day,
And thou soon must be his prey,
If the power that raised thee here
Hallow so thy watery bier.

A less drear ruin then than now,
With thy conquest-branded brow
Stooping to the slave of slaves
From thy throne among the waves
Wilt thou be when the sea-mew
Flies, as once before it flew,
O'er thine isles depopulate,
And all is in its ancient state,
Save where many a palace-gate
With green sea-flowers overgrown
Like a rock of ocean's own,
Topples o'er the abandoned sea
As the tides change sullenly.
The fisher on his watery way
Wandering at the close of day
Will spread his sail and seize his oar
Till he pass the gloomy shore,
Lest thy dead should, from their sleep
Bursting o'er the starlight deep,
Lead a rapid masque of death
O'er the waters of his path.

Those who alone thy towers behold
Quivering through aërial gold,
As I now behold them here,
Would imagine not they were
Sepulchres where human forms,
Like pollution-nourished worms,
To the corpse of greatness cling,
Murdered and now mouldering:
But, if Freedom should awake
In her omnipotence, and shake
From the Celtic Anarch's hold
All the keys of dungeons cold
Where a hundred cities lie
Chained like thee ingloriously,
Thou and all thy sister band

Might adorn this sunny land,
Twining memories of old time
With new virtues more sublime.
If not, perish thou and they;
Clouds which stain truth's rising day,
By her sun consumed away;
Earth can spare ye; while, like flowers,
In the waste of years and hours,
From your dust new nations spring
With more kindly blossoming.

Perish! Let there only be,
Floating o'er thy hearthless sea,
As the garment of thy sky
Clothes the world immortally,
One remembrance, more sublime
Than the tattered pall of Time
Which scarce hides thy visage wan:
That a tempest-cleaving swan
Of the songs of Albion,
Driven from his ancestral streams
By the might of evil dreams,
Found a nest in thee; and Ocean
Welcomed him with such emotion
That its joy grew his, and sprung
From his lips like music flung
O'er a mighty thunder-fit,
Chastening terror: what though yet
Poesy's unfailing river,
Which through Albion winds for ever,
Lashing with melodious wave
Many a sacred poet's grave,
Mourn its latest nursling fled!
What though thou with all thy dead
Scarce canst for this fame repay
Aught thine own,—oh! rather say,
Though thy sins and slaveries foul

Overcloud a sunlike soul!
As the ghost of Homer clings
Round Scamander's wasting springs;
As divinest Shakspeare's might
Fills Avon and the world with light,
Like Omniscient Power, which he
Imaged 'mid mortality;
As the love from Petrarch's urn
Yet amid yon hills doth burn,
A quenchless lamp by which the heart
Sees things unearthly;—so thou art,
Mighty spirit! so shall be
The city that did refuge thee!

Lo, the sun floats up the sky,
Like thought-wingèd Liberty,
Till the universal light
Seems to level plain and height.
From the sea a mist has spread,
And the beams of morn lie dead
On the towers of Venice now,
Like its glory long ago.
By the skirts of that grey cloud
Many-domèd Padua proud
Stands, a peopled solitude
'Mid the harvest-shining plain,
Where the peasant heaps his grain
In the garner of his foe,
And the milk-white oxen slow
With the purple vintage strain
Heaped upon the creaking wain,
That the brutal Celt may swill
Drunken sleep with savage will;
And the sickle to the sword
Lies unchanged, though many a lord,
Like a weed whose shade is poison,
Overgrows this region's foison,

Sheaves of whom are ripe to come
To destruction's harvest-home:
Men must reap the things they sow,
Force from force must ever flow,
Or worse; but 'tis a bitter woe
That love or reason cannot change
The despot's rage, the slave's revenge.

Padua! thou within whose walls
Those mute guests at festivals,
Son and Mother, Death and Sin,
Played at dice for Ezzelin,
Till Death cried, "I win, I win!"
And Sin cursed to lose the wager,
But Death promised, to assuage her,
That he would petition for
Her to be made Vice-Emperor,
When the destined years were o'er,
Over all between the Po
And the eastern Alpine snow,
Under the mighty Austrian:—
Sin smiled so as Sin only can;
And, since that time, ay long before,
Both have ruled from shore to shore,—
That incestuous pair who follow
Tyrants as the sun the swallow,
As repentance follows crime,
And as changes follow time.

In thine halls the lamp of learning,
Padua, now no more is burning;
Like a meteor whose wild way
Is lost over the grave of day,
It gleams betrayed and to betray;
Once remotest nations came
To adore that sacred flame,
When it lit not many a hearth
On this cold and gloomy earth;

Now new fires from antique light
Spring beneath the wide world's might;
But their spark lies dead in thee,
Trampled out by Tyranny.
As the Norway woodman quells,
In the depth of piny dells,
One light flame among the brakes,
While the boundless forest shakes,
And its mighty trunks are torn
By the fire thus lowly born;
The spark beneath his feet is dead,
He starts to see the flames it fed
Howling through the darkened sky
With myriad tongues victoriously,
And sinks down in fear: so thou,
O Tyranny! beholdest now
Light around thee, and thou hearest
The loud flames ascend, and fearest.
Grovel on the earth! ay, hide
In the dust thy purple pride!

Noon descends around me now:
'Tis the noon of autumn's glow,
When a soft and purple mist
Like a vaporous amethyst,
Or an air-dissolvèd star
Mingling light and fragrance, far
From the curved horizon's bound
To the point of heaven's profound,
Fills the overflowing sky;
And the plains that silent lie
Underneath; the leaves unsodden
Where the infant frost has trodden
With his morning-wingèd feet
Whose bright print is gleaming yet;
And the red and golden vines
Piercing with their trellised lines

The rough dark-skirted wilderness;
The dun and bladed grass no less,
Pointing from this hoary tower
In the windless air; the flower
Glimmering at my feet; the line
Of the olive-sandalled Apennine
In the south dimly islanded;
And the Alps, whose snows are spread
High between the clouds and sun;
And of living things each one;
And my spirit, which so long
Darkened this swift stream of song,—
Interpenetrated lie
By the glory of the sky;
Be it love, light, harmony,
Odour, or the soul of all
Which from heaven like dew doth fall
Or the mind which feeds this verse
Peopling the lone universe.

Noon descends, and after noon
Autumn's evening meets me soon,
Leading the infantine moon,
And that one star, which to her
Almost seems to minister
Half the crimson light she brings
From the sunset's radiant springs:
And the soft dreams of the morn
(Which like wingèd winds had borne,
To that silent isle, which lies
'Mid remembered agonies,
The frail bark of this lone being),
Pass, to other sufferers fleeing,
And its ancient pilot, Pain,
Sits beside the helm again.

Other flowering isles must be
In the sea of Life and Agony:

Other spirits float and flee
O'er that gulf: even now perhaps
On some rock the wild wave wraps,
With folded wings, they waiting sit
For my bark, to pilot it
To some calm and blooming cove,
Where for me, and those I love,
May a windless bower be built,
Far from passion, pain, and guilt,
In a dell 'mid lawny hills
Which the wild sea-murmur fills,
And soft sunshine, and the sound
Of old forests echoing round,
And the light and smell divine
Of all flowers that breathe and shine.
We may live so happy there
That the spirits of the air,
Envying us, may even entice
To our healing paradise
The polluting multitude;
But their rage would be subdued
By that clime divine and calm,
And the winds whose wings rain balm
On the uplifted soul, and leaves
Under which the bright sea heaves;
While each breathless interval
In their whisperings musical
The inspired soul supplies
With its own deep melodies,
And the love which heals all strife
Circling, like the breath of life,
All things in that sweet abode
With its own mild brotherhood.
They, not it, would change; and soon
Every sprite beneath the moon
Would repent its envy vain,
And the Earth grow young again.

October 1818.

LETTER TO MARIA GISBORNE.
LEGHORN, *July* 1, 1820.

THE spider spreads her webs, whether she be
In poet's tower, cellar, or barn, or tree;
The silkworm in the dark-green mulberry leaves
His winding-sheet and cradle ever weaves:
So I, a thing whom moralists call worm,
Sit spinning still round this decaying form,
From the fine threads of rare and subtle thought—
No net of words in garish colours wrought
To catch the idle buzzers of the day—
But a soft cell where, when that fades away,
Memory may clothe in wings my living name,
And feed it with the asphodels of fame
Which in those hearts which must remember me
Grow, making love an immortality.

Whoever should behold me now, I wist,
Would think I were a mighty mechanist,
Bent with sublime Archimedean art
To breathe a soul into the iron heart
Of some machine portentous, or strange gin,
Which by the force of figured spells might win
Its way over the sea, and sport therein;—
For round the walls are hung dread engines, such
As Vulcan never wrought for Jove to clutch
Ixion or the Titan; or the quick
Wit of that man of God, Saint Dominic,
To convince atheist, Turk, or heretic;
Or those in philanthropic councils met
Who thought to pay some interest for the debt
They owed to Jesus Christ for their salvation
By giving a faint foretaste of damnation
To Shakspeare, Sydney, Spenser, and the rest
Who made our land an island of the blessed,
(When lamp-like Spain, who now relumes her fire
On Freedom's hearth, grew dim with empire),—

With thumbscrews, wheels with tooth and spike and jag,
Which fishers found under the utmost crag
Of Cornwall, and the storm-encompassed isles
Where to the sky the rude sea seldom smiles
Unless in treacherous wrath, as on the morn
When the exulting elements in scorn,
Satiated with destroyed destruction, lay
Sleeping in beauty on their mangled prey,
As panthers sleep. And other strange and dread
Magical forms the brick floor overspread.
Proteus transformed to metal did not make
More figures, or more strange; nor did he take
Such shapes of unintelligible brass
Or heap himself in such a horrid mass
Of tin and iron not to be understood,
And forms of unimaginable wood,
To puzzle Tubal Cain and all his brood:
Great screws, and cones, and wheels, and groovèd blocks,
The elements of what will stand the shocks
Of wave and wind and time.—Upon the table
More knacks and quips there be than I am able
To catalogize in this verse of mine:
A pretty bowl of wood—not full of wine,
But quicksilver; that dew which the gnomes drink
When at their subterranean toil they swink,
Pledging the demons of the earthquake, who
Reply to them in lava, cry "halloo!"—
And call out to the cities o'er their head.
Roofs, towns, and shrines, the dying and the dead,
Crash through the chinks of earth: and then all quaff
Another rouse, and hold their sides and laugh.
This quicksilver no gnome has drunk: within
The walnut bowl it lies, veinèd and thin,
In colour like the wake of light that stains
The Tuscan deep when from the moist moon rains
The inmost shower of its white fire—the breeze
Is still—blue heaven smiles over the pale seas.

And in this bowl of quicksilver—for I
Yield to the impulse of an infancy
Outlasting manhood—I have made to float
A rude idealism of a paper boat,
A hollow screw with cogs: Henry will know
The thing I mean, and laugh at me. If so,
He fears not I should do more mischief.—Next
Lie bills and calculations much perplexed
With steam-boats, frigates, and machinery quaint,
Traced over them in blue and yellow paint.
Then comes a range of mathematical
Instruments, for plans nautical and statical;
A heap of rosin; a queer broken glass
With ink in it; a china cup that was
(What it will never be again, I think)
A thing from which sweet lips were wont to drink
The liquor doctors rail at—and which I
Will quaff in spite of them; and, when we die,
We'll toss up who died first of drinking tea,
And cry out "heads or tails!" where'er we be.
Near that, a dusty paint-box, some old hooks,
A half-burnt match, an ivory block, three books,
Where conic sections, spherics, logarithms,
To great Laplace from Saunderson and Sims,
Lie heaped in their harmonious disarray
Of figures,—disentangle them who may.
Baron de Tott's Memoirs beside them lie,
And some odd volumes of old chemistry.
Near them a most inexplicable thing,
With lead in the middle—I'm conjecturing
How to make Henry understand; but no!
I'll leave, as Spenser says "with many mo,"
This secret in the pregnant womb of Time,
Too vast a matter for so weak a rhyme.

And here like some weird archimage sit I,
Plotting dark spells and devilish enginery,—

The self-impelling steam-wheels of the mind,
Which pump up oaths from clergymen, and grind
The gentle spirit of our meek Reviews
Into a powdery foam of salt abuse,
Ruffling the ocean of their self-content.
I sit, and smile,—or sigh, as is my bent,
But not for them. Libeccio rushes round
With an inconstant and an idle sound;
I heed him more than them. The thunder-smoke
Is gathering on the mountains, like a cloak
Folded athwart their shoulders broad and bare;
The ripe corn under the undulating air
Undulates like an ocean; and the vines
Are trembling wide in all their trellised lines;
The murmur of the awakening sea doth fill
The empty pauses of the blast; the hill
Looks hoary through the white electric rain;
And from the glens beyond, in sullen strain,
The interrupted thunder howls; above
One chasm of heaven smiles, like the eye of Love
On the unquiet world;—while such things are,
How could one worth your friendship heed the war
Of worms,—the shriek of the world's carrion jays,
Their censure or their wonder or their praise?

You are not here! The quaint witch Memory sees
In vacant chairs your absent images,
And points where once you sat, and now should be,
But are not.—I demand if ever we
Shall meet as then we met;—and she replies,
Veiling in awe her second-sighted eyes,
"I know the past alone: but summon home
My sister Hope—she speaks of all to come."
But I, an old diviner who knew well
Every false verse of that sweet oracle,
Turned to the sad enchantress once again,
And sought a respite from my gentle pain

In citing every passage o'er and o'er
Of our communion:—How on the sea shore
We watched the ocean and the sky together,
Under the roof of blue Italian weather;
How I ran home through last year's thunder-storm,
And felt the transverse lightning linger warm
Upon my cheek; and how we often made
Treats for each other where good-will outweighed
The frugal luxury of our country cheer,
As it well might, were it less firm and clear
Than ours must ever be. And how we spun
A shroud of talk to hide us from the sun
Of this familiar life, which seems to be
But is not,—or is but quaint mockery
Of all we would believe; or sadly blame
The jarring and inexplicable frame
Of this wrong world, and then anatomize
The purposes and thoughts of men whose eyes
Were closed in distant years; or widely guess
The issue of the earth's great business,
When we shall be as we no longer are
Like babbling gossips safe, who hear the war
Of winds, and sigh, but tremble not; or how
You listened to some interrupted flow
Of visionary rhyme, in joy and pain
Struck from the inmost fountains of my brain,
With little skill perhaps; or how we sought
Those deepest wells of passion or of thought
Wrought by wise poets in the waste of years,
Staining the sacred waters with our tears,
Quenching a thirst ever to be renewed;
Or how I, wisest lady! then indued
The language of a land which now is free,
And, winged with thoughts of truth and majesty,
Flits round the tyrant's sceptre like a cloud,
And bursts the peopled prisons, and cries aloud
"My name is Legion!"—that majestic tongue

Which Calderon over the desert flung
Of ages and of nations, and which found
An echo in our hearts, and with the sound
Startled Oblivion. Thou wert then to me
As is a nurse when inarticulately
A child would talk as its grown parents do.
If living winds the rapid clouds pursue,
If hawks chase doves through the aërial way,
Huntsmen the innocent deer, and beasts their prey,
Why should not we rouse with the spirit's blast
Out of the forest of the pathless past
These recollected pleasures?

       You are now
In London; that great sea whose ebb and flow
At once is deaf and loud, and on the shore
Vomits its wrecks, and still howls on for more.
Yet in its depth what treasures! You will see
That which was Godwin,—greater none than he;
Though fallen, and fallen on evil times, to stand,
Among the spirits of our age and land,
Before the dread tribunal of To-come
The foremost, whilst Rebuke cowers pale and dumb.
You will see Coleridge; he who sits obscure
In the exceeding lustre and the pure
Intense irradiation of a mind
Which, with its own internal lightning blind,
Flags wearily through darkness and despair—
A cloud-encircled meteor of the air,
A hooded eagle among blinking owls.
You will see Hunt; one of those happy souls
Which are the salt of the earth, and without whom
This world would smell like what it is—a tomb;
Who is what others seem. His room no doubt
Is still adorned by many a cast from Shout;
With graceful flowers tastefully placed about,
And coronals of bay from ribbons hung,

And brighter wreaths in neat disorder flung,
The gifts of the most learned among some dozens
Of female friends, sisters-in-law, and cousins.
And there is he with his eternal puns,
Which beat the dullest brain for smiles, like duns
Thundering for money at a poet's door;
Alas! it is no use to say "I'm poor!"—
Or oft in graver mood, when he will look
Things wiser than were ever read in book,
Except in Shakspeare's wisest tenderness.
You will see Hogg; and I cannot express
His virtues (though I know that they are great),
Because he locks, then barricades, the gate
Within which they inhabit. Of his wit
And wisdom, you'll cry out when you are bit.
He is a pearl within an oyster-shell,
One of the richest of the deep. And there
Is English Peacock, with his mountain fair,—
Turned into a Flamingo, that shy bird
That gleams i' the Indian air. Have you not heard,
When a man marries, dies, or turns Hindoo,
His best friends hear no more of him? But you
Will see him, and will like him too, I hope,
With the milk-white Snowdonian antelope
Matched with this camelopard. His fine wit
Makes such a wound the knife is lost in it;
A strain too learned for a shallow age,
Too wise for selfish bigots;—let his page,
Which charms the chosen spirits of the time
Fold itself up for a serener clime
Of years to come, and find its recompense
In that just expectation. Wit and sense,
Virtue and human knowledge, all that might
Make this dull world a business of delight,
Are all combined in Horace Smith.—And these
(With some exceptions, which I need not teaze

Your patience by descanting on) are all
You and I know in London.

                    I recall
My thoughts, and bid you look upon the night.
As water does a sponge, so the moonlight
Fills the void, hollow, universal air.
What see you?—Unpavilioned heaven is fair;
Whether the moon, into her chamber gone,
Leaves midnight to the golden stars, or wan
Climbs with diminished beams the azure steep;
Or whether clouds sail o'er the inverse deep,
Piloted by the many-wandering blast,
And the rare stars rush through them, dim and fast.
All this is beautiful in every land.
But what see *you* beside? A shabby stand
Of hackney-coaches—a brick house or wall
Fencing some lonely court, white with the scrawl
Of our unhappy politics;—or worse—
A wretched woman reeling by, whose curse,
Mixed with the watchman's, partner of her trade,
You must accept in place of serenade,
Or yellow-haired Pollonia murmuring
To Henry some unutterable thing.

I see a chaos of green leaves and fruit
Built round dark caverns, even to the root
Of the living stems who feed them, in whose bowers
There sleep in their dark dew the folded flowers.
Beyond, the surface of the unsickled corn
Trembles not in the slumbering air; and, borne
In circles quaint and ever-changing dance,
Like wingèd stars the fireflies flash and glance,
Pale in the open moonshine, but each one
Under the dark trees seems a little sun,
A meteor tamed, a fixed star gone astray
From the silver regions of the milky way.
Afar the contadino's song is heard,

Rude but made sweet by distance, and a bird
Which cannot be a nightingale, and yet
I know none else that sings so sweet as it
At this late hour:—and then all is still.
Now, Italy or London, which you will!

Next winter you must pass with me. I'll have
My house by that time turned into a grave
Of dead despondence and low-thoughted care,
And all the dreams which our tormentors are.
Oh, that Hunt, Hogg, Peacock, and Smith, were there,
With everything belonging to them fair!
We will have books, Spanish, Italian, Greek;
And ask one week to make another week
As like his father as I'm unlike mine.
Though we eat little flesh and drink no wine,
Yet let's be merry. We'll have tea and toast;
Custards for supper; and an endless host
Of syllabubs and jellies and mince-pies,
And other such lady-like luxuries,—
Feasting on which we will philosophize.
And we'll have fires out of the Grand-Duke's wood,
To thaw the six weeks' winter in our blood.
And then we'll talk;—what shall we talk about?
Oh! there are themes enough for many a bout
Of thought-entangled descant! As to nerves—
With cones and parallelograms and curves
I've sworn to strangle them if once they dare
To bother me, when you are with me there;
And they shall never more sip laudanum
From Helicon or Himeros. Well, come,
And in despite of * * * and of the devil
We'll make our friendly philosophic revel
Outlast the leafless time; till buds and flowers
Warn the obscure inevitable hours
Sweet meeting by sad parting to renew:—
"To-morrow to fresh woods and pastures new."

TO ——

I.

THE serpent is shut out from paradise:
 The wounded deer must seek the herb no more
  In which its heart-cure lies:
 The widowed dove must cease to haunt a bower
Like that from which its mate with feignèd sighs
  Fled in the April hour.
 I too must seldom seek again
Near happy friends a mitigated pain.

II.

Of hatred I am proud,—with scorn content;
 Indifference, which once hurt me, is now grown
  Itself indifferent.
 But, not to speak of love, pity alone
Can break a spirit already more than bent.
  The miserable one
 Turns the mind's poison into food,—
Its medicine is tears,—its evil good.

III.

Therefore, if now I see you seldomer,
 Dear friends, dear *friend!* know that I only fly
  Your looks because they stir
 Griefs that should sleep, and hopes that cannot die
The very comfort that they minister
  I scarce can bear; yet I,
 So deeply is the arrow gone,
Should quickly perish if it were withdrawn.

IV.

When I return to my cold home, you ask
 Why I am not as I have lately been?
  You spoil me for the task
 Of acting a forced part in life's dull scene,—

Of wearing on my brow the idle mask
    Of author, great or mean,
        In the world's carnival. I sought
Peace thus, and but in you I found it not.

v.

Full half an hour, to-day, I tried my lot
    With various flowers, and every one still said,
        "She loves me,—loves me not."
And if this meant a vision long since fled—
If it meant fortune, fame, or peace of thought—
        If it meant—(but I dread
    To speak what you may know too well)—
Still there was truth in the sad oracle.

vi.

The crane o'er seas and forests seeks her home;
    No bird so wild but has its quiet nest
        When it no more would roam;
    The sleepless billows on the ocean's breast
Break like a bursting heart, and die in foam,
        And thus at length find rest:
    Doubtless there is a place of peace
Where *my* weak heart and all its throbs will cease.

vii.

I asked her yesterday if she believed
    That I had resolution. One who *had*
        Would ne'er have thus relieved
    His heart with words,—but what his judgment bade
Would do, and leave the scorner unrelieved.—
        These verses were too sad
    To send to you, but that I know,
Happy yourself, you feel another's woe.

THE AZIOLA.

"Do you not hear the Aziola cry?
  Methinks she must be nigh,"
    Said Mary, as we sate
In dusk, ere the stars were lit or candles brought.
    And I, who thought
  This Aziola was some tedious woman,
    Asked "Who is Aziola?" How elate
  I felt to know that it was nothing human,
    No mockery of myself to fear and hate!
      And Mary saw my soul,
And laughed and said, "Disquiet yourself not;
'Tis nothing but a little downy owl."

Sad Aziola! many an eventide
    Thy music I had heard
By wood and stream, meadow and mountain-side,
      And fields and marshes wide,—
Such as nor voice nor lute nor wind nor bird
      The soul ever stirred;
Unlike and far sweeter than they all.
Sad Aziola! from that moment I
      Loved thee and thy sad cry.

LINES TO A CRITIC.

Honey from silkworms who can gather,
  Or silk from the yellow bee?
The grass may grow in winter weather
  As soon as hate in me.

Hate men who cant, and men who pray,
  And men who rail, like thee;
An equal passion to repay
  They are not coy like me.

Or seek some slave of power and gold
  To be thy dear heart's mate;
Thy love will move that bigot cold
  Sooner than me thy hate.

A passion like the one I prove
  Cannot divided be;
I hate thy want of truth and love—
  How should I then hate thee?

December 1817.

AN EXHORTATION.

Chameleons feed on light and air;
  Poets' food is love and fame:
If in this wide world of care
  Poets could but find the same
With as little toil as they,
  Would they ever change their hue
  As the light chameleons do,
Suiting it to every ray
    Twenty times a-day?

Poets are on this cold earth
  As chameleons might be
Hidden from their early birth
  In a cave beneath the sea.
Where light is, chameleons change;
  Where love is not, poets do.
  Fame is love disguised: if few
Find either, never think it strange
    That poets range.

Yet dare not stain with wealth or power
  A poet's free and heavenly mind.
If bright chameleons should devour
  Any food but beams and wind,

They would grow as earthly soon
   As their brother lizards are.
Children of a sunnier star,
Spirits from beyond the moon,
   Oh! refuse the boon!

TO ——.

I FEAR thy kisses, gentle maiden;
   Thou needest not fear mine,—
My spirit is too deeply laden
   Ever to burthen thine.

I fear thy mien, thy tones, thy motion;
   Thou needest not fear mine,—
Innocent is the heart's devotion
   With which I worship thine

THE SENSITIVE PLANT.

PART I.

A SENSITIVE Plant in a garden grew,
And the young winds fed it with silver dew,
And it opened its fan-like leaves to the light,
And closed them beneath the kisses of night.

And the Spring arose on the garden fair,
Like the Spirit of Love felt everywhere;
And each flower and herb on earth's dark breast
Rose from the dreams of its wintry rest.

But none ever trembled and panted with bliss
In the garden, the field, or the wilderness,
Like a doe in the noontide with love's sweet want,
As the companionless Sensitive Plant.

The snowdrop, and then the violet,
Arose from the ground with warm rain wet;
And their breath was mixed with fresh odour sent
From the turf, like the voice and the instrument.

Then the pied wind-flowers and the tulip tall,
And narcissi, the fairest among them all,
Who gaze on their eyes in the stream's recess
Till they die of their own dear loveliness;

And the Naiad-like lily of the vale,
Whom youth makes so fair, and passion so pale,
That the light of its tremulous bells is seen
Through their pavilions of tender green;

And the hyacinth, purple, and white, and blue,
Which flung from its bells a sweet peal anew
Of music so delicate, soft, and intense,
It was felt like an odour within the sense;

And the rose, like a nymph to the bath addressed,
Which unveiled the depth of her glowing breast,
Till, fold after fold, to the fainting air
The soul of her beauty and love lay bare;

And the wand-like lily, which lifted up,
As a Mænad, its moonlight-coloured cup,
Till the fiery star which is its eye
Gazed through clear dew on the tender sky;

And the jessamine faint, and the sweet tuberose—
The sweetest flower for scent that blows—
And all rare blossoms from every clime,
Grew in that garden in perfect prime.

And on the stream whose inconstant bosom
Was pranked under boughs of embowering blossom,
With golden and green light slanting through
Their heaven of many a tangled hue,

Broad water-lilies lay tremulously,
And starry river-buds glimmered by;
And around them the soft stream did glide and dance
With a motion of sweet sound and radiance.

And the sinuous paths of lawn and of moss
Which led through the garden along and across,
Some open at once to the sun and the breeze,
Some lost among bowers of blossoming trees,

Were all paved with daisies and delicate bells
As fair as the fabulous asphodels,
And flowerets which, drooping as day drooped too,
Fell into pavilions, white, purple, and blue,
To roof the glow-worm from the evening dew.

And from this undefiled paradise
The flowers (as an infant's awakening eyes
Smile on its mother, whose singing sweet
Can first lull and at last must awaken it),

When heaven's blithe winds had unfolded them
As mine-lamps enkindle a hidden gem,
Shone smiling to heaven, and every one
Shared joy in the light of the gentle sun;—

For each one was interpenetrated
With the light and the odour its neighbour shed,
Like young lovers whom youth and love make dear,
Wrapped and filled by their mutual atmosphere.

But the Sensitive Plant, which could give small fruit
Of the love which it felt from the leaf to the root,
Received more than all; it loved more than ever,
Where none wanted but it, could belong to the giver:—

For the Sensitive Plant has no bright flower;
Radiance and odour are not its dower;
It loves even like Love,—its deep heart is full;
It desires what it has not, the beautiful.

The light winds which from unsustaining wings
Shed the music of many murmurings;
The beams which dart from many a star
Of the flowers whose hues they bear afar;

The plumèd insects swift and free,
Like golden boats on a sunny sea,
Laden with light and odour, which pass
Over the gleam of the living grass;

The unseen clouds of the dew which lie
Like fire in the flowers till the sun rides high,
Then wander like spirits among the spheres,
Each cloud faint with the fragrance it bears;

The quivering vapours of dim noontide,
Which like a sea o'er the warm earth glide,
In which every sound and odour and beam
Move as reeds in a single stream;—

Each and all like ministering angels were
For the Sensitive Plant sweet joy to bear,
Whilst the lagging hours of the day went by,
Like windless clouds o'er a tender sky.

And, when evening descended from heaven above,
And the earth was all rest, and the air was all love,
And delight, though less bright, was far more deep,
And the day's veil fell from the world of sleep,

And the beasts and the birds and the insects were drowned
In an ocean of dreams without a sound,
Whose waves never mark though they ever impress
The light sand which paves it, consciousness;

(Only overhead the sweet nightingale
Ever sang more sweet as the day might fail,
And snatches of its elysian chant
Were mixed with the dream of the Sensitive Plant);

The Sensitive Plant was the earliest
Upgathered into the bosom of rest;
A sweet child weary of its delight,
The feeblest and yet the favourite,
Cradled within the embrace of night.

PART II.

THERE was a power in this sweet place,
An Eve in this Eden; a ruling grace
Which to the flowers, did they waken or dream,
Was as God is to the starry scheme.

A Lady, the wonder of her kind,
Whose form was upborne by a lovely mind,
Which, dilating, had moulded her mien and motion
Like a sea-flower unfolded beneath the ocean,

Tended the garden from morn to even:
And the meteors of that sublunar heaven,
Like the lamps of the air when night walks forth,
Laughed round her footsteps up from the earth.

She had no companion of mortal race;
But her tremulous breath and her flushing face
Told, whilst the morn kissed the sleep from her eyes,
That her dreams were less slumber than paradise:

As if some bright Spirit for her sweet sake
Had deserted heaven while the stars were awake,
As if yet around her he lingering were,
Though the veil of daylight concealed him from her.

Her step seemed to pity the grass it pressed:
You might hear, by the heaving of her breast,
That the coming and going of the wind
Brought pleasure there, and left passion behind.

And, wherever her airy footstep trod,
Her trailing hair from the grassy sod
Erased its light vestige with shadowy sweep,
Like a sunny storm o'er the dark-green deep.

I doubt not the flowers of that garden sweet
Rejoiced in the sound of her gentle feet;
I doubt not they felt the spirit that came
From her glowing fingers through all their frame.

She sprinkled bright water from the stream
On those that were faint with the sunny beam;
And out of the cups of the heavy flowers
She emptied the rain of the thunder-showers.

She lifted their heads with her tender hands,
And sustained them with rods and osier bands;
If the flowers had been her own infants, she
Could never have nursed them more tenderly.

And all killing insects and gnawing worms,
And things of obscene and unlovely forms,
She bore in a basket of Indian woof
Into the rough woods far aloof;

In a basket of grasses and wild flowers full,
The freshest her gentle hands could pull
For the poor banished insects, whose intent,
Although they did ill, was innocent.

But the bee, and the beamlike ephemeris
Whose path is the lightning's, and soft moths that kiss
The sweet lips of the flowers, and harm not, did she
Make her attendant angels be.

And many an antenatal tomb
Where butterflies dream of the life to come
She left clinging round the smooth and dark
Edge of the odorous cedar bark.

This fairest creature from earliest Spring
Thus moved through the garden ministering
All the sweet season of summer tide:
And, ere the first leaf looked brown—she died.

PART III.

Three days the flowers of the garden fair
Like stars when the moon is awakened were,
Or the waves of Baiæ ere luminous
She floats up through the smoke of Vesuvius.

And on the fourth the Sensitive Plant
Felt the sound of the funeral chant;
And the steps of the bearers, heavy and slow;
And the sobs of the mourners, deep and low;

The weary sound and the heavy breath;
And the silent motions of passing death;
And the smell, cold, oppressive and dank,
Sent through the pores of the coffin plank.

The dark grass, and the flowers among the grass,
Were bright with tears as the crowd did pass;
From their sighs the wind caught a mournful tone,
And sate in the pines, and gave groan for groan.

The garden, once fair, became cold and foul,
Like the corpse of her who had been its soul:
Which at first was lovely as if in sleep,
Then slowly changed, till it grew a heap
To make men tremble who never weep.

Swift summer into the autumn flowed,
And frost in the mist of the morning rode,
Though the noonday sun looked clear and bright,
Mocking the spoil of the secret night.

The rose-leaves, like flakes of crimson snow,
Paved the turf and the moss below:
The lilies were drooping and white and wan,
Like the head and the skin of a dying man;

And Indian plants, of scent and hue
The sweetest that ever were fed on dew,
Leaf after leaf, day after day,
Were massed into the common clay.

And the leaves, brown, yellow, and grey, and red,
And white with the whiteness of what is dead,
Like troops of ghosts on the dry wind passed:
Their whistling noise made the birds aghast.

And the gusty winds waked the wingèd seeds
Out of their birthplace of ugly weeds,
Till they clung round many a sweet flower's stem,
Which rotted into the earth with them.

The water-blooms under the rivulet
Fell from the stalks on which they were set;
And the eddies drove them here and there,
As the winds did those of the upper air.

Then the rain came down; and the broken stalks
Were bent and tangled across the walks;
And the leafless network of parasite bowers
Massed into ruin, and all sweet flowers.

Between the time of the wind and the snow,
All loathliest weeds began to grow,
Whose coarse leaves were splashed with many a speck,
Like the water-snake's belly and the toad's back;

And thistles, and nettles, and darnels rank,
And the dock, and henbane; and hemlock dank
Stretched out its long and hollow shank,
And stifled the air till the dead wind stank.

And plants at whose names the verse feels loth
Filled the place with a monstrous undergrowth,
Prickly and pulpous and blistering and blue,
Livid, and starred with a lurid dew.

And agarics and fungi, with mildew and mould,
Started like mist from the wet ground cold;
Pale, fleshy, as if the decaying dead
With a spirit of growth had been animated.

Their moss rotted off them flake by flake,
Till the thick stalk stuck like a murderer's stake,
Where rags of loose flesh yet tremble on high,
Infecting the winds that wander by.

Spawn, weeds, and filth, a leprous scum,
Made the running rivulet thick and dumb,
And at its outlet flags huge as stakes
Dammed it up with roots knotted like water-snakes.

And hour by hour, when the air was still,
The vapours arose which have strength to kill:
At morn they were seen, at noon they were felt,
At night they were darkness no star could melt.

And unctuous meteors from spray to spray
Crept and flitted in broad noonday
Unseen; every branch on which they alit
By a venomous blight was burned and bit.

The Sensitive Plant, like one forbid,
Wept, and the tears within each lid
Of its folded leaves which together grew,
Were changed to a blight of frozen glue.

For the leaves soon fell, and the branches soon
By the heavy axe of the blast were hewn;
The sap shrank to the root through every pore,
As blood to a heart that will beat no more.

For Winter came: the wind was his whip;
One choppy finger was on his lip:
He had torn the cataracts from the hills,
And they clanked at his girdle like manacles.

His breath was a chain which without a sound
The earth and the air and the water bound;
He came, fiercely driven in his chariot-throne
By the tenfold blasts of the Arctic zone.

Then the weeds, which were forms of living death,
Fled from the frost to the earth beneath:
Their decay and sudden flight from frost
Was but like the vanishing of a ghost.

And under the roots of the Sensitive Plant
The moles and the dormice died for want:
The birds dropped stiff from the frozen air,
And were caught in the branches naked and bare.

First there came down a thawing rain,
And its dull drops froze on the boughs again;
Then there steamed up a freezing dew
Which to the drops of the thaw-rain grew;

And a northern whirlwind, wandering about
Like a wolf that had smelt a dead child out,
Shook the boughs, thus laden and heavy and stiff,
And snapped them off with his rigid griff.

When Winter had gone, and Spring came back,
The Sensitive Plant was a leafless wreck;
But the mandrakes and toadstools and docks and darnels
Rose like the dead from their ruined charnels.

CONCLUSION.

WHETHER the Sensitive Plant, or that
Which within its boughs like a spirit sat
Ere its outward form had known decay,
Now felt this change, I cannot say.

Whether that Lady's gentle mind,
No longer with the form combined
Which scattered love, as stars do light,
Found sadness, where it left delight,

I dare not guess; but in this life
Of error, ignorance, and strife,
Where nothing is but all things seem,
And we the shadows of the dream,

It is a modest creed, and yet
Pleasant if one considers it,
To own that death itself must be,
Like all the rest, a mockery.

That garden sweet, that Lady fair,
And all sweet shapes and odours there,
In truth have never passed away:
'Tis we, 'tis ours, are changed; not they.

For love, and beauty, and delight,
There is no death nor change; their might
Exceeds our organs, which endure
No light, being themselves obscure.

DIRGE FOR THE YEAR.

ORPHAN hours, the year is dead,
   Come and sigh, come and weep!
Merry hours, smile instead,
   For the year is but asleep:
See, it smiles as it is sleeping,
Mocking your untimely weeping.

As an earthquake rocks a corse
   In its coffin in the clay,
So white Winter, that rough nurse,
   Rocks the dead-cold year to-day;
Solemn hours! wail aloud
For your mother in her shroud.

As the wild air stirs and sways
   The tree-swung cradle of a child,
So the breath of these rude days
   Rocks the year:—be calm and mild,
Trembling hours; she will arise
With new love within her eyes.

January grey is here,
   Like a sexton by her grave;
February bears the bier,
   March with grief doth howl and rave;
And April weeps:—but O ye hours!
Follow with May's fairest flowers.

1 *January* 1821.

THE INVITATION.

BEST and brightest, come away,
Fairer far than this fair day,
Which, like thee to those in sorrow,
Comes to bid a sweet good-morrow
To the rough year just awake
In its cradle on the brake.
The brightest hour of unborn spring,
Through the winter wandering,
Found, it seems, the halcyon morn
To hoar February born.
Bending from heaven, in azure mirth,
It kissed the forehead of the earth,
And smiled upon the silent sea,
And bade the frozen streams be free,
And waked to music all their fountains,
And breathed upon the frozen mountains,
And like a prophetess of May
Strewed flowers upon the barren way,
Making the wintry world appear
Like one on whom thou smilest, dear.

THE INVITATION.

Away, away, from men and towns,
To the wild wood and the downs—
To the silent wilderness
Where the soul need not repress
Its music, lest it should not find
An echo in another's mind,
While the touch of Nature's art
Harmonizes heart to heart.
I leave this notice on my door
For each accustomed visitor:—
"I am gone into the fields
To take what this sweet hour yields.
Reflection, you may come to-morrow,
Sit by the fireside with Sorrow;
You with the unpaid bill, Despair,—
You tiresome verse-reciter, Care,—
I will pay you in the grave,—
Death will listen to your stave.
Expectation too, be off!
To-day is for itself enough.
Hope, in pity, mock not woe
With smiles, nor follow where I go;
Long having lived on thy sweet food,
At length I find one moment good
After long pain: with all your love,
This you never told me of."

Radiant Sister of the Day,
Awake! arise! and come away!
To the wild woods and the plains,
And the pools where winter rains
Image all their roof of leaves;
Where the pine its garland weaves
Of sapless green and ivy dun
Round stems that never kiss the sun;
Where the lawns and pastures be,
And the sandhills of the sea;

When the melting hoar-frost wets
The daisy-star that never sets,
And wind-flowers, and violets
Which yet join not scent to hue,
Crown the pale year weak and new;
When the night is left behind
In the deep east, dim and blind,
And the blue noon is over us,
And the multitudinous
Billows murmur at our feet
Where the earth and ocean meet,
And all things seem only one
In the universal Sun.

Pisa, February 1822.

THE RECOLLECTION.

Now the last day of many days,
All beautiful and bright as thou,
The loveliest and the last, is dead.
Rise, Memory, and write its praise!
Up—to thy wonted work! come, trace
The epitaph of glory fled,—
For now the Earth has changed its face,
A frown is on the Heaven's brow.

I.

We wandered to the Pine Forest
  That skirts the Ocean's foam;
The lightest wind was in its nest,
  The tempest in its home.
The whispering waves were half asleep,
  The clouds were gone to play,
And on the bosom of the deep
  The smile of Heaven lay;

It seemed as if the hour were one
   Sent from beyond the skies,
Which scattered from above the sun
   A light of Paradise.

II.

We paused amid the pines that stood
   The giants of the waste,
Tortured by storms to shapes as rude
   As serpents interlaced.
And soothed by every azure breath
   That under heaven is blown
To harmonies and hues beneath,
   As tender as its own;
Now all the tree-tops lay asleep
   Like green waves on the sea,
As still as in the silent deep
   The ocean woods may be.

III.

How calm it was!—The silence there
   By such a chain was bound
That even the busy woodpecker
   Made stiller with her sound
The inviolable quietness;
   The breath of peace we drew
With its soft motion made not less
   The calm that round us grew.
There seemed, from the remotest seat
   Of the white mountain waste,
To the soft flower beneath our feet,
   A magic circle traced,
A spirit interfused around,
   A thrilling silent life,
To momentary peace it bound
   Our mortal nature's strife;—

And still I felt, the centre of
  The magic circle there
Was one fair form that filled with love
  The lifeless atmosphere.

IV.

We paused beside the pools that lie
  Under the forest bough,
Each seemed as 'twere a little sky
  Gulfed in a world below;
A firmament of purple light
  Which in the dark earth lay,
More boundless than the depth of night,
  And purer than the day—
In which the lovely forests grew
  As in the upper air,
More perfect both in shape and hue
  Than any spreading there.
There lay the glade, the neighbouring lawn,
  And through the dark-green wood
The white sun twinkling like the dawn
  Out of a speckled cloud.
Sweet views which in our world above
  Can never well be seen
Were imaged by the water's love
  Of that fair forest green.
And all was interfused beneath
  With an Elysian glow,
An atmosphere without a breath,
  A softer day below.
Like one beloved, the scene had lent
  To the dark water's breast
Its every leaf and lineament
  With more than truth expressed;
Until an envious wind crept by,
  Like an unwelcome thought

Which from the mind's too faithful eye
    Blots one dear image out.
Though thou art ever fair and kind,
    The forests ever green,
Less oft is peace in Shelley's mind
    Than calm in waters seen.

2 February 1822.

TO A LADY WITH A GUITAR.

Ariel to Miranda:—Take
This slave of music, for the sake
Of him, who is the slave of thee;
And teach it all the harmony
In which thou canst, and only thou,
Make the delighted spirit glow,
Till joy denies itself again
And, too intense, is turned to pain.
For, by permission and command
Of thine own Prince Ferdinand,
Poor Ariel sends this silent token
Of more than ever can be spoken;
Your guardian spirit, Ariel, who
From life to life must still pursue
Your happiness, for thus alone
Can Ariel ever find his own.
From Prospero's enchanted cell,
As the mighty verses tell,
To the throne of Naples he
Lit you o'er the trackless sea,
Flitting on, your prow before,
Like a living meteor.
When you die, the silent Moon
In her interlunar swoon
Is not sadder in her cell
Than deserted Ariel.

TO A LADY WITH A GUITAR.

When you live again on earth,
Like an unseen star of birth
Ariel guides you o'er the sea
Of life from your nativity.
Many changes have been run
Since Ferdinand and you begun
Your course of love, and Ariel still
Has tracked your steps and served your will.
Now, in humbler, happier lot,
This is all remembered not;
And now, alas! the poor sprite is
Imprisoned for some fault of his
In a body like a grave—
From you he only dares to crave,
For his service and his sorrow,
A smile to-day, a song to-morrow.

The artist who this idol wrought,
To echo all harmonious thought,
Felled a tree while on the steep
The woods were in their winter sleep,
Rocked in that repose divine
On the wind-swept Apennine,
And dreaming, some of autumn past,
And some of spring approaching fast,
And some of April buds and showers,
And some of songs in July bowers,
And all of love; and so this tree—
Oh that such our death may be!—
Died in sleep, and felt no pain,
To live in happier form again:
From which, beneath heaven's fairest star,
The artist wrought this loved Guitar;
And taught it justly to reply,
To all who question skilfully,
In language gentle as thine own;
Whispering in enamoured tone

Sweet oracles of woods and dells,
And summer winds in sylvan cells;
—For it had learnt all harmonies
Of the plains and of the skies,
Of the forests and the mountains,
And the many-voicèd fountains;
The clearest echoes of the hills,
The softest notes of falling rills,
The melodies of birds and bees,
The murmuring of summer seas,
And pattering rain, and breathing dew,
And airs of evening; and it knew
That seldom-heard mysterious sound
Which, driven on its diurnal round,
As it floats through boundless day,
Our world enkindles on its way:
—All this it knows; but will not tell
To those who cannot question well
The Spirit that inhabits it;
It talks according to the wit
Of its companions; and no more
Is heard than has been felt before
By those who tempt it to betray
These secrets of an elder day.
But, sweetly as its answers will
Flatter hands of perfect skill,
It keeps its highest holiest tone
For our beloved Jane alone.

LINES WRITTEN IN THE BAY OF LERICI.

She left me at the silent time
When the moon had ceased to climb
The azure path of heaven's steep,
And, like an albatross asleep,

Balanced on her wings of light,
Hovered in the purple night,
Ere she sought her ocean nest
In the chambers of the west.
She left me; and I stayed alone,
Thinking over every tone,
Which, though silent to the ear,
The enchanted heart could hear,
Like notes which die when born, but still
Haunt the echoes of the hill,
And feeling ever—oh too much!—
The soft vibration of her touch,
As if her gentle hand even now
Lightly trembled on my brow,
And thus, although she absent were,
Memory gave me all of her
That even Fancy dares to claim:—
Her presence had made weak and tame
All passions, and I lived alone
In the time which is our own;
The past and future were forgot,
As they had been, and would be, not;
But soon, the guardian angel gone,
The dæmon reassumed his throne
In my faint heart. I dare not speak
My thoughts; but thus disturbed and weak
I sat, and saw the vessels glide
Over the ocean bright and wide,
Like spirit-wingèd chariots sent
O'er some serenest element
For ministrations strange and far,
As if to some Elysian star
Sailed for drink to medicine
Such sweet and bitter pain as mine.
And the wind that winged their flight
From the land came fresh and light;
And the scent of wingèd flowers,

And the coolness of the hours
Of dew, and sweet warmth left by day,
Were scattered o'er the twinkling bay;
And the fisher, with his lamp
And spear, about the low rocks damp
Crept, and struck the fish which came
To worship the delusive flame.
Too happy they, whose pleasure sought
Extinguishes all sense and thought
Of the regret that pleasure leaves,—
Destroying life alone, not peace!

TO ——.

ONE word is too often profaned
    For me to profane it;
One feeling too falsely disdained
    For thee to disdain it;
One hope is too like despair
    For prudence to smother;
And pity from thee more dear
    Than that from another.

I can give not what men call love:
    But wilt thou accept not
The worship the heart lifts above,
    And the Heavens reject not:
The desire of the moth for the star,
    Of the night for the morrow,
The devotion to something afar
    From the sphere of our sorrow?

THE INDIAN SERENADE.

I ARISE from dreams of thee
In the first sweet sleep of night,

LOVE'S PHILOSOPHY.

When the winds are breathing low,
And the stars are shining bright.
I arise from dreams of thee,
And a spirit in my feet
Has led me—who knows how?
To thy chamber window, sweet!

The wandering airs they faint
On the dark, the silent stream—
The champak odours fail
Like sweet thoughts in a dream;
The nightingale's complaint
It dies upon her heart,
As I must die on thine,
O belovèd as thou art!

O lift me from the grass!
I die, I faint, I fail!
Let thy love in kisses rain
On my lips and eyelids pale.
My cheek is cold and white, alas!
My heart beats loud and fast,
Oh! press it close to thine again,
Where it will break at last.

LOVE'S PHILOSOPHY.

THE fountains mingle with the river,
  And the rivers with the ocean;
The winds of heaven mix for ever
    With a sweet emotion;
Nothing in the world is single;
  All things by a law divine
In one another's being mingle—
    Why not I with thine?

See, the mountains kiss high heaven,
  And the waves clasp one another;

No sister flower would be forgiven
    If it disdained its brother;
And the sunlight clasps the earth,
    And the moonbeams kiss the sea;—
What are all these kissings worth,
    If thou kiss not me?

FROM THE ARABIC.

AN IMITATION.

My faint spirit was sitting in the light
    Of thy looks, my love;
It panted for thee like the hind at noon
    For the brooks, my love.
Thy barb, whose hoofs outspeed the tempest's flight,
    Bore thee far from me;
My heart, for my weak feet were weary soon,
    Did companion thee.

Ah! fleeter far than fleetest storm or steed,
    Or the death they bear,
The heart which tender thought clothes like a dove
    With the wings of care;
In the battle, in the darkness, in the need,
    Shall mine cling to thee,
Nor claim one smile for all the comfort, love,
    It may bring to thee.

TO EMILIA VIVIANI.

Madonna, wherefore hast thou sent to me
    Sweet-basil and mignonette?
Embleming love and health, which never yet
    In the same wreath might be.
Alas, and they are wet!

Is it with thy kisses or thy tears?
　For never rain or dew
　　　Such fragrance drew
From plant or flower—the very doubt endears
　My sadness ever new,
The sighs I breathe, the tears I shed, for thee.

THE DIRGE.

　　OLD winter was gone
In his weakness back to the mountains hoar;
　　And the spring came down
From the planet that hovers upon the shore
　Where the sea of sunlight encroaches
　　On the limits of wintry night;—
　　If the land and the air and the sea
Rejoice not when spring approaches,
　　We did not rejoice in thee,
　　　　Ginevra!

　　She is still, she is cold,
　　　On the bridal couch!
One step to the white death-bed,
　　　And one to the bier,
And one to the charnel, and one—oh where?
　　　The dark arrow fled
　　　　In the noon.
Ere the sun through heaven once more has rolled,
　　　The rats in her heart
　　　Will have made their nest,
And the worms be alive in her golden hair.
　　While the Spirit that guides the sun
　　Sits throned in his flaming chair,
　　　　She shall sleep.
　　　.　　.　　.　　.　　.　　.

SONNET.

Ye hasten to the dead: what seek ye there,
   Ye restless thoughts and busy purposes
Of the idle brain, which the world's livery wear?
   O thou quick heart, which pantest to possess
All that anticipation feigneth fair—
   Thou vainly curious mind which wouldest guess
Whence thou didst come and whither thou mayst go,
And that which never yet was known wouldst know—
   Oh! whither hasten ye, that thus ye press
   With such swift feet life's green and pleasant path,
Seeking alike from happiness and woe
   A refuge in the cavern of grey death?
O heart and mind and thoughts! what thing do you
Hope to inherit in the grave below?

TIME LONG PAST.

Like the ghost of a dear friend dead
    Is time long past.
A tone which is now forever fled,
A hope which is now forever past,
A love so sweet it could not last,
    Was time long past.

There were sweet dreams in the night
    Of time long past:
And, was it sadness or delight,
Each day a shadow onward cast
Which made us wish it yet might last—
    That time long past.

There is regret, almost remorse,
    For time long past.
'Tis like a child's belovèd corse
A father watches, till at last
Beauty is like remembrance cast
    From time long past.

TO-MORROW.

WHERE art thou, beloved To-morrow?
   When, young and old, and strong and weak,
Rich and poor, through joy and sorrow,
   Thy sweet smiles we ever seek,
In thy place—ah well-a-day!—
We find the thing we fled—To-day.

A BRIDAL SONG.

THE golden gates of Sleep unbar,
   Where Strength and Beauty, met together,
Kindle their image, like a star
   In a sea of glassy weather.
Night, with all thy stars look down—
   Darkness, weep thy holiest dew!
Never smiled the inconstant moon
     On a pair so true.
Let eyes not see their own delight:
Haste, swift Hour, and thy flight
     Oft renew.

Fairies, sprites, and angels, keep her!
   Holy stars, permit no wrong!
And return to wake the sleeper,
     Dawn,—ere it be long.
Oh joy! Oh fear! what will be done
In the absence of the sun? . . .
     Come along!

TO ——.

WHEN passion's trance is overpast
If tenderness and truth could last,
Or live whilst all wild feelings keep
Some mortal slumber, dark and deep,
I should not weep, I should not weep!

It were enough to feel, to see,
Thy soft eyes gazing tenderly,
And dream the rest—and burn, and be
The secret food of fires unseen—
Couldst thou but be as thou hast been.

After the slumber of the year
The woodland violets re-appear;
All things revive in field or grove,
And sky and sea,—but two, which move
And form all others, life and love.

LINES.

WHEN the lamp is shattered,
The light in the dust lies dead;
  When the cloud is scattered,
The rainbow's glory is shed;
  When the lute is broken,
Sweet notes are remembered not;
  When the lips have spoken,
Loved accents are soon forgot.

  As music and splendour
Survive not the lamp and the lute,
  The heart's echoes render
No song when the spirit is mute:—
  No song but sad dirges,
Like the wind in a ruined cell,
  Or the mournful surges
That ring the dead seaman's knell.

  When hearts have once mingled,
Love first leaves the well-built nest;
  The weak one is singled
To endure what it once possessed.

O Love! who bewailest
The frailty of all things here,
  Why choose you the frailest
For your cradle, your home, and your bier?

  Its passions will rock thee,
As the storms rock the ravens on high:
  Bright reason will mock thee,
Like the sun from a wintry sky:
  From thy nest every rafter
Will rot, and thine eagle home
  Leave thee naked to laughter
When leaves fall and cold winds come.

A LAMENT.

Swifter far than summer's flight,
Swifter far than youth's delight,
Swifter far than happy night,
    Art thou come and gone:
As the earth when leaves are dead,
As the night when sleep is sped,
As the heart when joy is fled,
    I am left lone, alone.

The swallow Summer comes again,
The owlet Night resumes her reign,
But the wild swan Youth is fain
    To fly with thee, false as thou:
My heart each day desires the morrow;
Sleep itself is turned to sorrow;
Vainly would my winter borrow
    Sunny leaves from any bough.

Lilies for a bridal bed,
Roses for a matron's head,
Violets for a maiden dead,
    Pansies let my flowers be:

On the living grave I bear
Scatter them without a tear,
Let no friend, however dear,
    Waste one hope, one fear, for me.

TO THE MOON.

ART thou pale for weariness
Of climbing heaven, and gazing on the earth,—
Wandering companionless
Among the stars that have a different birth,—
And ever changing like a joyless eye
That finds no object worth its constancy?

THE WANING MOON.

AND, like a dying lady, lean and pale,
Who totters forth, wrapped in a gauzy veil,
Out of her chamber, led by the insane
And feeble wanderings of her fading brain,
The moon arose up in the murky east
A white and shapeless mass. .

THE WORLD'S WANDERERS.

TELL me, thou star, whose wings of light
Speed thee in thy fiery flight,
In what cavern of the night
    Will thy pinions close now?

Tell me, moon, thou pale and grey
Pilgrim of heaven's homeless way,
In what depth of night or day
    Seekest thou repose now?

Weary wind, who wanderest
Like the world's rejected guest,
Hast thou still some secret nest
   On the tree or billow?

A DIRGE.

ROUGH wind that moanest loud
   Grief too sad for song;
Wild wind when sullen cloud
   Knells all the night long;
Sad storm, whose tears are vain,
Bare woods, whose branches stain,
Deep caves and dreary main,—
   Wail for the world's wrong!

SONG.

A WIDOW bird sate mourning for her Love
   Upon a wintry bough;
The frozen wind crept on above,
   The freezing stream below.

There was no leaf upon the forest bare,
   No flower upon the ground,
And little motion in the air
   Except the mill-wheel's sound.

A LAMENT.

O WORLD! O life! O time!
   On whose last steps I climb,
Trembling at that where I had stood before,—
When will return the glory of your prime?
   No more—Oh, never more!

Out of the day and night
A joy has taken flight:
Fresh spring, and summer, autumn, and winter hoar,
Move my faint heart with grief,—but with delight
No more—Oh, never more!

TO ——.

MUSIC, when soft voices die,
Vibrates in the memory—
Odours, when sweet violets sicken,
Live within the sense they quicken.

Rose leaves, when the rose is dead,
Are heaped for the beloved's bed;
And so thy thoughts, when thou art gone,
Love itself shall slumber on.

SELECTIONS FROM THE REVOLT OF ISLAM.

CANTO II.

The starlight smile of children, the sweet looks
   Of women, the fair breast from which I fed,
The murmur of the unreposing brooks,
   And the green light which, shifting overhead,
   Some tangled bower of vines around me shed,
The shells on the sea-sand, and the wild flowers,
   The lamplight through the rafters cheerly spread.
And on the twining flax—in life's young hours
These sights and sounds did nurse my spirit's folded powers.

In Argolis beside the echoing sea,
   Such impulses within my mortal frame
Arose, and they were dear to memory,
   Like tokens of the dead:—but others came
   Soon, in another shape: the wondrous fame
Of the past world, the vital words and deeds
   Of minds whom neither time nor change can tame,
Traditions dark and old whence evil creeds
Start forth, and whose dim shade a stream of poison feeds.

I heard, as all have heard, the various story
   Of human life, and wept unwilling tears.
Feeble historians of its shame and glory,
   False disputants on all its hopes and fears,
   Victims who worshipped ruin, chroniclers

Of daily scorn, and slaves who loathed their state,
  Yet, flattering Power, had given its ministers
  A throne of judgment in the grave—'twas fate
That among such as these my youth should seek its mate.

    . . . .

An orphan with my parents lived, whose eyes
  Were lodestars of delight which drew me home
When I might wander forth; nor did I prize
  Aught human thing beneath heaven's mighty dome
  Beyond this child. So, when sad hours were come,
And baffled hope like ice still clung to me,
  Since kin were cold, and friends had now become
Heartless and false, I turned from all to be,
Cythna, the only source of tears and smiles to thee.

What wert thou then? A child most infantine,
  Yet wandering far beyond that innocent age
In all but its sweet looks and mien divine;
  Even then, methought, with the world's tyrant rage
  A patient warfare thy young heart did wage,
When those soft eyes of scarcely conscious thought
  Some tale or thine own fancies would engage
To overflow with tears, or converse fraught
With passion o'er their depths its fleeting light had wrought.

She moved upon this earth a shape of brightness,
  A power that from its objects scarcely drew
One impulse of her being—in her lightness
  Most like some radiant cloud of morning dew
  Which wanders through the waste air's pathless blue,
To nourish some far desert; she did seem,
  Beside me, gathering beauty as she grew,
Like the bright shade of some immortal dream
Which walks when tempest sleeps the wave of life's dark stream.

As mine own shadow was this child to me,
  A second self, far dearer and more fair,

Which clothed in undissolving radiancy
  All those steep paths which languor and despair
Of human things had made so dark and bare.
But which I trod alone; nor, till bereft
  Of friends, and overcome by lonely care,
Knew I what solace for that loss was left,
Though by a bitter wound my trusting heart was cleft.

Once she was dear; now she was all I had
  To love in human life—this playmate sweet,
This child of twelve years old. So she was made
  My sole associate, and her willing feet
Wandered with mine where earth and ocean meet,
Beyond the aërial mountains whose vast cells
  The unreposing billows ever beat.
Through forests wide and old, and lawny dells
Where boughs of incense droop over the emerald wells.

And warm and light I felt her clasping hand
  When twined in mine: she followed where I went,
Through the lone paths of our immortal land.
  It had no waste but some memorial lent
Which strung me to my toil—some monument
Vital with mind: then Cythna by my side,
  Until the bright and beaming day were spent,
Would rest, with looks entreating to abide,
Too earnest and too sweet ever to be denied.

And soon I could not have refused her. Thus,
  For ever, day and night, we two were ne'er
Parted, but when brief sleep divided us:
  And, when the pauses of the lulling air
Of noon beside the sea had made a lair
For her soothed senses, in my arms she slept;
  And I kept watch over her slumbers there,
While, as the shifting visions o'er her swept,
Amid her innocent rest by turns she smiled and wept:—

And in the murmur of her dreams was heard
　　Sometimes the name of Laon:—suddenly
She would arise, and, like the secret bird
　　Whom sunset wakens, fill the shore and sky
　　With her sweet accents—a wild melody—
Hymns which my soul had woven to freedom. Strong
　　The source of passion whence they rose, to be
Triumphant strains which, like a spirit's tongue,
To the enchanted waves that child of glory sung—

Her white arms lifted through the shadowy stream
　　Of her loose hair. Oh excellently great
Seemed to me then my purpose, the vast theme
　　Of those impassioned songs! when Cythna sate
　　Amid the calm which rapture doth create
After its tumult; her heart vibrating,
　　Her spirit o'er the ocean's floating state
From her deep eyes far wandering, on the wing
Of visions that were mine, beyond its utmost spring.

For, before Cythna loved it, had my song
　　Peopled with thoughts the boundless universe,
A mighty congregation, which were strong,
　　Where'er they trod the darkness, to disperse
　　The cloud of that unutterable curse
Which clings upon mankind:—all things became
　　Slaves to my holy and heroic verse,
Earth, sea, and sky, the planets, life, and fame,
And fate, or whate'er else binds the world's wondrous frame.

And this beloved child thus felt the sway
　　Of my conceptions, gathering like a cloud
The very wind on which it rolls away.
　　Hers too were all my thoughts ere yet, endowed
　　With music and with light, their fountains flowed
In poesy; and her still and earnest face,
　　Pallid with feelings which intensely glowed

Within, was turned on mine with speechless grace,
Watching the hopes which there her heart had learned to trace.

. . . .

Within that fairest form the female mind,
   Untainted by the poison clouds which rest
On the dark world, a sacred home did find:
   But else, from the wide earth's maternal breast,
   Victorious Evil, which had dispossessed
All native power, had those fair children torn,
   And made them slaves to soothe his vile unrest,
   And minister to lust its joys forlorn,
Till they had learned to breathe the atmosphere of scorn.

This misery was but coldly felt, till she
   Became my only friend, who had endued
My purpose with a wider sympathy.
   Thus, Cythna mourned with me the servitude
   In which the half of humankind were mewed,
Victims of lust and hate, the slaves of slaves:
   She mourned that grace and power were thrown as food
   To the hyæna Lust, who among graves,
Over his loathed meal, laughing in agony, raves.

And I, still gazing on that glorious child,
   Even as these thoughts flushed o'er her:— "Cythna sweet,
Well with the world art thou unreconciled;
   Never will peace and human nature meet,
   Till free and equal man and woman greet
Domestic peace; and, ere this power can make
   In human hearts its calm and holy seat,
   This slavery must be broken." As I spake,
From Cythna's eyes a light of exultation brake.

CANTO V.

YET need was none for rest or food to care,
   Even though that multitude was passing great,
Since each one for the other did prepare

All kindly succour. Therefore to the gate
　　Of the Imperial House, now desolate,
I passed, and there was found aghast, alone,
　　The fallen Tyrant.—Silently he sate
Upon the footstool of his golden throne,
Which, starred with sunny gems, in its own lustre shone.

Alone, but for one child who led before him
　　A graceful dance: the only living thing,
Of all the crowd which thither to adore him
　　Flocked yesterday, who solace sought to bring
　　In his abandonment.—She knew the king
Had praised her dance of yore; and now she wove
　　Its circles, aye weeping and murmuring,
'Mid her sad task of unregarded love,
That to no smiles it might his speechless sadness move.

She fled to him, and wildly clasped his feet,
　　When human steps were heard:—he moved nor spoke,
Nor changed his hue, nor raised his looks to meet
　　The gaze of strangers.—Our loud entrance woke
　　The echoes of the hall, which circling broke
The calm of its recesses,—like a tomb,
　　Its sculptured walls vacantly to the stroke
Of footfalls answered, and the twilight's gloom
Lay like a charnel's mist within the radiant dome.

The little child stood up when we came nigh;
　　Her lips and cheeks seemed very pale and wan,
But on her forehead and within her eye
　　Lay beauty, which makes hearts that feed thereon
　　Sick with excess of sweetness;—on the throne
She leaned. The king, with gathered brow and lips
　　Wreathed by long scorn, did inly sneer and frown,
With hue like that when some great painter dips
His pencil in the gloom of earthquake and eclipse.

She stood beside him like a rainbow braided
　　Within some storm when scarce its shadows vast

From the blue paths of the swift sun have faded.
  A sweet and solemn smile, like Cythna's, cast
  One moment's light, which made my heart beat fast,
O'er that child's parted lips—a gleam of bliss,
  A shade of vanished days. As the tears passed
Which wrapped it, even as with a father's kiss
I pressed those softest eyes in trembling tenderness.

The sceptred wretch then from that solitude
  I drew, and, of his change compassionate,
With words of sadness soothed his rugged mood.
  But he, while pride and fear held deep debate,
  With sullen guile of ill-dissembled hate
Glared on me as a toothless snake might glare.
  Pity, not scorn, I felt, though desolate
The desolator now, and unaware
The curses which he mocked had caught him by the hair.

I led him forth from that which now might seem
  A gorgeous grave: through portals sculptured deep
With imagery beautiful as dream
  We went, and left the shades which tend on sleep
  Over its unregarded gold to keep
Their silent watch.—The child trod faintingly,
  And, as she went, the tears which she did weep
Glanced in the starlight; wildered seemèd she,
And, when I spake, for sobs she could not answer me.

At last the tyrant cried, "She hungers, slave!
  Stab her, or give her bread!"—It was a tone
Such as sick fancies in a new-made grave
  Might hear. I trembled, for the truth was known:
  He with this child had thus been left alone,
And neither had gone forth for food,—but he,
  In mingled pride and awe, cowered near his throne.
And she, a nursling of captivity,
Knew nought beyond those walls, nor what such change
    might be.

    .   .   .   .

The dawn flowed forth, and from its purple fountains
   I drank those hopes which make the spirit quail,
As to the plain between the misty mountains
   And the great city, with a countenance pale,
   I went. It was a sight which might avail
To make men weep exulting tears, for whom
   Now first from human power the reverend veil
Was torn, to see Earth from her general womb
Pour forth her swarming sons to a fraternal doom;

To see far glancing in the misty morning
   The signs of that innumerable host;
To hear one sound of many made, the warning
   Of earth to heaven from its free children tossed;
   While the eternal hills, and the sea lost
In wavering light, and, starring the blue sky,
   The city's myriad spires of gold, almost
With human joy made mute society—
Its witnesses with men who must hereafter be;

To see, like some vast island from the ocean,
   The Altar of the Federation rear
Its pile i' the midst,—a work which the devotion
   Of millions in one night created there,
   Sudden as when the moonrise makes appear
Strange clouds in the east; a marble pyramid
   Distinct with steps: that mighty shape did wear
The light of genius; its still shadow hid
Far ships: to know its height the morning mists forbid:—

To hear the restless multitudes for ever
   Around the base of that great altar flow,
As on some mountain islet burst and shiver
   Atlantic waves; and solemnly and slow,
   As the wind bore that tumult to and fro,
To feel the dreamlike music, which did swim
   Like beams through floating clouds on waves below,
Falling in pauses from that altar dim,
As silver-sounding tongues breathed an aërial hymn.

To hear, to see, to live, was on that morn
   Lethean joy, so that all those assembled
Cast off their memories of the past outworn.
   Two only bosoms with their own life trembled,
   And mine was one,—and we had both dissembled.
So with a beating heart I went, and one
   Who, having much, covets yet more, resembled,—
   A lost and dear possession, which not won,
He walks in lonely gloom beneath the noonday sun.

To the great pyramid I came: its stair
   With female choirs was thronged, the loveliest
Among the free, grouped with its sculptures rare.
   As I approached, the morning's golden mist,
   Which now the wonder-stricken breezes kissed
With their cold lips, fled, and the summit shone
   Like Athos seen from Samothracia, dressed
   In earliest light, by vintagers. And one
Sate there, a female shape upon an ivory throne:

A form most like the imagined habitant
   Of silver exhalations sprung from dawn,
By winds which feed on sunrise woven, to enchant
   The faiths of men. All mortal eyes were drawn—
   As famished mariners, through strange seas gone,
Gaze on a burning watch-tower—by the light
   Of those divinest lineaments. Alone
   With thoughts which none could share, from that fair sight
I turned in sickness, for a veil shrouded her countenance bright

And neither did I hear the acclamations
   Which, from brief silence bursting, filled the air
With her strange name and mine, from all the nations
   Which we, they said, in strength had gathered there
   From the sleep of bondage; nor the vision fair
Of that bright pageantry beheld;—but blind
   And silent as a breathing corpse did fare,
Leaning upon my friend, till, like a wind
To fevered cheeks, a voice flowed o'er my troubled mind.

Like music of some minstrel heavenly-gifted
  To one whom fiends enthrall, this voice to me;
Scarce did I wish her veil to be uplifted,
  I was so calm and joyous.—I could see
  The platform where we stood, the statues three
Which kept their marble watch on that high shrine,
  The multitudes, the mountains, and the sea;—
As, when eclipse hath passed, things sudden shine
To men's astonished eyes most clear and crystalline.

CANTO VI.

THE few who yet survived, resolute and firm,
  Around me fought. At the decline of day,
Winding above the mountain's snowy term,
  New banners shone: they quivered in the ray
  Of the sun's unseen orb. Ere night the array
Of fresh troops hemmed us in. Of those brave bands
  I soon survived alone:—and now I lay
Vanquished and faint, the grasp of bloody hands
I felt, and saw on high the glare of falling brands,

When on my foes a sudden terror came,
  And they fled, scattering.—Lo! with reinless speed
A black Tartarian horse of giant frame
  Comes trampling o'er the dead; the living bleed
  Beneath the hoofs of that tremendous steed,
On which, like to an angel, robed in white,
  Sate one waving a sword. The hosts recede
And fly, as through their ranks with awful might
Sweeps in the shadow of eve that phantom swift and bright.

And its path made a solitude.—I rose
  And marked its coming; it relaxed its course
As it approached me, and the wind that flows
  Through night bore accents to mine ear whose force
  Might create smiles in death.—The Tartar horse

Paused, and I saw the shape its might which swayed,
  And heard her musical pants, like the sweet source
Of waters in the desert, as she said,
"Mount with me, Laon, now!"—I rapidly obeyed.

Then "Away! away!" she cried, and stretched her sword
  As 'twere a scourge over the courser's head,
And lightly shook the reins.—We spake no word,
  But like the vapour of the tempest fled
  Over the plain; her dark hair was dispread
Like the pine's locks upon the lingering blast;
  Over mine eyes its shadowy strings it spread
Fitfully, and the hills and streams fled fast,
As o'er their glimmering forms the steed's broad shadow passed.

And his hoofs ground the rocks to fire and dust,
  His strong sides made the torrents rise in spray
And turbulence, as if a whirlwind's gust
  Surrounded us;—and still away, away,
  Through the desert night we sped, while she alway
Gazed on a mountain which we neared, whose crest
  Crowned with a marble ruin, in the ray
Of the obscure stars gleamed;—its rugged breast
The steed strained up, and then his impulse did arrest.

A rocky hill which overhung the ocean:—
  From that lone ruin, when the steed that panted
Paused, might be heard the murmur of the motion
  Of waters, as in spots for ever haunted
  By the choicest winds of heaven, which are enchanted
To music by the wand of solitude,
  That wizard wild, and the far tents implanted
Upon the plain be seen by those who stood
Thence marking the dark shore of ocean's curved flood.

One moment these were heard and seen—another
  Passed; and the two who stood beneath that night

Each only heard, or saw, or felt, the other.
　As from the lofty steed she did alight,
　Cythna (for, from the eyes whose deepest light
Of love and sadness made my lips feel pale
　With influence strange of mournfullest delight,
My own sweet Cythna looked) with joy did quail,
And felt her strength in tears of human weakness fail.

And for a space in my embrace she rested,
　Her head on my unquiet heart reposing,
While my faint arms her languid frame invested.
　At length she looked on me, and, half unclosing
　Her tremulous lips, said: "Friend, thy bands were losing,
The battle, as I stood before the king
　In bonds.—I burst them then, and swiftly choosing
The time, did seize a Tartar's sword, and spring
Upon his horse, and, swift as on the whirlwind's wing,

"Have thou and I been borne beyond pursuer,—
　And we are here."—Then, turning to the steed,
She pressed the white moon on his front with pure
　And rose-like lips, and many a fragrant weed
　From the green ruin plucked, that he might feed;—
But I to a stone seat that Maiden led,
　And, kissing her fair eyes, said "Thou hast need
Of rest;" and I heaped up the courser's bed
In a green mossy nook, with mountain flowers dispread.

Within that ruin, where a shattered portal
　Looks to the eastern stars (abandoned now
By man, to be the home of things immortal,
　Memories like awful ghosts which come and go,
　And must inherit all he builds below,
When he is gone), a hall stood; o'er whose roof
　Fair clinging weeds with ivy pale did grow,
Clasping its grey rents with a verdurous woof,
A hanging dome of leaves, a canopy moon-proof.

The autumnal winds, as if spell-bound, had made
 A natural couch of leaves in that recess,
Which seasons none disturbed,—but, in the shade
 Of flowering parasites, did spring love to dress
 With their sweet blooms the wintry loneliness
Of those dead leaves, shedding their stars whene'er
 The wandering wind her nurslings might caress;
 Whose intertwining fingers ever there
Made music wild and soft that filled the listening air.

We know not where we go, or what sweet dream
 May pilot us through caverns strange and fair
Of far and pathless passion, while the stream
 Of life our bark doth on its whirlpools bear,
 Spreading swift wings as sails to the dim air:
Nor should we seek to know, so the devotion
 Of love and gentle thoughts be heard still there
 Louder and louder from the utmost Ocean
Of universal life, attuning its commotion.

To the pure all things are pure. Oblivion wrapped
 Our spirits, and the fearful overthrow
Of public hope was from our being snapped,
 Though linked years had bound it there; for now
 A power, a thirst, a knowledge, which below
All thoughts (like light beyond the atmosphere,
 Clothing its clouds with grace) doth ever flow,
 Came on us, as we sate in silence there,
Beneath the golden stars of the clear azure air:—

In silence which doth follow talk that causes
 The baffled heart to speak with sighs and tears,
When wildering passion swalloweth up the pauses
 Of inexpressive speech. The youthful years
 Which we together passed, their hopes and fears,
The blood itself which ran within our frames,
 That likeness of the features which endears
 The thoughts expressed by them, our very names,
And all the wingèd hours which speechless memory claims,

Had found a voice:—and, ere that voice did pass,
    The night grew damp and dim, and, through a rent
Of the ruin where we sate, from the morass,
    A wandering meteor by some wild wind sent,
    Hung high in the green dome, to which it lent
A faint and pallid lustre; while the song
    Of blasts, in which its blue hair quivering bent,
Strewed strangest sounds the moving leaves among;
A wondrous light, the sound as of a spirit's tongue.

The Meteor showed the leaves on which we sate,
    And Cythna's glowing arms, and the thick ties
Of her soft hair which bent with gathered weight
    My neck near hers; her dark and deepening eyes,
    Which, as twin phantoms of one star that lies
O'er a dim well move though the star reposes,
    Swam in our mute and liquid ecstacies;
Her marble brow; and eager lips, like roses,
With their own fragrance pale, which spring but half uncloses

The Meteor to its far morass returned:
    The beating of our veins one interval
Made still; and then I felt the blood that burned
    Within her frame mingle with mine, and fall
    Around my heart like fire; and over all
A mist was spread, the sickness of a deep
    And speechless swoon of joy, as might befall
Two disunited spirits when they leap
In union from this earth's obscure and fading sleep.

Was it one moment that confounded thus
    All thought, all sense, all feeling, into one
Unutterable power, which shielded us
    Even from our own cold looks, when we had gone
    Into a wide and wild oblivion
Of tumult and of tenderness? or now
    Had ages, such as make the moon and sun,
The seasons and mankind, their changes know,
Left fear and time unfelt by us alone below?

I know not. What are kisses whose fire clasps
  The failing heart in languishment, or limb
Twined within limb? or the quick dying gasps
  Of the life meeting, when the faint eyes swim
  Through tears of a wide mist boundless and dim,
In one caress? What is the strong control
  Which leads the heart that dizzy steep to climb
Where far over the world those vapours roll
Which blend two restless frames in one reposing soul?

It is the shadow which doth float unseen,
  But not unfelt, o'er blind mortality,
Whose divine darkness fled not from that green
  And lone recess, where lapped in peace did lie
  Our linkèd frames, till from the changing sky
That night and still another day had fled;
  And then I saw and felt. The moon was high,
And clouds, as of a coming storm, were spread
Under its orb,—loud winds were gathering overhead.

Cythna's sweet lips seemed lurid in the moon,
  Her fairest limbs with the night-wind were chill,
And her dark tresses were all loosely strewn
  O'er her pale bosom:—all within was still,
  And the sweet peace of joy did almost fill
The depth of her unfathomable look;—
  And we sate calmly, though that rocky hill
The waves contending in its caverns strook,
For they foreknew the storm, and the grey ruin shook.

There we unheeding sate, in the communion
  Of interchangèd vows which, with a rite
Of faith most sweet and sacred, stamped our union.—
  Few were the living hearts which could unite
  Like ours, or celebrate a bridal night
With such close sympathies; for they had sprung
  From linkèd youth, and from the gentle might
Of earliest love, delayed and cherished long,
Which common hopes and fears made, like a tempest, strong.

And such is Nature's law divine that those
　　Who grow together cannot choose but love,
If faith or custom do not interpose,
　　Or common slavery mar what else might move
　　All gentlest thoughts. As, in the sacred grove
Which shades the springs of Ethiopian Nile,
　　That living tree which if the arrowy dove
Strike with her shadow shrinks in fear awhile;
But its own kindred leaves clasps while the sunbeams smile,

And clings to them when darkness may dissever
　　The close caresses of all duller plants
Which bloom on the wide earth;—thus we for ever
　　Were linked, for love had nursed us in the haunts
　　Where knowledge from its secret source enchants
Young hearts with the fresh music of its springing,
　　Ere yet its gathered flood feeds human wants,—
As the great Nile feeds Egypt, ever flinging
Light on the woven boughs which o'er its waves are swinging.

The tones of Cythna's voice like echoes were
　　Of those far murmuring streams; they rose and fell,
Mixed with mine own in the tempestuous air,—
　　And so we sate, until our talk befell
　　Of the late ruin, swift and horrible,
And how those seeds of hope might yet be sown
　　Whose fruit is evil's mortal poison. Well
For us, this ruin made a watch-tower lone;
But Cythna's eyes looked faint, and now two days were gone

Since she had food:—therefore I did awaken
　　The Tartar steed, who, from his ebon mane
Soon as the clinging slumbers he had shaken,
　　Bent his thin head to seek the brazen rein, .
　　Following me obediently. With pain
Of heart so deep and dread that one caress,
　　When lips and heart refuse to part again
Till they have told their fill, could scarce express
The anguish of her mute and fearful tenderness,

Cythna beheld me part, as I bestrode
    That willing steed. The tempest and the night,
Which gave my path its safety as I rode
    Down the ravine of rocks, did soon unite
    The darkness and the tumult of their might
Borne on all winds.—Far through the streaming rain
    Floating, at intervals the garments white
Of Cythna gleamed, and her voice once again
Came to me on the gust, and soon I reached the plain.

I dreaded not the tempest, nor did he
    Who bore me, but his eyeballs wide and red
Turned on the lightning's cleft exultingly;
    And, when the earth beneath his tameless tread
    Shook with the sullen thunder, he would spread
His nostrils to the blast, and joyously
    Mock the fierce peal with neighings;—thus we sped
O'er the lit plain, and soon I could descry
Where Death and Fire had gorged the spoil of victory.

There was a desolate village in a wood,
    Whose bloom-inwoven leaves now scattering fed
The hungry storm; it was a place of blood,
    A heap of heartless walls;—the flames were dead
    Within those dwellings now,—the life had fled
From all those corpses now,—but the wide sky,
    Flooded with lightning, was ribbed overhead
By the black rafters, and around did lie
Women and babes and men slaughtered confusedly.

Beside the fountain in the market-place
    Dismounting, I beheld those corpses stare
With horny eyes upon each other's face,
    And on the earth, and on the vacant air,
    And upon me, close to the waters where
I stooped to slake my thirst.—I shrank to taste,
    For the salt bitterness of blood was there;
But tied the steed beside, and sought in haste
If any yet survived amid that ghastly waste.

No living thing was there beside one woman
  Whom I found wandering in the streets, and she
Was withered from a likeness of aught human
  Into a fiend, by some strange misery.
  Soon as she heard my steps, she leaped on me,
And glued her burning lips to mine, and laughed
  With a loud, long, and frantic laugh of glee,
And cried, "Now, Mortal, thou hast deeply quaffed
The Plague's blue kisses—soon millions shall pledge the
    draught!

"My name is Pestilence—this bosom dry
  Once fed two babes—a sister and a brother—
When I came home, one in the blood did lie
  Of three death-wounds—the flames had ate the other!
  Since then I have no longer been a mother,
But I am Pestilence;—hither and thither
  I flit about, that I may slay and smother;—
All lips which I have kissed must surely wither,
But Death's—if thou art he, we'll go to work together!

"What seek'st thou here? the moonlight comes in
    flashes,—
  The dew is rising dankly from the dell;
'Twill moisten her! and thou shalt see the gashes
  In my sweet boy—now full of worms—But tell
  First what thou seek'st."—"I seek for food."—"'Tis well,
Thou shalt have food; Famine, my paramour,
  Waits for us at the feast—cruel and fell
Is Famine, but he drives not from his door
Those whom these lips have kissed, alone. No more, no
    more!"

As thus she spake, she grasped me with the strength
  Of madness, and by many a ruined hearth
She led, and over many a corpse. At length
  We came to a lone hut, where, on the earth
  Which made its floor, she in her ghastly mirth,

Gathering from all those homes now desolate,
  Had piled three heaps of loaves, making a dearth
Among the dead—round which she set in state
A ring of cold stiff babes; silent and stark they sate.

She leaped upon a pile, and lifted high
  Her mad looks to the lightning, and cried: "Eat!
Share the great feast—to-morrow we must die!"
  And then she spurned the loaves with her pale feet,
  Towards her bloodless guests. That sight to meet,
Mine eyes and my heart ached, and, but that she
  Who loved me did with absent looks defeat
Despair, I might have raved in sympathy;
But now I took the food that woman offered me;

And, vainly having with her madness striven
  If I might win her to return with me,
Departed. In the eastern beams of heaven
  The lightning now grew pallid—rapidly
  As by the shore of the tempestuous sea
The dark steed bore me: and the mountain grey
  Soon echoed to his hoofs, and I could see
Cythna among the rocks, where she alway
Had sate with anxious eyes fixed on the lingering day.

And joy was ours to meet: she was most pale,
  Famished, and wet, and weary; so I cast
My arms around her, lest her steps should fail
  As to our home we went,—and, thus embraced,
  Her full heart seemed a deeper joy to taste
Than e'er the prosperous know; the steed behind
  Trod peacefully along the mountain waste:
We reached our home ere morning could unbind
Night's latest veil, and on our bridal couch reclined.

Her chilled heart having cherished in my bosom,
  And sweetest kisses passed, we two did share
Our peaceful meal:—as an autumnal blossom
  Which spreads its shrunk leaves in the sunny air

After cold showers, like rainbows woven there,—
Thus in her lips and cheeks the vital spirit
  Mantled, and in her eyes an atmosphere
Of health and hope; and sorrow languished near it,
And fear, and all that dark despondence doth inherit.

CANTO IX.

"The rest thou knowest.—Lo!—we two are here—
  We have survived a ruin wide and deep.
Strange thoughts are mine.—I cannot grieve nor fear;
  Sitting with thee upon this lonely steep,
  I smile, though human love should make me weep.
We have survived a joy that knows no sorrow,
  And I do feel a mighty calmness creep
Over my heart, which can no longer borrow
Its hues from chance or change, dark children of to-morrow.

"We know not what will come.—Yet, Laon dearest,
  Cythna shall be the prophetess of love;
Her lips shall rob thee of the grace thou wearest,
  To hide thy heart, and clothe the shapes which rove
  Within the homeless future's wintry grove;
For I now, sitting thus beside thee, seem
  Even with thy breath and blood to live and move,
And violence and wrong are as a dream
Which rolls from steadfast truth,—an unreturning stream.

"The blasts of Autumn drive the wingèd seeds
  Over the earth,—next come the snows, and rain,
And frosts, and storms, which dreary Winter leads
  Out of his Scythian cave, a savage train;
  Behold! Spring sweeps over the world again,
Shedding soft dews from her etherial wings;
  Flowers on the mountains, fruits over the plain,
And music on the waves and woods, she flings,
And love on all that lives, and calm on lifeless things.

"O Spring! of hope and love and youth and gladness
    Wind-wingèd emblem! brightest, best, and fairest!
Whence comest thou when with dark Winter's sadness
    The tears that fade in sunny smiles thou sharest?
    Sister of joy! thou art the child who wearest
Thy mother's dying smile, tender and sweet;
    Thy mother Autumn, for whose grave thou bearest
Fresh flowers, and beams like flowers, with gentle feet
Disturbing not the leaves which are her winding-sheet.

"Virtue, and hope, and love, like light and heaven,
    Surround the world. We are their chosen slaves.
Has not the whirlwind of our spirit driven
    Truth's deathless germs to thought's remotest caves?
    Lo, winter comes!—the grief of many graves,
The frost of death, the tempest of the sword,
    The flood of tyranny, whose sanguine waves
Stagnate like ice at Faith the enchanter's word,
And bind all human hearts in its repose abhorred!

"The seeds are sleeping in the soil. Meanwhile
    The tyrant peoples dungeons with his prey;
Pale victims on the guarded scaffold smile
    Because they cannot speak; and, day by day,
    The moon of wasting science wanes away
Among her stars; and in that darkness vast
    The sons of earth to their foul idols pray;
And grey priests triumph; and like blight or blast
A shade of selfish care o'er human looks is cast.

"This is the Winter of the world;—and here
    We die, even as the winds of autumn fade,
Expiring in the frore and foggy air.—
    Behold! Spring comes, though we must pass who made
    The promise of its birth, even as the shade
Which from our death, as from a mountain, flings
    The future, a broad sunrise; thus arrayed
As with the plumes of overshadowing wings,
From its dark gulf of chains earth like an eagle springs.

"O dearest love! we shall be dead and cold
   Before this morn may on the world arise:
Wouldst thou the glory of its dawn behold?
   Alas! gaze not on me, but turn thine eyes
   On thine own heart—it is a paradise
Which everlasting Spring has made its own:
   And, while drear winter fills the naked skies,
Sweet streams of sunny thought, and flowers fresh blown,
Are there, and weave their sounds and odours into one.

"In their own hearts the earnest of the hope
   Which made them great the good will ever find;
And, though some envious shade may interlope
   Between the effect and it, one comes behind
   Who aye the future to the past will bind—
Necessity, whose sightless strength for ever
   Evil with evil, good with good, must wind
In bands of union which no power may sever;
They must bring forth their kind, and be divided never!

"The good and mighty of departed ages
   Are in their graves,—the innocent and free,
Heroes, and Poets, and prevailing Sages,
   Who leave the vesture of their majesty
   To adorn and clothe this naked world;—and we
Are like to them—such perish, but they leave
   All hope or love or truth or liberty
Whose forms their mighty spirits could conceive,
To be a rule and law to ages that survive.

"So be the turf heaped over our remains
   Even in our happy youth, and that strange lot,
Whate'er it be, when in these mingling veins
   The blood is still, be ours; let sense and thought
   Pass from our being, or be numbered not
Among the things that are; let those who come
   Behind, for whom our steadfast will has bought
A calm inheritance, a glorious doom,
Insult with careless tread our undivided tomb.

"Our many thoughts and deeds, our life and love,
   Our happiness, and all that we have been,
Immortally must live and burn and move
   When we shall be no more. The world has seen
   A type of peace; and,—as some most serene
And lovely spot to a poor maniac's eye,
   After long years, some sweet and moving scene
Of youthful hope, returning suddenly,
Quells his long madness—thus man shall remember thee.

"And calumny meanwhile shall feed on us
   As worms devour the dead, and near the throne
And at the altar most accepted thus
   Shall sneers and curses be;—what we have done
   None shall dare vouch, though it be truly known.
That record shall remain when they must pass
   Who built their pride on its oblivion,
And fame, in human hope which sculptured was,
Survive the perished scrolls of unenduring brass:—

"The while we two, beloved, must depart,
   And Sense and Reason, those enchanters fair
Whose wand of power is hope, would bid the heart
   That gazed beyond the wormy grave despair:
   These eyes, these lips, this blood, seem darkly there
To fade in hideous ruin; no calm sleep,
   Peopling with golden dreams the stagnant air,
Seems our obscure and rotting eyes to steep
In joy;—but senseless death—a ruin dark and deep.

"These are blind fancies. Reason cannot know
   What sense can neither feel nor thought conceive;
There is delusion in the world, and woe,
   And fear, and pain. We know not whence we live,
   Or why, or how; or what mute Power may give
Their being to each plant and star and beast,
   Or even these thoughts.—Come near me! I do weave
A chain I cannot break—I am possessed
With thoughts too swift and strong for one lone human breast.

"Yes, yes—thy kiss is sweet, thy lips are warm!
   Oh willingly, beloved, would these eyes,
Might they no more drink being from thy form,
   Even as to sleep whence we again arise,
   Close their faint orbs in death. I fear nor prize
Aught that can now betide, unshared by thee.
   Yes, Love, when wisdom fails, makes Cythna wise;
Darkness and death, if death be true, must be
Dearer than life and hope if unenjoyed with thee.

"Alas! our thoughts flow on with stream whose waters
   Return not to their fountain: earth and heaven,
The ocean and the sun, the clouds their daughters,
   Winter and Spring, and morn and noon and even,
   All that we are or know, is darkly driven
Towards one gulf.—Lo! what a change is come
   Since I first spake—but time shall be forgiven,
Though it change all but thee!" She ceased—night's gloom
Meanwhile had fallen on earth from the sky's sunless dome.

Though she had ceased, her countenance, uplifted
   To heaven, still spake, with solemn glory bright;
Her dark deep eyes, her lips whose motions gifted
   The air they breathed with love, her locks undight.
   "Fair star of life and love," I cried, "my soul's delight,
Why lookest thou on the crystalline skies?
   Oh that my spirit were yon Heaven of night
Which gazes on thee with its thousand eyes!"
She turned to me and smiled—that smile was Paradise!

CANTO X.

PEACE in the desert fields and villages,
   Between the glutted beasts and mangled dead;
Peace in the silent streets, save when the cries
   Of victims, to their fiery judgment led,
   Made pale their voiceless lips who seemed to dread,

Even in their dearest kindred, lest some tongue
    Be faithless to the fear yet unbetrayed:
Peace in the tyrant's palace, where the throng
Waste the triumphal hours in festival and song.

Day after day the burning Sun rolled on
    Over the death-polluted land. It came
Out of the east like fire, and fiercely shone
    A lamp of autumn, ripening with its flame
    The few lone ears of corn;—the sky became
Stagnate with heat, so that each cloud and blast
    Languished and died; the thirsting air did claim
All moisture, and a rotting vapour passed
From the unburied dead, invisible and fast.

First want, then plague, came on the beasts; their food
    Failed, and they drew the breath of its decay.
Millions on millions, whom the scent of blood
    Had lured, or who from regions far away
    Had tracked the hosts in festival array,
From their dark deserts, gaunt and wasting now,
    Stalked like fell shades among their perished prey;
In their green eyes a strange disease did glow,—
They sank in hideous spasm, or pains severe and slow.

The fish were poisoned in the streams; the birds
    In the green woods perished; the insect race
Was withered up; the scattered flocks and herds
    Who had survived the wild beasts' hungry chase
    Died moaning, each upon the other's face
In helpless agony gazing; round the city
    All night the lean hyænas their sad case
Like starving infants wailed—a woeful ditty—
And many a mother wept, pierced with unnatural pity.

Amid the aërial minarets on high
    The Ethiopian vultures fluttering fell
From their long line of brethren in the sky,
    Startling the concourse of mankind.—Too well

These signs the coming mischief did foretell:—
Strange panic first, a deep and sickening dread,
   Within each heart, like ice, did sink and dwell,—
A voiceless thought of evil, which did spread
With the quick glance of eyes, like withering lightnings shed.

Day after day, when the year wanes, the frosts
   Strip its green crown of leaves, till all is bare;
So on those strange and congregated hosts
   Came Famine, a swift shadow, and the air
   Groaned with the burthen of a new despair;
Famine, than whom Misrule no deadlier daughter
   Feeds from her thousand breasts, though sleeping there
With lidless eyes lie Faith and Plague and Slaughter,
A ghastly brood conceived of Lethe's sullen water.

There was no food. The corn was trampled down,
   The flocks and herds had perished; on the shore
The dead and putrid fish were ever thrown:
   The deeps were foodless, and the winds no more
   Creaked with the weight of birds, but, as before
Those wingèd things sprang forth, were void of shade;
   The vines and orchards, autumn's golden store,
Were burned; so that the meanest food was weighed
With gold, and avarice died before the god it made.

There was no corn—in the wide market-place
   All loathliest things, even human flesh, was sold;
They weighed it in small scales—and many a face
   Was fixed in eager horror then. His gold
   The miser brought; the tender maid, grown bold
Through hunger, bared her scorned charms in vain;
   The mother brought her eldest-born, controlled
By instinct blind as love, but turned again,
And bade her infant suck, and died in silent pain.

Then fell blue Plague upon the race of man.
   "Oh for the sheathed steel, so late which gave

Oblivion to the dead, when the streets ran
  With brothers' blood! Oh that the earthquake's grave
  Would gape, or ocean lift its stifling wave!"
Vain cries! Throughout the streets, thousands, pursued
  Each by his fiery torture, howl and rave,
Or sit in frenzy's unimagined mood
Upon fresh heaps of dead—a ghastly multitude.

It was not hunger now, but thirst. Each well
  Was choked with rotting corpses, and became
A cauldron of green mist made visible
  At sunrise. Thither still the myriads came,
  Seeking to quench the agony of the flame
Which raged like poison through their bursting veins;
  Naked they were from torture, without shame,
Spotted with nameless scars and lurid blains,
Childhood and youth and age writhing in savage pains.

It was not thirst but madness. Many saw
  Their own lean image everywhere; it went
A ghastlier self beside them, till the awe
  Of that dread sight to self-destruction sent
  Those shrieking victims. Some, ere life was spent,
Sought, with a horrid sympathy, to shed
  Contagion on the sound; and others rent
Their matted hair, and cried aloud, "We tread
On fire! the avenging Power his hell on earth has spread!"

Sometimes the living by the dead were hid.
  Near the great fountain in the public square,
Where corpses made a crumbling pyramid
  Under the sun, was heard one stifled prayer
  For life, in the hot silence of the air;
And strange 'twas 'mid that hideous heap to see
  Some shrouded in their long and golden hair,
As if not dead but slumbering quietly,
Like forms which sculptors carve, then love to agony.

CANTO XI.

She saw me not—she heard me not—alone
    Upon the mountain's dizzy brink she stood;
She spake not, breathed not, moved not—there was thrown
    Over her look the shadow of a mood
    Which only clothes the heart in solitude,
A thought of voiceless death.—She stood alone.
    Above, the heavens were spread;—below, the flood
Was murmuring in its caves;—the wind had blown
Her hair apart, through which her eyes and forehead shone.

A cloud was hanging o'er the western mountains;
    Before its blue and moveless depth were flying
Grey mists poured forth from the unresting fountains
    Of darkness in the north:—the day was dying:—
    Sudden, the sun shone forth; its beams were lying
Like boiling gold on ocean, strange to see,
    And on the shattered vapours which, defying
The power of light in vain, tossed restlessly
In the red heaven, like wrecks in a tempestuous sea.

It was a stream of living beams, whose bank
    On either side by the cloud's cleft was made;
And, where its chasms that flood of glory drank,
    Its waves gushed forth like fire, and, as if swayed
    By some mute tempest, rolled on her. The shade
Of her bright image floated on the river
    Of liquid light, which then did end and fade—
Her radiant shape upon its verge did shiver;
Aloft, her flowing hair like strings of flame did quiver.

I stood beside her, but she saw me not—
    She looked upon the sea, and skies, and earth.
Rapture and love and admiration wrought
    A passion deeper far than tears or mirth,
    Or speech or gesture, or whate'er has birth

From common joy; which with the speechless feeling
    That led her there united, and shot forth
From her far eyes a light of deep revealing,
All but her dearest self from my regard concealing.

Her lips were parted, and the measured breath
    Was now heard there;—her dark and intricate eyes,
Orb within orb, deeper than sleep or death,
    Absorbed the glories of the burning skies,
    Which, mingling with her heart's deep ecstasies,
Burst from her looks and gestures;—and a light
    Of liquid tenderness, like love, did rise
From her whole frame,—an atmosphere which quite
Arrayed her in its beams, tremulous and soft and bright.

She would have clasped me to her glowing frame;
    Those warm and odorous lips might soon have shed
On mine the fragrance and the invisible flame
    Which now the cold winds stole;—she would have laid
    Upon my languid heart her dearest head;
I might have heard her voice, tender and sweet;
    Her eyes, mingling with mine, might soon have fed
My soul with their own joy.—One moment yet
I gazed—we parted then, never again to meet!

PROMETHEUS UNBOUND:

A LYRICAL DRAMA.

ACT I.

SCENE—*A Ravine of Icy Rocks in the Indian Caucasus.* PROMETHEUS *is discovered bound to the Precipice.* PANTHEA *and* IONE *are seated at his feet. Time, Night. During the Scene, Morning slowly breaks.*

Prometheus. Monarch of Gods and Dæmons, and all Spirits
But One, who throng those bright and rolling worlds
Which thou and I alone of living things
Behold with sleepless eyes! regard this Earth
Made multitudinous with thy slaves, whom thou
Requitest for knee-worship, prayer, and praise,
And toil, and hecatombs of broken hearts,
With fear and self-contempt and barren hope.
Whilst me who am thy foe, eyeless in hate
Hast thou made reign and triumph, to thy scorn,
O'er mine own misery and thy vain revenge.
Three thousand years of sleep-unsheltered hours,
And moments aye divided by keen pangs
Till they seemed years, torture and solitude,
Scorn and despair—these are mine empire:—
More glorious far than that which thou surveyest
From thine unenvied throne, O Mighty God!
Almighty, had I deigned to share the shame
Of thine ill tyranny, and hung not here
Nailed to this wall of eagle-baffling mountain,

Black, wintry, dead, unmeasured; without herb,
Insect, or beast, or shape or sound of life.
Ah me! alas! pain, pain ever, for ever!

No change, no pause, no hope! Yet I endure.
I ask the Earth, have not the mountains felt?
I ask yon Heaven, the all-beholding Sun,
Has it not seen? The Sea, in storm or calm,
Heaven's ever-changing Shadow spread below,
Have its deaf waves not heard my agony?
Ah me! alas! pain, pain ever, for ever!

The crawling glaciers pierce me with the spears
Of their moon-freezing crystals; the bright chains
Eat with their burning cold into my bones;
Heaven's wingèd hound, polluting from thy lips
His beak in poison not his own, tears up
My heart; and shapeless sights come wandering by,
The ghastly people of the realm of dream,
Mocking me: and the Earthquake-fiends are charged
To wrench the rivets from my quivering wounds
When the rocks split and close again behind:
While from their loud abysses howling throng
The Genii of the Storm, urging the rage
Of whirlwind, and afflict me with keen hail.
And yet to me welcome is day and night;
Whether one breaks the hoar-frost of the morn,
Or, starry, dim, and slow, the other climbs
The leaden-coloured east; for then they lead
The wingless crawling Hours, one among whom
—As some dark priest hales the reluctant victim—
Shall drag thee, cruel King, to kiss the blood
From these pale feet, which then might trample thee
If they disdained not such a prostrate slave.
Disdain! Ah no! I pity thee. What ruin
Will hunt thee undefended through the wide Heaven!
How will thy soul, cloven to its depth with terror,
Gape like a hell within! I speak in grief,

Not exultation; for I hate no more,
As then ere misery made me wise. The curse
Once breathed on thee I would recall. Ye Mountains,
Whose many-voicèd Echoes through the mist
Of cataracts flung the thunder of that spell!
Ye icy Springs, stagnant with wrinkling frost,
Which vibrated to hear me, and then crept
Shuddering through India! thou serenest Air,
Through which the Sun walks burning without beams!
And ye swift Whirlwinds who on poised wings
Hung mute and moveless o'er yon hushed abyss,
As thunder, louder than your own, made rock
The orbèd world! if then my words had power,—
Though I am changed so that aught evil wish
Is dead within, although no memory be
Of what is hate,—let them not lose it now!
What was that curse? for ye all heard me speak.

   FIRST VOICE, *from the Mountains.*
Thrice three hundred thousand years
 O'er the Earthquake's couch we stood:
Oft, as men convulsed with fears,
 We trembled in our multitude:—

   SECOND VOICE, *from the Springs.*
Thunderbolts had parched our water,
 We had been stained with bitter blood,
And had run mute, 'mid shrieks of slaughter,
 Through a city and a solitude:—

   THIRD VOICE, *from the Air.*
I had clothed since Earth uprose
 Its wastes in colours not their own;
And oft had my serene repose
 Been cloven by many a rending groan:—

   FOURTH VOICE, *from the Whirlwinds.*
We had soared beneath these mountains
 Unresting ages; nor had thunder,
Nor yon volcano's flaming fountains,

Nor any power above or under,
Ever made us mute with wonder:—
   FIRST VOICE.
But never bowed our snowy crest
As at the voice of thine unrest.
   SECOND VOICE.
Never such a sound before
To the Indian waves we bore.
A pilot asleep on the howling sea
Leaped up from the deck in agony,
And heard, and cried "Ah! woe is me!"
And died as mad as the wild waves be.
   THIRD VOICE.
By such dread words from Earth to Heaven
My still realm was never riven:
When its wound was closed, there stood
Darkness o'er the day like blood.
   FOURTH VOICE.
And we shrank back: for dreams of ruin
To frozen caves our flight pursuing
Made us keep silence—thus—and thus—
Though silence is a hell to us.

The Earth. The tongueless Caverns of the craggy hills
Cried "Misery!" then; the hollow Heaven replied
"Misery!" and the Ocean's purple waves,
Climbing the land, howled to the lashing winds,
And the pale nations heard it, "Misery!"

Prometheus. I hear a sound of voices: not the voice
Which I gave forth. Mother, thy sons and thou
Scorn him without whose all-enduring will
Beneath the fierce omnipotence of Jove
Both they and thou had vanished, like thin mist
Unrolled on the morning wind. Know ye not me,
The Titan? he who made his agony
The barrier to your else all-conquering Foe?
O rock-embosomed lawns and snow-fed streams,

Now seen athwart frore vapours, deep below,
Through whose o'ershadowing woods I wandered once
With Asia, drinking life from her loved eyes:
Why scorns the spirit which informs ye now
To commune with me? me alone who checked,
As one who checks a fiend-drawn charioteer,
The falsehood and the force of him who reigns
Supreme, and with the groans of pining slaves
Fills your dim glens and liquid wildernesses.
Why answer ye not, still, Brethren?
   The Earth.   They dare not.
   Prometheus. Who dares? for I would hear that curse again.—
Ha! what an awful whisper rises up!
'Tis scarce like sound: it tingles through the frame
As lightning tingles, hovering ere it strike.
Speak, Spirit! From thine inorganic voice,
I only know that thou art moving near,
And love. How cursed I him?
   The Earth.   How canst thou hear,
Who knowest not the language of the dead?
   Prometheus. Thou art a living spirit; speak as they.
   The Earth. I dare not speak like life, lest heaven's fell King
Should hear, and link me to some wheel of pain
More torturing than the one whereon I roll.
Subtle thou art and good; and, though the Gods
Hear not this voice, yet thou art more than God,
Being wise and kind: earnestly hearken now.
   Prometheus. Obscurely through my brain, like shadows dim,
Sweep awful thoughts, rapid and thick. I feel
Faint, like one mingled in entwining love;
Yet 'tis not pleasure.
   The Earth.   No, thou canst not hear:
Thou art immortal, and this tongue is known
Only to those who die.
   Prometheus.   And what art thou,
O melancholy Voice?
   The Earth.   I am the Earth,

Thy mother; she within whose stony veins,
To the last fibre of the loftiest tree
Whose thin leaves trembled in the frozen air,
Joy ran, as blood within a living frame,
When thou didst from her bosom like a cloud
Of glory arise,—a spirit of keen joy!
And at thy voice her pining sons uplifted
Their prostrate brows from the polluting dust;
And our almighty Tyrant with fierce dread
Grew pale,—until his thunder chained thee here.
Then,—see those million worlds which burn and roll
Around us—their inhabitants beheld
My sphered light wane in wide heaven; the sea
Was lifted by strange tempest, and new fire
From earthquake-rifted mountains of bright snow
Shook its portentous hair beneath heaven's frown;
Lightning and Inundation vexed the plains;
Blue thistles bloomed in cities, foodless toads
Within voluptuous chambers panting crawled,
When Plague had fallen on man and beast and worm,
And Famine; and black blight on herb and tree;
And in the corn and vines and meadow-grass
Teemed ineradicable poisonous weeds,
Draining their growth,—for my wan breast was dry
With grief; and the thin air, my breath, was stained
With the contagion of a mother's hate
Breathed on her child's destroyer. Aye, I heard
Thy curse, the which, if thou rememberest not,
Yet my innumerable seas and streams,
Mountains and caves and winds, and yon wide air,
And the inarticulate people of the dead,
Preserve, a treasured spell. We meditate
In secret joy and hope those dreadful words,
But dare not speak them.
   Prometheus.   Venerable Mother!
All else who live and suffer take from thee
Some comfort; flowers and fruits and happy sounds,

And love, though fleeting: these may not be mine.
But mine own words, I pray, deny me not.

    The Earth.   They shall be told.   Ere Babylon was dust,
The Magus Zoroaster, my dead child,
Met his own image walking in the garden:
That apparition, sole of men, he saw.
For know, there are two worlds of life and death:—
One, that which thou beholdest; but the other
Is underneath the grave, where do inhabit
The shadows of all forms that think and live,
Till death unite them and they part no more;
Dreams and the light imaginings of men,
And all that faith creates or love desires,
Terrible, strange, sublime, and beauteous shapes.
There thou art, and dost hang, a writhing shade,
'Mid whirlwind-peopled mountains. All the Gods
Are there; and all the Powers of nameless worlds—
Vast, sceptred phantoms; heroes, men, and beasts;
And Demogorgon, a tremendous gloom;
And he, the Supreme Tyrant, on his throne
Of burning gold. Son, one of these shall utter
The curse which all remember. Call at will
Thine own ghost, or the ghost of Jupiter,
Hades or Typhon, or what mightier Gods
From all-prolific Evil, since thy ruin,
Have sprung, and trampled on my prostrate sons.
Ask, and they must reply: so the revenge
Of the Supreme may sweep through vacant shades,
As rainy wind through the abandoned gate
Of a fallen palace.

    Prometheus.   Mother, let not aught
Of that which may be evil pass again
My lips, or those of aught resembling me.
Phantasm of Jupiter, arise, appear!

                    IONE.
    My wings are folded o'er mine ears:
      My wings are crossèd o'er mine eyes:

Yet through their silver shade appears,
  And through their lulling plumes arise,
    A Shape, a throng of sounds.
May it be no ill to thee
  O thou of many wounds,
Near whom, for our sweet Sister's sake,
Ever thus we watch and wake!

    PANTHEA.
The sound is of whirlwind underground,
  Earthquake, and fire, and mountains cloven!
The shape is awful like the sound,
  Clothed in dark purple, star-inwoven.
    A sceptre of pale gold,
To stay steps proud o'er the slow cloud,
    His veined hand doth hold.
Cruel he looks, but calm and strong,
Like one who does, not suffers, wrong.

 Phantasm of Jupiter. Why have the secret powers of this
  strange world
Driven me, a frail and empty phantom, hither
On direst storms? What unaccustomed sounds
Are hovering on my lips, unlike the voice
With which our pallid race hold ghastly talk
In darkness? And, proud sufferer, who art thou?
 Prometheus. Tremendous Image! as thou art must be
He whom thou shadowest forth. I am his foe,
The Titan. Speak the words which I would hear,
Although no thought inform thine empty voice.
 The Earth. Listen! and, though your echoes must be mute,
Grey mountains, and old woods, and haunted springs,
Prophetic caves, and isle-surrounding streams,
Rejoice to hear what yet ye cannot speak!
 Phantasm. A spirit seizes me and speaks within:
It tears me as fire tears a thunder-cloud.
 Panthea. See how he lifts his mighty looks! the Heaven
Darkens above!

Ione.   He speaks! Oh shelter me!
Prometheus. I see the curse, on gestures proud and cold,
And looks of firm defiance and calm hate,
And such despair as mocks itself with smiles,
Written as on a scroll. Yet speak! Oh speak!

PHANTASM.

"Fiend, I defy thee! with a calm fixed mind,
　All that thou canst inflict I bid thee do;
Foul Tyrant both of Gods and Humankind,
　One only being shalt thou not subdue.
　　　Rain then thy plagues upon me here,
　　　Ghastly disease and frenzying fear;
　　　And let alternate frost and fire
　　　Eat into me, and be thine ire
Lightning, and cutting hail, and legioned forms
Of Furies driving by upon the wounding storms.

"Ay, do thy worst. Thou art omnipotent.
　O'er all things but thyself I gave thee power,
And my own will. Be thy swift mischiefs sent
　To blast mankind, from yon etherial tower
　　　Let thy malignant spirit move
　　　In darkness over those I love:
　　　On me and mine I imprecate
　　　The utmost torture of thy hate;
And thus devote to sleepless agony
This undeclining head while thou must reign on high.

"But thou, who art the God and Lord: Oh thou
　Who fillest with thy soul this world of woe,
To whom all things of Earth and Heaven do bow
　In fear and worship, all-prevailing foe!
　　　I curse thee! Let a sufferer's curse
　　　Clasp thee, his torturer, like remorse!
　　　Till thine Infinity shall be
　　　A robe of envenomed agony;
And thine Omnipotence a crown of pain,
To cling like burning gold round thy dissolving brain.

"Heap on thy soul, by virtue of this curse,
　Ill deeds,—then be thou damned, beholding good
Both infinite as is the universe,
　And thou, and thy self-torturing solitude.
　　An awful image of calm Power
　　Though now thou sittest, let the hour
　　Come when thou must appear to be
　　That which thou art internally:
And, after many a false and fruitless crime,
Scorn track thy lagging fall through boundless space and time!"

Prometheus.　Were these my words, O Parent?
The Earth.　　　　　　　　　They were thine.
Prometheus.　It doth repent me: words are quick and vain:
Grief for awhile is blind, and so was mine.
I wish no living thing to suffer pain.
The Earth.　Misery, Oh misery to me,
　　That Jove at length should vanquish thee!
　　Wail, howl aloud, Land and Sea,—
　　The Earth's rent heart shall answer ye!
Howl, Spirits of the living and the dead,
Your refuge, your defence, lies fallen and vanquishèd!

　　　　　FIRST ECHO.
　　Lies fallen and vanquishèd?
　　　　　SECOND ECHO.
　　Fallen and vanquishèd!
　　　　　IONE.
Fear not: 'tis but some passing spasm,
　The Titan is unvanquished still.
But see where through the azure chasm
　Of yon forked and snowy hill,
Trampling the slant winds on high
　With golden-sandalled feet that glow
Under plumes of purple dye
Like rose-ensanguined ivory,
　　　　A Shape comes now,

    Stretching on high from his right hand
     A serpent-cinctured wand.
Panthea. 'Tis Jove's world-wandering herald, Mercury.
       IONE.
  And who are those with hydra tresses
    And iron wings that climb the wind,
  Whom the frowning God represses,
    Like vapours steaming up behind,
  Clanging loud, an endless crowd?
      PANTHEA.
  These are Jove's tempest-walking hounds,
  Whom he gluts with groans and blood
  When, charioted on sulphurous cloud,
    He bursts heaven's bounds.
      IONE.
  Are they now led from the thin dead,
    On new pangs to be fed?
Panthea. The Titan looks, as ever, firm, not proud.
First Fury. Ha! I scent life!
Second Fury. Let me but look into his eyes!
Third Fury. The hope of torturing him smells like a heap
Of corpses to a death-bird after battle!
 First Fury. Darest thou delay, O Herald! Take cheer,
    Hounds
Of Hell! What if the Son of Maia soon
Should make us food and sport?—Who can please long
The Omnipotent?
 Mercury.   Back to your towers of iron,
And gnash, beside the streams of fire and wail,
Your foodless teeth!—Geryon, arise! and Gorgon,
Chimæra, and thou Sphinx, subtlest of fiends,
Who ministered to Thebes heaven's poisoned wine—
Unnatural love, and more unnatural hate!—
These shall perform your task.
 First Fury.   Oh! mercy! mercy!
We die with our desire: drive us not back!

Mercury.   Crouch then in silence.
                              Awful Sufferer!
To thee unwilling, most unwillingly
I come, by the Great Father's will driven down,
To execute a doom of new revenge.
Alas! I pity thee, and hate myself
That I can do no more.   Aye from thy sight
Returning, for a season heaven seems hell,
So thy worn form pursues me night and day,
Smiling reproach.   Wise art thou, firm, and good,
But vainly wouldst stand forth alone in strife
Against the Omnipotent; as yon clear lamps
That measure and divide the weary years,
From which there is no refuge, long have taught,
And long must teach.   Even now thy Torturer arms
With the strange might of unimagined pains
The powers who scheme slow agonies in hell;
And my commission is to lead them here,
Or what more subtle, foul, or savage fiends
People the abyss, and leave them to their task.
Be it not so!   There is a secret known
To thee, and to none else of living things,
Which may transfer the sceptre of wide heaven,
The fear of which perplexes the Supreme;—
Clothe it in words, and bid it clasp his throne
In intercession; bend thy soul in prayer,
And, like a suppliant in some gorgeous fane,
Let the will kneel within thy haughty heart:
For benefits and meek submission tame
The fiercest and the mightiest.
   Prometheus.   Evil minds
Change good to their own nature.   I gave all
He has; and in return he chains me here,
Years, ages, night and day; whether the Sun
Split my parched skin, or in the moony night
The crystal-winged snow cling round my hair;
Whilst my beloved race is trampled down

By his thought-executing ministers.
Such is the Tyrant's recompense. 'Tis just:
He who is evil can receive no good
And for a world bestowed or a friend lost
He can feel hate, fear, shame; not gratitude.
He but requites me for his own misdeed.
Kindness to such is keen reproach, which breaks
With bitter stings the light sleep of Revenge.
Submission thou dost know I cannot try;
For what submission but that fatal word,
The death-seal of mankind's captivity,
Like the Sicilian's hair-suspended sword
Which trembles o'er his crown, would he accept,
Or could I yield? Which yet I will not yield.
Let others flatter Crime where it sits throned
In brief omnipotence! Secure are they:
For Justice, when triumphant, will weep down
Pity, not punishment, on her own wrongs,
Too much avenged by those who err. I wait,
Enduring thus, the retributive hour
Which since we spake is even nearer now.
But hark, the Hell-hounds clamour. Fear delay!
Behold! Heaven lours under thy Father's frown!
   Mercury. Oh that we might be spared—I to inflict,
And thou to suffer! Once more answer me:
Thou knowest not the period of Jove's power?
   Prometheus. I know but this, that it must come.
   Mercury.   Alas!
Thou canst not count thy years to come of pain!
   Prometheus. They last while Jove must reign; nor more
       nor less
Do I desire or fear.
   Mercury.   Yet pause, and plunge
Into eternity, where recorded time—
Even all that we imagine, age on age—
Seems but a point, and the reluctant mind
Flags wearily in its unending flight,

Till it sink, dizzy, blind, lost, shelterless.
Perchance it has not numbered the slow years
Which thou must spend in torture, unreprieved?
   Prometheus. Perchance no thought can count them, yet
      they pass.
   Mercury. If thou mightst dwell among the Gods the while,
Lapped in voluptuous joy?
   Prometheus.   I would not quit
This bleak ravine, these unrepentant pains.
   Mercury. Alas! I wonder at, yet pity thee.
   Prometheus. Pity the self-despising slaves of Heaven,—
Not me, within whose mind sits peace serene,
As light in the sun, throned. How vain is talk!
Call up the fiends.
   Ione.   O sister, look! White fire
Has cloven to the roots yon huge snow-loaded cedar!
How fearfully God's thunder howls behind!
   Mercury. I must obey his words and thine: alas!
Most heavily remorse hangs at my heart!
   Panthea. See where the child of Heaven, with wingèd
      feet,
Runs down the slanted sunlight of the dawn.
   Ione. Dear sister, close thy plumes over thine eyes,
Lest thou behold and die. They come, they come,
Blackening the birth of day with countless wings,
And hollow underneath like death.
   First Fury.   Prometheus!
   Second Fury. Immortal Titan!
   Third Fury.   Champion of Heaven's slaves!
   Prometheus. He whom some dreadful voice invokes is here,
Prometheus, the chained Titan. Horrible forms,
What and who are ye? Never yet there came
Phantasms so foul through monster-teeming Hell
From the all-miscreative brain of Jove.
Whilst I behold such execrable shapes,
Methinks I grow like what I contemplate,
And laugh and stare in loathsome sympathy.

First Fury. We are the ministers of pain and fear,
And disappointment and mistrust and hate,
And clinging crime; and, as lean dogs pursue
Through wood and lake some struck and sobbing fawn,
We track all things that weep and bleed and live,
When the great King betrays them to our will.
   Prometheus. O many fearful natures in one name!
I know ye; and these lakes and echoes know
The darkness and the clangour of your wings.
But why more hideous than your loathed selves
Gather ye up in legions from the deep?
   Second Fury. We knew not that. Sisters, rejoice, rejoice!
   Prometheus. Can aught exult in its deformity?
   Second Fury. The beauty of delight makes lovers glad,
Gazing on one another: so are we.
As from the rose which the pale priestess kneels
To gather for her festal crown of flowers
The aërial crimson falls, flushing her cheek,
So from our victim's destined agony
The shade which is our form invests us round,—
Else we are shapeless as our mother Night.
   Prometheus. I laugh your power, and his who sent you here,
To lowest scorn. Pour forth the cup of pain.
   First Fury. Thou thinkest we will rend thee bone from bone,
And nerve from nerve, working like fire within?
   Prometheus. Pain is my element, as hate is thine.
Ye rend me now: I care not.
   Second Fury.   Dost imagine
We will but laugh into thy lidless eyes?
   Prometheus. I weigh not what ye do, but what ye suffer,
Being evil. Cruel was the power which called
You, or aught else so wretched, into light.
   Third Fury. Thou think'st we will live through thee, one
        by one,
Like animal life; and, though we can obscure not
The soul which burns within, that we will dwell
Beside it, like a vain loud multitude

Vexing the self-content of wisest men;
That we will be dread thought beneath thy brain,
And foul desire round thine astonished heart,
And blood within thy labyrinthine veins
Crawling like agony.
   Prometheus.   Why, ye are thus now:--
Yet am I king over myself, and rule
The torturing and conflicting throngs within,
As Jove rules you when Hell grows mutinous.

Chorus of Furies.

From the ends of the earth, from the ends of the earth,
Where the night has its grave and the morning its birth,
   Come, come, come!
O ye who shake hills with the scream of your mirth
When cities sink howling in ruin! and ye
Who with wingless footsteps trample the sea,
And close upon Shipwreck and Famine's track
Sit chattering with joy on the foodless wreck,
   Come, come, come!
Leave the bed, low, cold, and red,
Strewed beneath a nation dead;
Leave the hatred, as in ashes
  Fire is left for future burning—
It will burst in bloodier flashes
  When ye stir it, soon returning:
Leave the self-contempt implanted
In young spirits, sense-enchanted,
  Misery's yet unkindled fuel:
Leave Hell's secrets half unchanted
  To the maniac dreamer,—cruel,
More than ye can be with hate,
     Is he with fear.
   Come, come, come!
We are steaming up from Hell's wide gate,
And we burthen the blasts of the atmosphere,
But vainly we toil till ye come here!

Ione. Sister, I hear the thunder of new wings.
Panthea. These solid mountains quiver with the sound,
Even as the tremulous air: their shadows make
The space within my plumes more black than night.

FOURTH FURY.
Your call was as a wingèd car
Driven on whirlwinds fast and far;
It rapt us from red gulfs of war;

FIFTH FURY.
From wide cities famine-wasted;

SIXTH FURY.
Groans half heard, and blood untasted;

SEVENTH FURY.
Kingly conclaves, stern and cold,
Where blood with gold is bought and sold;

EIGHTH FURY.
From the furnace, white and hot,
In which—

A FURY.
Speak not, whisper not!
I know all that ye would tell,
But to speak might break the spell
Which must bend the Invincible,
The stern of thought;
He yet defies the deepest power of Hell.

A FURY.
Tear the veil!

ANOTHER FURY.
It is torn.

CHORUS.
The pale stars of the morn
Shine on a misery dire to be borne.
Dost thou faint, mighty Titan? We laugh thee to scorn!
Dost thou boast the clear knowledge thou wakenedst for
man?
Then was kindled within him a thirst which outran
Those perishing waters; a thirst of fierce fever,

Hope, love, doubt, desire, which consume him for ever.
One came forth of gentle worth,
Smiling on the sanguine earth:
His words outlived him, like swift poison
   Withering up truth, peace, and pity.
Look! where round the wide horizon
   Many a million-peopled city
Vomits smoke in the bright air!
Mark that outcry of despair!
'Tis his mild and gentle ghost
   Wailing for the faith he kindled.
Look again! the flames almost
   To a glow-worm's lamp have dwindled:
The survivors round the embers
      Gather in dread.
     Joy, joy, joy!
Past ages crowd on thee, but each one remembers;
And the future is dark, and the present is spread
Like a pillow of thorns for thy slumberless head!
      SEMICHORUS I.
Drops of bloody agony flow
From his white and quivering brow.
Grant a little respite now.
See! a disenchanted nation
Springs like day from desolation;
To Truth its state is dedicate,
And Freedom leads it forth, her mate;—
A legioned band of linked brothers,
Whom Love calls children—
      SEMICHORUS II.
                'Tis another's!
See how kindred murder kin!
'Tis the vintage-time for Death and Sin.
Blood, like new wine, bubbles within:
   Till despair smothers
The struggling world, which slaves and tyrants win.
      [*All the* FURIES *vanish, except one.*

Ione. Hark, sister! what a low yet dreadful groan,
Quite unsuppressed, is tearing up the heart
Of the good Titan, as storms tear the deep,
And beasts hear the sea moan in inland caves.
Darest thou observe how the fiends torture him?
   Panthea. Alas! I looked forth twice, but will no more.
   Ione. What didst thou see?
   Panthea.   A woful sight: a youth
With patient looks nailed to a crucifix.
   Ione. What next?
   Panthea.   The heaven around, the earth below,
Was peopled with thick shapes of human death,
All horrible, and wrought by human hands:
And some appeared the work of human hearts,
For men were slowly killed by frowns and smiles.
And other sights too foul to speak and live
Were wandering by. Let us not tempt worse fear
By looking forth: those groans are grief enough.
   Fury. Behold an emblem: those who do endure
Deep wrongs for man, and scorn, and chains, but heap
Thousandfold torment on themselves and him.
   Prometheus. Remit the anguish of that lighted stare:
Close those wan lips; let that thorn-wounded brow
Stream not with blood; it mingles with thy tears!
Fix, fix those tortured orbs in peace and death,—
So thy sick throes shake not that crucifix,
So those pale fingers play not with thy gore.
Oh horrible! Thy name I will not speak,
It hath become a curse. I see, I see
The wise, the mild, the lofty, and the just,
Whom thy slaves hate for being like to thee,
Some hunted by foul lies from their heart's home,
An early-chosen, late-lamented home,—
As hooded ounces cling to the driven hind;
Some linked to corpses in unwholesome cells;
Some—hear I not the multitude laugh loud?—
Impaled in lingering fire: and mighty realms

Float by my feet, like sea-uprooted isles,
Whose sons are kneaded down in common blood
By the red light of their own burning homes.
   Fury. Blood thou canst see, and fire; and canst hear
        groans:—
Worse things, unheard, unseen, remain behind.
   Prometheus. Worse?
   Fury.   In each human heart terror survives
The ravin it has gorged. The loftiest fear
All that they would disdain to think were true:
Hypocrisy and custom make their minds
The fanes of many a worship now outworn.
They dare not devise good for man's estate,
And yet they know not that they do not dare.
The good want power but to weep barren tears:
The powerful goodness want,—worse need for them:
The wise want love: and those who love want wisdom:
And all best things are thus confused to ill.
Many are strong and rich, and would be just,
But live among their suffering fellow-men
As if none felt: they know not what they do.
   Prometheus. Thy words are like a cloud of wingèd snakes;
And yet I pity those they torture not.
   Fury. Thou pitiest them? I speak no more!   [*Vanishes.*
   Prometheus.   Ah woe!
Ah woe! Alas! pain, pain ever, for ever!
I close my tearless eyes, but see more clear
Thy works within my woe-illumined mind,
Thou subtle Tyrant! Peace is in the grave:
The grave hides all things beautiful and good.
I am a God, and cannot find it there,
Nor would I seek it: for, though dread revenge,
This is defeat, fierce king! not victory.
The sights with which thou torturest gird my soul
With new endurance, till the hour arrives
When they shall be no types of things which are.
   Panthea. Alas! what sawest thou?

Prometheus.   There are two woes
To speak, and to behold:—thou spare me one.
Names are there, Nature's sacred watchwords: they
Were borne aloft in bright emblazonry;
The nations thronged around, and cried aloud,
As with one voice, "Truth, Liberty, and Love!"
Suddenly fierce confusion fell from heaven
Among them: there was strife, deceit, and fear:
Tyrants rushed in, and did divide the spoil.
This was the shadow of the truth I saw.
   The Earth. I felt thy torture, son, with such mixed joy
As pain and virtue give. To cheer thy state,
I bid ascend those subtle and fair Spirits
Whose homes are the dim caves of human thought,
And who inhabit, as birds wing the wind,
Its world-surrounding ether. They behold
Beyond that twilight realm, as in a glass,
The future: may they speak comfort to thee!
   Panthea. Look, sister, where a troop of Spirits gather,
Like flocks of clouds in Spring's delightful weather
Thronging in the blue air!
   Ione.   And see! more come,
Like fountain-vapours when the winds are dumb,
That climb up the ravine in scattered lines.
And hark! is it the music of the pines?
Is it the lake? is it the waterfall?
   Panthea. 'Tis something sadder, sweeter, far than all.

CHORUS OF SPIRITS OF THE MIND.

From unremembered ages we
Gentle guides and guardians be
Of Heaven-oppressed Mortality.
And we breathe, and sicken not,
The atmosphere of human thought:
Be it dim and dank and grey,
Like a storm-extinguished day
Travelled o'er by dying gleams;

Be it bright as all between
Cloudless skies and windless streams,
　Silent, liquid, and serene.
As the birds within the wind,
　As the fish within the wave,
As the thoughts of man's own mind
　Float through all above the grave:
We make there our liquid lair,
Voyaging cloudlike and unpent
Through the boundless element.
Thence we bear the prophecy
Which begins and ends in thee!

Ione.　More yet come, one by one: the air around them
Looks radiant as the air around a star.

FIRST SPIRIT.
On a battle-trumpet's blast
I fled hither, fast, fast, fast,
'Mid the darkness upward cast.
From the dust of creeds outworn,
From the tyrant's banner torn,
Gathering round me, onward borne,
There was mingled many a cry—
"Freedom! Hope! Death! Victory!"
Till they faded through the sky.
And one sound above, around,
One sound beneath, around, above,
Was moving; 'twas the soul of Love;
'Twas the hope, the prophecy,
Which begins and ends in thee.

SECOND SPIRIT.
A rainbow's arch stood on the sea,
Which rocked beneath, immovably;
And the triumphant storm did flee
(Like a conqueror, swift and proud)
Between,—with many a captive cloud,
A shapeless, dark, and rapid crowd,

Each by lightning riven in half.
I heard the thunder hoarsely laugh:
Mighty fleets were strewn like chaff,
And spread beneath, a hell of death,
O'er the white waters. I alit
On a great ship lightning-split;
And speeded hither on the sigh
Of one who gave an enemy
His plank, then plunged aside to die.

THIRD SPIRIT.
I sate beside a sage's bed,
And the lamp was burning red
Near the book where he had fed;
When a Dream with plumes of flame
To his pillow hovering came.
And I knew it was the same
Which had kindled long ago
Pity, eloquence, and woe;
And the world awhile below
Wore the shade its lustre made.
It has borne me here as fleet
As Desire's lightning feet:
I must ride it back ere morrow,
Or the sage will wake in sorrow.

FOURTH SPIRIT.
On a poet's lips I slept,
Dreaming like a love-adept
In the sound his breathing kept;
Nor seeks nor finds he mortal blisses,
But feeds on the aërial kisses
Of shapes that haunt thought's wildernesses.
He will watch from dawn to gloom
The lake-reflected sun illume
The yellow bees in the ivy-bloom,
Nor heed nor see what things they be;
But from these create he can

Forms more real than living man,
Nurslings of immortality!
One of these awakened me,
And I sped to succour thee.

Ione. Behold'st thou not two shapes from the east and west
Come? as two doves to one beloved nest,
Twin nurslings of the all-sustaining air,
On swift still wings glide down the atmosphere.
And hark! their sweet sad voices! 'tis despair
Mingled with love, and then dissolved in sound.
    Panthea. Canst thou speak, sister? all my words are
        drowned.
    Ione. Their beauty gives me voice. See how they float
On their sustaining wings of skiey grain,
Orange and azure deepening into gold:
Their soft smiles light the air like a star's fire.

Chorus of Spirits.

Hast thou beheld the form of Love?

Fifth Spirit.

                      As over wide dominions
  I sped, like some swift cloud that wings the wide air's
     wildernesses,
That planet-crested shape swept by on lightning-braided
     pinions,
  Scattering the liquid joy of life from his ambrosial tresses:
His footsteps paved the world with light; but, as I passed,
     'twas fading,
  And hollow ruin yawned behind: great sages bound in
     madness,
And headless patriots, and pale youths who perished unup-
     braiding,
  Gleamed in the night. I wandered o'er, till thou, O King
     of Sadness,
  Turn'st by thy smile the worst I saw to recollected glad-
     ness.

Sixth Spirit.

Ah Sister! Desolation is a delicate thing:
  It walks not on the earth, it floats not on the air,
But treads with killing footstep, and fans with silent wing,
The tender hopes which in their hearts the best and gentlest
    bear;
  Who, soothed to false repose by the fanning plumes
    above,
And the music-stirring motion of its soft and busy feet,
  Dream visions of aërial joy, and call the monster Love,
And wake, and find the shadow Pain, as he whom now we greet.

Chorus.

Though Ruin now Love's shadow be
Following him destroyingly
  On Death's white and winged steed
Which the fleetest cannot flee,
  Trampling down both flower and weed,
Man and beast, and foul and fair,
Like a tempest through the air;
Thou shalt quell this horseman grim,
Woundless though in heart or limb.

Prometheus.

Spirits! how know ye this shall be?

Chorus.

In the atmosphere we breathe,
As buds grow red when the snow-storms flee
  From spring gathering up beneath,
Whose mild winds shake the elder-brake,
And the wandering herdsmen know
That the white-thorn soon will blow:
Wisdom, Justice, Love, and Peace,
When they struggle to increase,
Are to us as soft winds be
To shepherd boys, the prophecy
Which begins and ends in thee.

Ione. Where are the Spirits fled?
Panthea.   Only a sense
Remains of them; like the omnipotence
Of music when the inspired voice and lute
Languish, ere yet the responses are mute
Which through the deep and labyrinthine soul,
Like echoes through long caverns, wind and roll.
Prometheus. How fair these air-born shapes! And yet I feel
Most vain all hope but love! And thou art far,
Asia! who, when my being overflowed,
Wert like a golden chalice to bright wine
Which else had sunk into the thirsty dust.
All things are still. Alas! how heavily
This quiet morning weighs upon my heart;
Though I should dream I could even sleep with grief,
If slumber were denied not. I would fain
Be what it is my destiny to be,
The saviour and the strength of suffering man,
Or sink into the original gulf of things:
There is no agony and no solace left;
Earth can console, Heaven can torment, no more.
Panthea. Hast thou forgotten one who watches thee
The cold dark night, and never sleeps but when
The shadow of thy spirit falls on her?
Prometheus. I said all hope was vain but love: thou lovest.
Panthea. Deeply in truth; but the eastern star looks white,
And Asia waits in that far Indian vale,
The scene of her sad exile; rugged once
And desolate and frozen, like this ravine;
But now invested with fair flowers and herbs,
And haunted by sweet airs and sounds, which flow
Among the woods and waters, from the ether
Of her transforming presence, which would fade
If it were mingled not with thine. Farewell!

ACT IV.

SCENE.—*A part of the Forest near the Cave of* PROMETHEUS. PANTHEA *and* IONE *are sleeping: they awaken gradually during the first Song.*

VOICE OF UNSEEN SPIRITS.

The pale stars are gone,
   For the Sun, their swift shepherd,
   To their folds them compelling
In the depths of the dawn,
Hastes in meteor-eclipsing array; and they flee
   Beyond his blue dwelling,
   As fawns flee the leopard,
But where are ye?

A train of dark Forms and Shadows passes by confusedly, singing.

   Here, oh here
   We bear the bier
Of the Father of many a cancelled year.
   Spectres we
   Of the dead Hours be,
We bear Time to his tomb in Eternity.

   Strew, oh strew
   Hair, not yew!
Wet the dusty pall with tears, not dew!
   Be the faded flowers
   Of Death's bare bowers
Spread on the corpse of the King of Hours!

   Haste, oh haste!
   As shades are chased,
Trembling, by day, from heaven's blue waste,

We melt away,
Like dissolving spray,
From the children of a diviner day,
With the lullaby
Of winds that die
On the bosom of their own harmony.

IONE.
What dark forms were they?

PANTHEA.
The past Hours weak and grey,
With the spoil which their toil
Raked together
From the conquest but One could foil.

IONE.
Have they passed?

PANTHEA.
They have passed;
They outspeeded the blast.
While 'tis said, they are fled.

IONE.
Whither, oh! whither?

PANTHEA.
To the dark, to the past, to the dead.

VOICE OF UNSEEN SPIRITS.
Bright clouds float in heaven,
Dew-stars gleam on earth,
Waves assemble on ocean,
They are gathered and driven
By the storm of delight, by the panic of glee,
They shake with emotion,
They dance in their mirth.
But where are ye?

                The pine-boughs are singing
                    Old songs with new gladness,
                The billows and fountains
                    Fresh music are flinging,
            Like the notes of a spirit, from land and from sea;
                The storms mock the mountains
                    With the thunder of gladness.
            But where are ye?

Ione. What charioteers are these?
Panthea.   Where are their chariots?

Semichorus I. of Hours.
The voice of the Spirits of Air and of Earth
    Has drawn back the figured curtain of sleep,
Which covered our being and darkened our birth
    In the deep.

A Voice.
In the deep?

Semichorus II.
             Oh! below the deep.

Semichorus I.
An hundred ages we had been kept
    Cradled in visions of hate and care,
And each one who waked as his brother slept
    Found the truth—

Semichorus II.
         Worse than his visions were!

Semichorus I.
We have heard the lute of Hope in sleep;
    We have known the voice of Love in dreams;
We have felt the wand of Power, and leap—

Semichorus II.
As the billows leap in the morning beams,

CHORUS.
Weave the dance on the floor of the breeze,
  Pierce with song heaven's silent light,
Enchant the Day, that too swiftly flees,
  To check its flight ere the cave of Night.

Once the hungry Hours were hounds
  Which chased the Day like a bleeding deer,
And it limped and stumbled with many wounds
  Through the nightly dells of the desert year.

But now—oh! weave the mystic measure
  Of music and dance and shapes of light!
Let the Hours, and the Spirits of might and pleasure,
  Like the clouds and sunbeams, unite.

A VOICE.
                    Unite.

Panthea. See where the Spirits of the Human Mind,
Wrapped in sweet sounds as in bright veils, approach.

CHORUS OF SPIRITS OF THE MIND.
    We join the throng
    Of the dance and the song
By the whirlwind of gladness borne along;
    As the flying-fish leap
    From the Indian deep,
And mix with the sea-birds half asleep.

CHORUS OF HOURS.
Whence come ye, so wild and so fleet,
For sandals of lightning are on your feet,
And your wings are soft and swift as thought,
And your eyes are as love which is veiled not?

CHORUS OF SPIRITS OF THE MIND.
    We come from the mind
    Of humankind,
Which was late so dusk and obscene and blind:—

Now 'tis an ocean
Of clear emotion,
A heaven of serene and mighty motion:—

From that deep abyss
Of wonder and bliss
Whose caverns are crystal palaces;
From those skiey towers
Where thought's crowned powers
Sit watching your dance, ye happy Hours:—

From the dim recesses
Of woven caresses,
Where lovers catch ye by your loose tresses;
From the azure isles
Where sweet Wisdom smiles,
Delaying your ships with her siren wiles:—

From the temples high
Of Man's ear and eye,
Roofed over Sculpture and Poesy;
From the murmurings
Of the unsealed springs
Where Science bedews his dædal wings.

Years after years,
Through blood and tears,
And a thick hell of hatreds and hopes and fears,
We waded and flew,—
And the islets were few
Where the bud-blighted flowers of happiness grew.

Our feet now, every palm,
Are sandalled with calm,
And the dew of our wings is a rain of balm;
And beyond our eyes
The human love lies
Which makes all it gazes on paradise.

Chorus of Spirits and Hours.
Then weave the web of the mystic measure;
  From the depths of the sky and the ends of the earth,
Come, swift Spirits of might and of pleasure,
  Fill the dance and the music of mirth,—
As the waves of a thousand streams rush by
To an ocean of splendour and harmony!

Chorus of Spirits of the Mind.
    Our spoil is won,
    Our task is done,
We are free to dive, or soar, or run;
    Beyond and around,
    Or within the bound
Which clips the world with darkness round.

    We'll pass the eyes
    Of the starry skies
Into the hoar deep to colonize:
    Death, Chaos, and Night,
    From the sound of our flight
Shall flee, like mist from a tempest's might.

    And Earth, Air, and Light,
    And the Spirit of Might
Which drives round the stars in their fiery flight,
    And Love, Thought, and Breath,
    The powers that quell Death,
Wherever we soar shall assemble beneath.

    And our singing shall build
    In the void's loose field
A world for the Spirit of Wisdom to wield;
    We will take our plan
    From the new world of man,
And our work shall be called the Promethean.

Chorus of Hours.
Break the dance, and scatter the song;
  Let some depart, and some remain.

SEMICHORUS I.
We beyond heaven are driven along:

SEMICHORUS II.
Us the enchantments of earth retain:

SEMICHORUS I.
Ceaseless and rapid and fierce and free,
With the Spirits which build a new earth and sea,
And a heaven where yet heaven could never be.

SEMICHORUS II.
Solemn and slow and serene and bright,
Leading the day, and outspeeding the night,
With the powers of a world of perfect light.

SEMICHORUS I.
We whirl, singing loud, round the gathering sphere,
Till the trees and the beasts and the clouds appear
From its chaos, made calm by love, not fear.

SEMICHORUS II.
We encircle the ocean and mountains of earth,
And the happy forms of its death and birth
Change to the music of our sweet mirth.

CHORUS OF HOURS AND SPIRITS.
Break the dance, and scatter the song;
  Let some depart and some remain.
Wherever we fly, we lead along
In leashes like star-beams, soft yet strong,
  The clouds that are heavy with love's sweet rain.

Panthea. Ha! they are gone!
Ione.   Yet feel you no delight
From the past sweetness?
Panthea.   As the bare green hill,
When some soft cloud vanishes into rain,
Laughs with a thousand drops of sunny water
To the unpavilioned sky!

Ione.   Even whilst we speak,
New notes arise. What is that awful sound?
   Panthea. 'Tis the deep music of the rolling world,
Kindling within the strings of the waved air
Æolian modulations.
   Ione.   Listen too
How every pause is filled with under-notes,
Clear, silver, icy, keen, awakening tones,
Which pierce the sense, and live within the soul,
As the sharp stars pierce winter's crystal air,
And gaze upon themselves within the sea.
   Panthea. But see where, through two openings in the forest
Which hanging branches overcanopy,
And where two runnels of a rivulet
Between the close moss, violet-inwoven,
Have made their path of melody, like sisters
Who part with sighs that they may meet in smiles
Turning their dear disunion to an isle
Of lovely grief, a wood of sweet sad thoughts,
Two visions of strange radiance float upon
The ocean-like enchantment of strong sound,
Which flows intenser, keener, deeper yet,
Under the ground and through the windless air.
   Ione. I see a chariot like that thinnest boat
In which the Mother of the Months is borne
By ebbing night into her western cave,
When she upsprings from interlunar dreams,
O'er which is curved an orblike canopy
Of gentle darkness, and the hills and woods,
Distinctly seen through that dusk airy veil,
Regard like shapes in an enchanter's glass;
Its wheels are solid clouds, azure and gold,
Such as the genii of the thunder-storm
Pile on the floor of the illumined sea
When the sun rushes under it; they roll
And move and grow as with an inward wind;
Within it sits a wingèd infant, white

Its countenance, like the whiteness of bright snow,
Its plumes are as feathers of sunny frost,
Its limbs gleam white through the wind-flowing folds
Of its white robe, woof of etherial pearl.
Its hair is white, the brightness of white light
Scattered in strings; yet its two eyes are heavens
Of liquid darkness, which the Deity
Within seems pouring, as a storm is poured
From jagged clouds, out of their arrowy lashes,
Tempering the cold and radiant air around
With fire that is not brightness; in its hand
It sways a quivering moonbeam, from whose point
A guiding power directs the chariot's prow
Over its wheeled clouds, which, as they roll
Over the grass and flowers and waves, wake sounds
Sweet as a singing rain of silver dew.

Panthea. And from the other opening in the wood
Rushes, with loud and whirlwind harmony,
A sphere which is as many thousand spheres,
Solid as crystal, yet through all its mass
Flow, as through empty space, music and light:
Ten thousand orbs involving and involved,
Purple and azure, white and green and golden,
Sphere within sphere; and every space between
Peopled with unimaginable shapes,
Such as ghosts dream dwell in the lampless deep,
Yet each inter-transpicuous. And they whirl
Over each other with a thousand motions,
Upon a thousand sightless axles spinning;
And, with the force of self-destroying swiftness,
Intensely, slowly, solemnly, roll on,
Kindling with mingled sounds, and many tones,
Intelligible words and music wild.
With mighty whirl the multitudinous orb
Grinds the bright brook into an azure mist
Of elemental subtlety, like light;
And the wild odour of the forest flowers,

The music of the living grass and air,
The emerald light of leaf-entangled beams,
Round its intense yet self-conflicting speed
Seem kneaded into one aërial mass
Which drowns the sense. Within the orb itself,
Pillowed upon its alabaster arms,
Like to a child o'erwearied with sweet toil,
On its own folded wings and wavy hair
The Spirit of the Earth is laid asleep;
And you can see its little lips are moving,
Amid the changing light of their own smiles,
Like one who talks of what he loves in dream.
   Ione. 'Tis only mocking the orb's harmony.
   Panthea. And from a star upon its forehead shoot,
Like swords of azure fire, or golden spears
With tyrant-quelling myrtle overtwined,
Embleming heaven and earth united now,
Vast beams like spokes of some invisible wheel:
Which whirl as the orb whirls, swifter than thought,
Filling the abyss with sun-like lightenings,
And, perpendicular now and now transverse,
Pierce the dark soil, and, as they pierce and pass,
Make bare the secrets of the earth's deep heart;
Infinite mine of adamant and gold,
Valueless stones and unimagined gems,
And caverns on crystalline columns poised,
With vegetable silver overspread,
Wells of unfathomed fire, and water-springs
Whence the great sea even as a child is fed,
Whose vapours clothe earth's monarch mountain tops
With kingly ermine snow. The beams flash on,
And make appear the melancholy ruins
Of cancelled cycles; anchors, beaks of ships;
Planks turned to marble; quivers, helms, and spears,
And gorgon-headed targes, and the wheels
Of scythed chariots; and the emblazonry
Of trophies, standards, and armorial beasts,

Round which Death laughed, sepulchred emblems
Of dead destruction, ruin within ruin!
The wrecks beside of many a city vast,
Whose population, which the earth grew over,
Was mortal, but not human. See, they lie,
Their monstrous works and uncouth skeletons,
Their statues, homes, and fanes; prodigious shapes
Huddled in grey annihilation, split,
Jammed in the hard black deep: and over these,
The anatomies of unknown winged things,
And fishes which were isles of living scale,
And serpents, bony chains twisted around
The iron crags, or within heaps of dust
To which the tortuous strength of their last pangs
Had crushed the iron crags; and over these,
The jagged alligator, and the might
Of earth-convulsing behemoth, which once
Were monarch beasts, and on the slimy shores
And weed-overgrown continents of earth
Increased and multiplied like summer worms
On an abandoned corpse,—till the blue globe
Wrapped deluge round it like a cloak, and they
Yelled, gasped, and were abolished; or some God
Whose throne was in a comet passed, and cried
"Be not!" and like my words they were no more.

The Earth.

The joy, the triumph, the delight, the madness!
The boundless, overflowing, bursting gladness,
The vaporous exultation not to be confined!
Ha! ha! the animation of delight
Which wraps me like an atmosphere of light,
And bears me as a cloud is borne by its own wind!

The Moon.

Brother mine, calm wanderer,
Happy globe of land and air,
Some spirit is darted like a beam from thee,

Which penetrates my frozen frame,
And passes, with the warmth of flame,
With love and odour and deep melody,
    Through me, through me!

The Earth.
Ha! ha! the caverns of my hollow mountains,
My cloven fire-crags, sound-exulting fountains,
Laugh with a vast and inextinguishable laughter!
    The oceans, and the deserts, and the abysses,
    And the deep air's unmeasured wildernesses,
Answer from all their clouds and billows, echoing after.

They cry aloud as I do:—"Sceptred Curse,
Who all our green and azure universe
Threatenedst to muffle round with black destruction, sending
    A solid cloud to rain hot thunder-stones,
    And splinter and knead down my children's bones,
All I bring forth to one void mass battering and blending—

"Until each crag-like tower and storied column,
Palace and obelisk and temple solemn,
My imperial mountains crowned with cloud, and snow, and fire;
    My sea-like forests, every blade and blossom
    Which finds a grave or cradle in my bosom,
Were stamped by thy strong hate into a lifeless mire—

"How art thou sunk, withdrawn, covered, drunk up
By thirsty nothing, as the brackish cup
Drained by a desert-troop, a little drop for all!
    And from beneath, around, within, above,
    Filling thy void annihilation, Love
Bursts in like light on caves cloven by the thunder-ball!"

The Moon.
The snow upon my lifeless mountains
Is loosened into living fountains,
My solid oceans flow and sing and shine:
    A spirit from my heart bursts forth,
    It clothes with unexpected birth

My cold bare bosom: Oh! it must be thine
  On mine, on mine!
 Gazing on thee, I feel, I know,
 Green stalks burst forth, and bright flowers grow,
And living shapes upon my bosom move:
 Music is in the sea and air,
 Winged clouds soar here and there,
Dark with the rain new buds are dreaming of:
  'Tis Love, all Love!

THE EARTH.

It interpenetrates my granite mass;
Through tangled roots and trodden clay doth pass
Into the utmost leaves and delicatest flowers;
 Upon the winds, among the clouds, 'tis spread,
 It wakes a life in the forgotten dead,
They breathe a spirit up from their obscurest bowers.

 And, like a storm bursting its cloudy prison
 With thunder, and with whirlwind, has arisen.
Out of the lampless caves of unimagined being:—
 With earthquake shock and swiftness making shiver
 Thought's stagnant chaos, unremoved for ever:—
Till hate, and fear, and pain, light-vanquished shadows, fleeing,

 Leave Man, who was a many-sided mirror,
 Which could distort to many a shape of error
This true fair world of things, a sea reflecting love;
 Which over all his kind—as the sun's heaven
 Gliding o'er ocean, smooth, serene, and even—
Darting from starry depths radiance and life, doth move:—

 Leave man, even as a leprous child is left
 Who follows a sick beast to some warm cleft
Of rocks through which the might of healing springs is poured,—
 Then when it wanders home with rosy smile,
 Unconscious, and its mother fears awhile
It is a spirit,—then, weeps on her child restored.

Man,—oh, not men! a chain of linked thought,
Of love and might to be divided not,
Compelling the elements with adamantine stress;
  As the Sun rules, even with a tyrant's gaze,
  The unquiet republic of the maze
Of Planets, struggling fierce towards heaven's free wilderness.

  Man, one harmonious soul of many a soul,
  Whose nature is its own divine control,
Where all things flow to all, as rivers to the sea;
  Familiar acts are beautiful through love;
  Labour and pain and grief, in life's green grove,
Sport like tame beasts,—none knew how gentle they could be!

  His will, with all mean passions, bad delights,
  And selfish cares, its trembling satellites,
A spirit ill to guide, but mighty to obey,—
  Is as a tempest-winged ship, whose helm
  Love rules, through waves which dare not overwhelm,
Forcing life's wildest shores to own its sovereign sway.

  All things confess his strength. Through the cold mass
  Of marble and of colour his dreams pass,—
Bright threads whence mothers weave the robes their children wear;
  Language is a perpetual Orphic song
  Which rules with Dædal harmony a throng
Of thoughts and forms, which else senseless and shapeless were.

  The lightning is his slave; heaven's utmost deep
  Gives up her stars, and like a flock of sheep
They pass before his eye, are numbered, and roll on.
  The tempest is his steed; he strides the air,
  And the abyss shouts from her depth laid bare,
"Heaven, hast thou secrets? Man unveils me; I have none."

THE MOON.

  The shadow of white death has passed
  From my path in heaven at last,
A clinging shroud of solid frost and sleep;

  And through my newly-woven bowers
   Wander happy paramours,
 Less mighty, but as mild as those who keep
   Thy vales more deep.

THE EARTH.

—As the dissolving warmth of dawn may fold
A half infrozen dew-globe, green and gold
And crystalline, till it becomes a winged mist,
 And wanders up the vault of the blue day,
 Outlives the noon, and on the sun's last ray'
Hangs o'er the sea, a fleece of fire and amethyst.

THE MOON.

  Thou art folded, thou art lying,
  In the light which is undying
 Of thine own joy and heaven's smile divine;
  All suns and constellations shower
  On thee a light, a life, a power,
 Which doth array thy sphere; thou pourest thine
   On mine, on mine!

THE EARTH.

I spin beneath my pyramid of night,
 Which points into the heavens,—dreaming delight,
Murmuring victorious joy in my enchanted sleep;
 As a youth lulled in love-dreams faintly sighing,
 Under the shadow of his beauty lying,
Which round his rest a watch of light and warmth doth keep.

THE MOON.

  As in the soft and sweet eclipse
  When soul meets soul on lovers' lips,
 High hearts are calm, and brightest eyes are dull;
  So, when thy shadow falls on me,
  Then am I mute and still, by thee
 Covered; of thy love, Orb most beautiful,
   Full, oh! too full!

Thou art speeding round the sun,
Brightest world of many a one;
Green and azure sphere which shinest
With a light which is divinest
Among all the lamps of Heaven
To whom life and light is given;
I, thy crystal paramour,
Borne beside thee by a power
Like the polar paradise,
Magnet-like, of lovers' eyes;
I, a most enamoured maiden
Whose weak brain is overladen
With the pleasure of her love,
Maniac-like around thee move
Gazing, an insatiate bride,
On thy form from every side,
Like a Mænad round the cup
Which Agave lifted up
In the weird Cadmæan forest.
Brother, wheresoe'er thou soarest,
I must hurry, whirl, and follow,
Through the heavens wide and hollow,
Sheltered by the warm embrace
Of thy soul from hungry space,
Drinking from thy sense and sight
Beauty, majesty, and might;
As a lover or chameleon
Grows like what it looks upon;
As a violet's gentle eye
Gazes on the azure sky
Until its hue grows like what it beholds;
As a grey and watery mist
Glows like solid amethyst
Athwart the western mountain it enfolds,
  When the sunset sleeps
   Upon its snow.

THE EARTH.
And the weak day weeps
That it should be so.
O gentle Moon, the voice of thy delight
Falls on me like thy clear and tender light
Soothing the seaman borne the summer night
Through isles for ever calm;
O gentle Moon, thy crystal accents pierce
The caverns of my pride's deep universe,
Charming the tiger joy, whose tramplings fierce
Made wounds which need thy balm.

Panthea. I rise as from a bath of sparkling water,
A bath of azure light among dark rocks,
Out of the stream of sound.
Ione. Ah me! sweet sister,
The stream of sound has ebbed away from us,
And you pretend to rise out of its wave,
Because your words fall like the clear soft dew
Shaken from a bathing wood-nymph's limbs and hair.
Panthea. Peace, peace! A mighty Power which is as
darkness
Is rising out of earth, and from the sky
Is showered like night, and from within the air
Bursts, like eclipse which had been gathered up
Into the pores of sunlight. The bright visions,
Wherein the singing Spirits rode and shone,
Gleam like pale meteors through a watery night.
Ione. There is a sense of words upon mine ear.
Panthea. An universal sound like words. Oh! list!

DEMOGORGON.
Thou Earth, calm empire of a happy soul,
Sphere of divinest shapes and harmonies,
Beautiful orb! gathering as thou dost roll
The love which paves thy path along the skies:

THE EARTH.
I hear: I am as a drop of dew that dies.

DEMOGORGON.
Thou Moon which gazest on the nightly Earth
  With wonder, as it gazes upon thee;
Whilst each, to men and beasts and the swift birth
  Of birds, is beauty, love, calm, harmony:

THE MOON.
I hear: I am a leaf shaken by thee.

DEMOGORGON.
Ye Kings of Suns and Stars! Dæmons and Gods,
  Etherial Dominations! who possess
Elysian, windless, fortunate abodes
  Beyond Heaven's constellated wilderness:

A VOICE FROM ABOVE.
Our great Republic hears; we are blessed, and bless.

DEMOGORGON.
Ye happy Dead: whom beams of brightest verse
  Are clouds to hide, not colours to pourtray,
Whether your nature is that universe
  Which once ye saw and suffered—

A VOICE FROM BENEATH.
                              Or, as they
Whom we have left, we change and pass away—

DEMOGORGON.
Ye elemental Genii, who have homes
  From man's high mind even to the central stone
Of sullen lead; from Heaven's star-fretted domes
  To the dull weed some sea-worm battens on:

A CONFUSED VOICE.
We hear: thy words waken Oblivion.

DEMOGORGON.
Spirits! whose homes are flesh: ye beasts and birds,
  Ye worms and fish, ye living leaves and buds;
Lightning and wind; and ye untameable herds,
  Meteors and mists, which throng air's solitudes!

A Voice.
Thy voice to us is wind among still woods.

Demogorgon.
Man, who wert once a despot and a slave;
  A dupe and a deceiver; a decay;
A traveller from the cradle to the grave
  Through the dim night of this immortal day!

All.
Speak! thy strong words may never pass away.

Demogorgon.
This is the day which down the void abysm,
At the Earth-born's spell, yawns for Heaven's despotism.
  And Conquest is dragged captive through the deep.
Love, from its awful throne of patient power
In the wise heart, from the last giddy hour
  Of dread endurance, from the slippery, steep,
And narrow verge of crag-like agony, springs,
And folds over the world its healing wings.

Gentleness, Virtue, Wisdom, and Endurance,
These are the seals of that most firm assurance
  Which bars the pit over Destruction's strength;
And, if with infirm hand Eternity,
Mother of many acts and hours, should free
  The serpent that would clasp her with his length,
These are the spells by which to re-assume
An empire o'er the disentangled doom.

To suffer woes which hope thinks infinite;
To forgive wrongs darker than death or night;
  To defy Power which seems omnipotent;
To love, and bear; to hope till hope creates
From its own wreck the thing it contemplates;
  Neither to change, nor falter, nor repent;
This, like thy glory, Titan! is to be
Good, great, and joyous, beautiful and free;
This is alone Life, Joy, Empire, and Victory!

THE CENCI.

A TRAGEDY IN FIVE ACTS.

DRAMATIS PERSONÆ.

COUNT FRANCESCO CENCI.
GIACOMO, } *his Sons.*
BERNARDO,
CARDINAL CAMILLO.
ORSINO, *a Prelate.*
SAVELLA, *the Pope's Legate.*
OLIMPIO, } *Assassins.*
MARZIO,
ANDREA, *Servant to* CENCI.
Nobles, Judges, Guards, Servants.
LUCRETIA, *Wife of* CENCI, *and stepmother of his children.*
BEATRICE, *his daughter.*
The SCENE *lies principally in Rome, but changes during the Fourth Act to Petrella, a Castle among the Apulian Apennines.*
TIME.—During the Pontificate of Clement VIII.

ACT I.

SCENE I.—*An Apartment in the Cenci Palace.*

Enter COUNT CENCI *and* CARDINAL CAMILLO.

Camillo. That matter of the murder is hushed up
If you consent to yield his Holiness
Your fief that lies beyond the Pincian gate.
It needed all my interest in the conclave
To bend him to this point. He said that you
Bought perilous impunity with your gold;
That crimes like yours, if once or twice compounded,
Enriched the Church, and respited from hell

An erring soul which might repent and live;
But that the glory and the interest
Of the high throne he fills little consist
With making it a daily mart of guilt
So manifold and hideous as the deeds
Which you scarce hide from men's revolted eyes.
    Cenci. The third of my possessions—let it go!
Ay, I once heard the nephew of the Pope
Had sent his architect to view the ground,
Meaning to build a villa on my vines
The next time I compounded with his uncle:
I little thought he should outwit me so!
Henceforth no witness—not the lamp—shall see
That which the vassal threatened to divulge
Whose throat is choked with dust for his reward.
The deed he saw could not have rated higher
Than his most worthless life:—it angers me!
"Respited me from hell!"—So may the Devil
Respite their souls from heaven! No doubt Pope Clement
And his most charitable nephews pray
That the Apostle Peter and the saints
Will grant for their sakes that I long enjoy
Strength, wealth, and pride, and lust, and length of days
Wherein to act the deeds which are the stewards
Of their revenue.—But much yet remains
To which they show no title.
    Camillo.   O Count Cenci!
So much that you might honourably live,
And reconcile yourself with your own heart,
And with your God, and with the offended world.
How hideously look deeds of lust and blood
Through those snow-white and venerable hairs!
Your children should be sitting round you now,
But that you fear to read upon their looks
The shame and misery you have written there.
Where is your wife? Where is your gentle daughter?
Methinks her sweet looks, which make all things else

Beauteous and glad, might kill the fiend within you.
Why is she barred from all society
But her own strange and uncomplaining wrongs?
Talk with me, Count; you know I mean you well.
I stood beside your dark and fiery youth,
Watching its bold and bad career, as men
Watch meteors,—but it vanished not; I marked
Your desperate and remorseless manhood; now
Do I behold you, in dishonoured age,
Charged with a thousand unrepented crimes.
Yet I have ever hoped you would amend,
And in that hope have saved your life three times.
    Cenci. For which Aldobrandino owes you now
My fief beyond the Pincian.—Cardinal,
One thing, I pray you, recollect henceforth,
And so we shall converse with less restraint.
A man you knew spoke of my wife and daughter.
He was accustomed to frequent my house;
So the next day *his* wife and daughter came,
And asked if I had seen him; and I smiled:—
I think they never saw him any more.
    Camillo. Thou execrable man, beware!—
    Cenci.   Of thee?
Nay, this is idle:—We should know each other.
As to my character for what men call crime,
Seeing I please my senses as I list,
And vindicate that right with force or guile,
It is a public matter, and I care not
If I discuss it with you.   I may speak
Alike to you and my own conscious heart;
For you give out that you have half reformed me,
Therefore strong vanity will keep you silent,
If fear should not; both will, I do not doubt.
All men delight in sensual luxury,
All men enjoy revenge; and most exult
Over the tortures they can never feel,
Flattering their secret peace with others' pain.

But I delight in nothing else. I love
The sight of agony, and the sense of joy,—
When this shall be another's, and that mine.
And I have no remorse, and little fear,
Which are, I think, the checks of other men.
This mood has grown upon me, until now
Any design my captious fancy makes
The picture of its wish (and it forms none
But such as men like you would start to know)
Is as my natural food and rest debarred
Until it be accomplished.
  Camillo.   Art thou not
Most miserable?
  Cenci. Why miserable?
No. I am what your theologians call
"Hardened;" which they must be in impudence,
So to revile a man's peculiar taste.
True, I was happier than I am, while yet
Manhood remained to act the thing I thought,—
While lust was sweeter than revenge. And now
Invention palls; ay, we must all grow old.
But that there yet remains a deed to act
Whose horror might make sharp an appetite
Duller than mine, I'd do—I know not what.
When I was young, I thought of nothing else
But pleasure, and I fed on honey sweets.
Men, by St. Thomas! cannot live like bees,
And I grew tired: yet, till I killed a foe,
And heard his groans, and heard his children's groans,
Knew I not what delight was else on earth,—
Which now delights me little. I the rather
Look on such pangs as terror ill conceals;
The dry fixed eyeball, the pale quivering lip,
Which tell me that the spirit weeps within
Tears bitterer than the bloody sweat of Christ.
I rarely kill the body, which preserves,
Like a strong prison, the soul within my power,

Wherein I feed it with the breath of fear
For hourly pain.
 Camillo.   Hell's most abandoned fiend
Did never, in the drunkenness of guilt,
Speak to his heart as now you speak to me!
I thank my God that I believe you not.

      Enter ANDREA.
 Andrea. My lord, a gentleman from Salamanca
Would speak with you.
 Cenci.   Bid him attend me in
The grand saloon.   [*Exit* ANDREA.
 Camillo.   Farewell; and I will pray
Almighty God that thy false impious words
Tempt not his Spirit to abandon thee. [*Exit* CAMILLO.
 Cenci. The third of my possessions!—I must use
Close husbandry, or gold, the old man's sword,
Falls from my withered hand. But yesterday
There came an order from the Pope to make
Fourfold provision for my cursed sons;
Whom I have sent from Rome to Salamanca,—
Hoping some accident might cut them off,
And meaning, if I could, to starve them there.
I pray thee, God, send some quick death upon them!
Bernardo and my wife could not be worse
If dead and damned. Then, as to Beatrice—
      [*Looking around him suspiciously.*
I think they cannot hear me at that door;
What if they should? And yet I need not speak,
Though the heart triumphs with itself in words.
O thou most silent air, that shalt not hear
What now I think! thou pavement, which I tread
Towards her chamber! let your echoes talk
Of my imperious step, scorning surprise,
But not of my intent!—Andrea!

      Enter ANDREA.
 Andrea.   My lord.

Cenci. Bid Beatrice attend me in her chamber
This evening—no, at midnight; and alone.   [*Exeunt.*

SCENE II.—*A Garden of the Cenci Palace.*

Enter BEATRICE *and* ORSINO, *as in conversation.*

Beatrice.   Pervert not truth,
Orsino.   You remember where we held
That conversation;—nay, we see the spot
Even from this cypress.   Two long years are past
Since on an April midnight, underneath
The moonlight ruins of Mount Palatine,
I did confess to you my secret mind.
   Orsino.   You said you loved me then.
   Beatrice.   You are a priest:
Speak to me not of love.
   Orsino.   I may obtain
The dispensation of the Pope to marry.
Because I am a priest, do you believe
Your image, as the hunter some struck deer,
Follows me not whether I wake or sleep?
   Beatrice.   As I have said, speak to me not of love.
Had you a dispensation, I have not;
Nor will I leave this home of misery
Whilst my poor Bernard, and that gentle lady
To whom I owe life and these virtuous thoughts,
Must suffer what I still have strength to share.
Alas, Orsino! all the love that once
I felt for you is turned to bitter pain.
Ours was a youthful contract, which you first
Broke by assuming vows no Pope will loose.
And yet I love you still, but holily,
Even as a sister or a spirit might;
And so I swear a cold fidelity.
And it is well perhaps we shall not marry:
You have a sly equivocating vein
That suits me not.—Ah! wretched that I am!

Where shall I turn? Even now you look on me
As you were not my friend, and as if you
Discovered that I thought so, with false smiles
Making my true suspicion seem your wrong.
Ah no! Forgive me, Sorrow makes me seem
Sterner than else my nature might have been:
I have a weight of melancholy thoughts,
And they forebode—but what can they forebode
Worse than I now endure?
   Orsino. All will be well.
Is the petition yet prepared? You know
My zeal for all you wish, sweet Beatrice;
Doubt not but I will use my utmost skill
So that the Pope attend to your complaint.
   Beatrice. Your zeal for all I wish!—Ah me! you are cold!
Your utmost skill!—Speak but one word—(*Aside*)—Alas!
Weak and deserted creature that I am,
Here I stand bickering with my only friend!
(*To* ORSINO.) This night my father gives a sumptuous feast,
Orsino; he has heard some happy news
From Salamanca, from my brothers there,
And with this outward show of love he mocks
His inward hate. 'Tis bold hypocrisy,
For he would gladlier celebrate their deaths,
Which I have heard him pray for on his knees.
Great God! that such a father should be mine!—
But there is mighty preparation made,
And all our kin, the Cenci, will be there,
And all the chief nobility of Rome.
And he has bidden me and my pale mother
Attire ourselves in festival array.
Poor lady! she expects some happy change
In his dark spirit from this act; I, none.
At supper I will give you the petition:
Till when—farewell.
   Orsino. Farewell. [*Exit* BEATRICE.
               I know the Pope

Will ne'er absolve me from my priestly vow
But by absolving me from the revenue
Of many a wealthy see; and, Beatrice,
I think to win thee at an easier rate.
Nor shall he read her eloquent petition:
He might bestow her on some poor relation
Of his sixth cousin, as he did her sister,
And I should be debarred from all access.
Then, as to what she suffers from her father,
In all this there is much exaggeration.
Old men are testy, and will have their way.
A man may stab his enemy or his vassal,
And live a free life as to wine or women,
And with a peevish temper may return
To a dull home, and rate his wife and children;
Daughters and wives call this foul tyranny.
I shall be well content if on my conscience
There rest no heavier sin than what they suffer
From the devices of my love—a net
From which she shall escape not. Yet I fear
Her subtle mind, her awe-inspiring gaze,
Whose beams anatomize me nerve by nerve,
And lay me bare, and make me blush to see
My hidden thoughts.—Ah no! A friendless girl,
Who clings to me as to her only hope:—
I were a fool, not less than if a panther
Were panic-stricken by the antelope's eye,
If she escape me. [*Exit*.

SCENE III.—*A magnificent Hall in the Cenci Palace.*
A Banquet. Enter CENCI, LUCRETIA, BEATRICE, ORSINO,
CAMILLO, NOBLES.

Cenci. Welcome, my friends and kinsmen; welcome ye,
Princes and Cardinals, pillars of the church,
Whose presence honours our festivity.
I have too long lived like an anchorite,
And, in my absence from your merry meetings,

An evil word is gone abroad of me;
But I do hope that you, my noble friends,
When you have shared the entertainment here,
And heard the pious cause for which 'tis given,
And we have pledged a health or two together,
Will think me flesh and blood as well as you;
Sinful indeed, for Adam made all so,
But tender-hearted, meek, and pitiful.
   First Guest. In truth, my lord, you seem too light of heart,
Too sprightly and companionable a man,
To act the deeds that rumour pins on you.
(*To his Companion.*) I never saw such blithe and open cheer
In any eye.
   Second Guest. Some most desired event,
In which we all demand a common joy,
Has brought us hither; let us hear it, Count.
   Cenci. It is indeed a most desired event.
If, when a parent, from a parent's heart,
Lifts from this earth to the great Father of all
A prayer, both when he lays him down to sleep,
And when he rises up from dreaming it,—
One supplication, one desire, one hope,—
That he would grant a wish for his two sons,
Even all that he demands in their regard;
And suddenly, beyond his dearest hope,
It is accomplished—he should then rejoice,
And call his friends and kinsmen to a feast,
And task their love to grace his merriment—
Then honour me thus far—for I am he.
   Beatrice (*to* LUCRETIA). Great God! how horrible! Some
        dreadful ill
Must have befallen my brothers!
   Lucretia.   Fear not, child;
He speaks too frankly.
   Beatrice.   Ah! my blood runs cold.
I fear that wicked laughter round his eye,
Which wrinkles up the skin even to the hair.

Cenci. Here are the letters brought from Salamanca;
Beatrice, read them to your mother. God,
I thank thee! In one night didst thou perform,
By ways inscrutable, the thing I sought.
My disobedient and rebellious sons
Are dead.—Why, dead.—What means this change of cheer
You hear me not, I tell you they are dead:
And they will need no food or raiment more;
The tapers that did light them the dark way
Are their last cost. The Pope, I think, will not
Expect I should maintain them in their coffins.
Rejoice with me—my heart is wondrous glad!
(LUCRETIA *sinks, half fainting;* BEATRICE *supports her*).

Beatrice. It is not true!—Dear lady, pray look up.
Had it been true,—there is a God in Heaven,
He would not live to boast of such a boon.
Unnatural man, thou know'st that it is false!

Cenci. Ay, as the word of God; whom here I call
To witness that I speak the sober truth:
And whose most favouring providence was shown
Even in the manner of their deaths. For Rocco
Was kneeling at the mass, with sixteen others,
When the church fell and crushed him to a mummy;
The rest escaped unhurt. Cristofano
Was stabbed in error by a jealous man,
Whilst she he loved was sleeping with his rival.
All in the self-same hour of the same night;
Which shows that Heaven has special care of me.
I beg those friends who love me that they mark
The day a feast upon their calendars.
It was the twenty-seventh of December:
Ay, read the letters if you doubt my oath.

[*The assembly appears confused; several of the guests rise.*
First Guest. Oh horrible! I will depart!
Second Guest.   And I!
Third Guest. No, stay!
I do believe it is some jest; though, faith!

'Tis mocking us somewhat too solemnly.
I think his son has married the Infanta,
Or found a mine of gold in El Dorado.
'Tis but to season some such news; stay, stay!
I see 'tis only raillery by his smile.
 Cenci (filling a bowl of wine, and lifting it up).
O thou bright wine, whose purple splendour leaps
And bubbles gaily in this golden bowl
Under the lamplight, as my spirits do
To hear the death of my accursed sons!
Could I believe thou wert their mingled blood,
Then would I taste thee like a sacrament,
And pledge with thee the mighty Devil in hell;
Who, if a father's curses, as men say,
Climb with swift wings after their children's souls,
And drag them from the very throne of heaven,
Now triumphs in my triumph!—But thou art
Superfluous; I have drunken deep of joy,
And I will taste no other wine to-night.
Here, Andrea! Bear the bowl around.
 A Guest (rising).   Thou wretch!
Will none among this noble company
Check the abandoned villain?
 Camillo.   For God's sake,
Let me dismiss the guests! You are insane!
Some ill will come of this.
 Second Guest. Seize, silence him!
 First Guest. I will!
 Third Guest. And I!
 Cenci (addressing those who rise with a threatening gesture).
  Who moves? Who speaks? [*Turning to the company.*
          'Tis nothing,
Enjoy yourselves.—Beware! for my revenge
Is as the sealed commission of a king,
That kills, and none dare name the murderer.
 [*The banquet is broken up; several of the guests are departing.*
 Beatrice. I do entreat you, go not, noble guests.

What although tyranny and impious hate
Stand sheltered by a father's hoary hair?
What if 'tis he who clothed us in these limbs
Who tortures them and triumphs? What if we,
The desolate and the dead, were his own flesh,
His children and his wife, whom he is bound
To love and shelter? Shall we therefore find
No refuge in this merciless wide world?
Oh think what deep wrongs must have blotted out
First love, then reverence, in a child's prone mind,
Till it thus vanquish shame and fear! Oh think!
I have borne much, and kissed the sacred hand
Which crushed us to the earth, and thought its stroke
Was perhaps some paternal chastisement;
Have excused much; doubted; and, when no doubt
Remained, have sought by patience, love, and tears,
To soften him; and, when this could not be,
I have knelt down through the long sleepless nights,
And lifted up to God the Father of all
Passionate prayers; and, when these were not heard,
I have still borne;—until I meet you here,
Princes and kinsmen, at this hideous feast
Given at my brothers' deaths. Two yet remain,
His wife remains and I,—whom if ye save not,
Ye may soon share such merriment again
As fathers make over their children's graves.
O Prince Colonna, thou art our near kinsman;
Cardinal, thou art the Pope's chamberlain;
Camillo, thou art chief Justiciary;—
Take us away!—

    Cenci. (*He has been conversing with* CAMILLO *during the first part of* BEATRICE's *speech; he hears the conclusion, and now advances.*)
                  I hope my good friends here
Will think of their own daughters—or perhaps
Of their own throats—before they lend an ear
To this wild girl.

Beatrice (not noticing the words of CENCI).
                    Dare not one look on me?
None answer? Can one tyrant overbear
The sense of many best and wisest men?
Or is it that I sue not in some form
Of scrupulous law, that ye deny my suit?
O God! that I were buried with my brothers!
And that the flowers of this departed Spring
Were fading on my grave! and that my father
Were celebrating now one feast for all!
    Camillo. A bitter wish for one so young and gentle;
Can we do nothing?
    Colonna.   Nothing that I see.
Count Cenci were a dangerous enemy:
Yet I would second any one.
    A Cardinal.   And I.
    Cenci. Retire to your chamber, insolent girl!
    Beatrice. Retire thou, impious man! Ay, hide thyself
Where never eye can look upon thee more!
Wouldst thou have honour and obedience,
Who art a torturer? Father, never dream,
Though thou mayst overbear this company,
But ill must come of ill.—Frown not on me!
Haste, hide thyself, lest with avenging looks
My brothers' ghosts should hunt thee from thy seat!
Cover thy face from every living eye,
And start if thou but hear a human step:
Seek out some dark and silent corner; there
Bow thy white head before offended God,—
And we will kneel around, and fervently
Pray that he pity both ourselves and thee!
    Cenci. My friends, I do lament this insane girl
Has spoilt the mirth of our festivity.
Good night, farewell; I will not make you longer
Spectators of our dull domestic quarrels.
Another time.—   [*Exeunt all but* CENCI *and* BEATRICE.
                My brain is swimming round;

Give me a bowl of wine.
             (*To* BEATRICE).   Thou painted viper!
Beast that thou art! fair and yet terrible!
I know a charm shall make thee meek and tame.
Now get thee from my sight!   [*Exit* BEATRICE.
                    Here, Andrea,
Fill up this goblet with Greek wine.   I said
I would not drink this evening, but I must;
For, strange to say, I feel my spirits fail
With thinking what I have decreed to do. [*Drinking the wine.*
Be thou the resolution of quick youth
Within my veins, and manhood's purpose stern,
And age's firm, cold, subtle villany;
As if thou wert indeed my children's blood
Which I did thirst to drink.   The charm works well;—
It must be done, it shall be done, I swear!   [*Exit.*

ACT II.

SCENE I.—*An Apartment in the Cenci Palace.*
Enter LUCRETIA *and* BERNARDO.

Lucretia.   Weep not, my gentle boy; he struck but me,
Who have borne deeper wrongs.   In truth, if he
Had killed me, he had done a kinder deed.
O God Almighty, do thou look upon us!
We have no other friend but only thee.
Yet weep not; though I love you as my own,
I am not your true mother.
    Bernardo.   Oh! more, more
Than ever mother was to any child,
That have you been to me!   Had he not been
My father, do you think that I should weep?
    Lucretia. Alas! poor boy, what else couldst thou have done?
           Enter BEATRICE.
    Beatrice (*in a hurried voice*).   Did he pass this way?   Have
       you seen him, brother?

Ah! no, that is his step upon the stairs;
'Tis nearer now; his hand is on the door!
Mother, if I to thee have ever been
A duteous child, now save me! Thou great God
Whose image upon earth a father is,
Dost thou indeed abandon me? He comes—
The door is opening now! I see his face;
He frowns on others, but he smiles on me,
Even as he did after the feast last night!   [*Enter a Servant.*
Almighty God, how merciful thou art!
'Tis but Orsino's servant.—Well, what news?
    Servant. My master bids me say the Holy Father
Has sent back your petition thus unopened. [*Giving a paper.*
And he demands at what hour 'twere secure
To visit you again.
    Lucretia.   At the Ave Mary.   [*Exit Servant.*
So, daughter, our last hope has failed. Ah me!
How pale you look! you tremble, and you stand
Rapt in some fixed and fearful meditation,
As if one thought were over-strong for you.
Your eyes have a chill glare! Oh! dearest child,
Are you gone mad? If not, pray speak to me.
    Beatrice. You see I am not mad; I speak to you.
    Lucretia. You talked of something that your father did
After that dreadful feast. Could it be worse
Than when he smiled, and cried "My sons are dead!"
And every one looked in his neighbour's face
To see if others were as white as he?
At the first word he spoke, I felt the blood
Rush to my heart, and fell into a trance.
And, when it passed, I sat all weak and wild;
Whilst you alone stood up, and with strong words
Checked his unnatural pride; and I could see
The devil was rebuked that lives in him.
Until this hour thus you have ever stood
Between us and your father's moody wrath
Like a protecting presence: your firm mind

Has been our only refuge and defence.
What can have thus subdued it? What can now
Have given you that cold melancholy look,
Succeeding to your unaccustomed fear?

   Beatrice. What is it that you say? I was just thinking
'Twere better not to struggle any more.
Men, like my father, have been dark and bloody,
Yet never—Oh! before worse comes of it,
'Twere wise to die! it ends in that at last.

   Lucretia. Oh! talk not so, dear child! Tell me at once
What did your father do or say to you?
He stayed not, after that accursèd feast,
One moment in your chamber.—Speak to me.

   Bernardo. Oh sister, sister, prithee speak to us!

   Beatrice (*speaking very slowly with a forced calmness*). It was
      one word, mother, one little word;
One look, one smile.   [*Wildly*
              Oh! he has trampled me
Under his feet, and made the blood stream down
My pallid cheeks. And he has given us all
Ditch-water, and the fever-stricken flesh
Of buffaloes, and bade us eat or starve,
And we have eaten. He has made me look
On my beloved Bernardo, when the rust
Of heavy chains has gangrened his sweet limbs,—
And I have never yet despaired—But now!
What would I say?   [*Recovering herself.*
              Ah! no, 'tis nothing new.
The sufferings we all share have made me wild.
He only struck and cursed me as he passed:
He said, he looked, he did—nothing at all
Beyond his wont, yet it disordered me.
Alas! I am forgetful of my duty:
I should preserve my senses for your sake.

   Lucretia. Nay, Beatrice; have courage, my sweet girl.
If any one despairs, it should be I,
Who loved him once, and now must live with him

Till God in pity call for him or me.
For you may, like your sister, find some husband,
And smile, years hence, with children round your knees;
Whilst I, then dead, and all this hideous coil,
Shall be remembered only as a dream.

Beatrice. Talk not to me, dear lady, of a husband.
Did you not nurse me when my mother died?
Did you not shield me and that dearest boy?
And had we any other friend but you
In infancy, with gentle words and looks,
To win our father not to murder us?
And shall I now desert you? May the ghost
Of my dead mother plead against my soul,
If I abandon her who filled the place
She left, with more even than a mother's love!

Bernardo. And I am of my sister's mind. Indeed,
I would not leave you in this wretchedness,
Even though the Pope should make me free to live
In some blithe place, like others of my age,
With sports, and delicate food, and the fresh air.
Oh never think that I will leave you, mother!

Lucretia. My dear, dear children!

Enter CENCI, *suddenly.*

Cenci. What! Beatrice here!
Come hither. [*She shrinks back, and covers her face.*
Nay, hide not your face, 'tis fair;
Look up! Why, yesternight you dared to look
With disobedient insolence upon me,
Bending a stern and an enquiring brow
On what I meant; whilst I then sought to hide
That which I came to tell you—but in vain.

Beatrice (*wildly staggering towards the door*). Oh that the earth
would gape! Hide me, O God!

Cenci. Then it was I whose inarticulate words
Fell from my lips, and who with tottering steps
Fled from your presence, as you now from mine.

Stay, I command you! From this day and hour,
Never again, I think, with fearless eye,
And brow superior, and unaltered cheek,
And that lip made for tenderness or scorn,
Shalt thou strike dumb the meanest of mankind:
Me least of all. Now get thee to thy chamber,
Thou too,[*To* BERNARDO]loathed image of thy cursed mother,
Thy milky meek face makes me sick with hate!
      [*Exeunt* BEATRICE *and* BERNARDO.
(*Aside.*) So much has passed between us as must make
Me bold, her fearful. 'Tis an awful thing
To touch such mischief as I now conceive:
So men sit shivering on the dewy bank,
And try the chill stream with their feet; once in—
How the delighted spirit pants for joy!
 Lucretia (*advancing timidly towards him*). O husband! Pray
   forgive poor Beatrice,—
She meant not any ill.
  Cenci.   Nor you perhaps?
Nor that young imp whom you have taught by rote
Parricide with his alphabet? Nor Giacomo?
Nor those two most unnatural sons who stirred
Enmity up against me with the Pope?
Whom in one night merciful God cut off:
Innocent lambs! they thought not any ill!
You were not here conspiring? You said nothing
Of how I might be dungeoned as a madman;
Or be condemned to death for some offence,
And you would be the witnesses?—This failing,
How just it were to hire assassins, or
Put sudden poison in my evening drink?
Or smother me when overcome by wine?—
Seeing we had no other judge but God,
And he had sentenced me, and there were none
But you to be the executioners
Of his decree enregistered in heaven.
Oh no! You said not this?

Lucretia. So help me God,
I never thought the things you charge me with!
Cenci. If you dare speak that wicked lie again,
I'll kill you. What! it was not by your counsel
That Beatrice disturbed the feast last night?
You did not hope to stir some enemies
Against me, and escape, and laugh to scorn
What every nerve of you now trembles at?
You judged that men were bolder than they are;
Few dare to stand between their grave and me!
Lucretia. Look not so dreadfully! By my salvation,
I knew not aught that Beatrice designed;
Nor do I think she designed anything
Until she heard you talk of her dead brothers.
Cenci. Blaspheming liar! You are damned for this!
But I will take you where you may persuade
The stones you tread on to deliver you:
For men shall there be none but those who dare
All things,—not question that which I command.
On Wednesday next I shall set out. You know
That savage rock, the Castle of Petrella.
'Tis safely walled, and moated round about:
Its dungeons underground and its thick towers
Never told tales; though they have heard and seen
What might make dumb things speak. Why do you linger?
Make speediest preparation for the journey. [*Exit* LUCRETIA.
The all-beholding sun yet shines; I hear
A busy stir of men about the streets;
I see the bright sky through the window-panes.
It is a garish, broad, and peering day;
Loud, light, suspicious, full of eyes and ears;
And every little corner, nook, and hole,
Is penetrated with the insolent light.
Come, darkness! Yet what is the day to me?
And wherefore should I wish for night, who do
A deed which shall confound both night and day?
'Tis she shall grope through a bewildering mist

Of horror: if there be a sun in heaven,
She shall not dare to look upon its beams,
Nor feel its warmth. Let her, then, wish for night.
The act I think shall soon extinguish all
For me: I bear a darker deadlier gloom
Than the earth's shade, or interlunar air,
Or constellations quenched in murkiest cloud,
In which I walk secure and unbeheld
Towards my purpose.—Would that it were done! [*Exit.*

SCENE II.—*A Chamber in the Vatican.*

Enter CAMILLO *and* GIACOMO, *in conversation.*

Camillo. There is an obsolete and doubtful law,
By which you might obtain a bare provision
Of food and clothing.
   Giacomo. Nothing more? Alas!
Bare must be the provision which strict law
Awards, and aged sullen avarice pays.
Why did my father not apprentice me
To some mechanic trade? I should have then
Been trained in no highborn necessities
Which I could meet not by my daily toil.
The eldest son of a rich nobleman
Is heir to all his incapacities;
He has wide wants, and narrow powers. If you,
Cardinal Camillo, were reduced at once
From thrice-driven beds of down, and delicate food,
An hundred servants and six palaces,
To that which nature doth indeed require?—
   Camillo. Nay, there is reason in your plea; 'twere hard.
   Giacomo. 'Tis hard for a firm man to bear. But I
Have a dear wife, a lady of high birth,
Whose dowry in ill hour I lent my father
Without a bond or witness to the deed;
And children, who inherit her fine senses,

The fairest creatures in this breathing world;
And she and they reproach me not. Cardinal,
Do you not think the Pope would interpose,
And stretch authority beyond the law?
    Camillo. Though your peculiar case is hard, I know
The Pope will not divert the course of law.
After that impious feast the other night
I spoke with him, and urged him then to check
Your father's cruel hand. He frowned and said:
"Children are disobedient, and they sting
Their fathers' hearts to madness and despair,
Requiting years of care with contumely.
I pity the Count Cenci from my heart;
His outraged love perhaps awakened hate,
And thus he is exasperated to ill.
In the great war between the old and young,
I, who have white hairs and a tottering body,
Will keep at least blameless neutrality."   [*Enter* ORSINO.
You, my good lord Orsino, heard those words.
    Orsino. What words?
    Giacomo.   Alas! repeat them not again.—
There then is no redress for me; at least
None but that which I may achieve myself,
Since I am driven to the brink. But say,—
My innocent sister and my only brother
Are dying underneath my father's eye.
The memorable torturers of this land,
Galeaz Visconti, Borgia, Ezzelin,
Never inflicted on their meanest slave
What these endure; shall they have no protection?
    Camillo. Why, if they would petition to the Pope,
I see not how he could refuse it. Yet
He holds it of most dangerous example
In aught to weaken the paternal power,
Being, as 'twere, the shadow of his own.—
I pray you now excuse me. I have business
That will not bear delay.   [*Exit* CAMILLO.

Giacomo.   But you, Orsino,
Have the petition; wherefore not present it?
    Orsino.   I have presented it, and backed it with
My earnest prayers and urgent interest;
It was returned unanswered. I doubt not
But that the strange and execrable deeds
Alleged in it—in truth, they might well baffle
Any belief—have turned the Pope's displeasure
Upon the accusers from the criminal:
So I should guess from what Camillo said.
    Giacomo.   My friend, that palace-walking devil, Gold,
Has whispered silence to his Holiness.
And we are left as scorpions ringed with fire:
What should we do but strike ourselves to death?
For he who is our murderous persecutor
Is shielded by a father's holy name,
Or I would—   [*Stops abruptly.*
    Orsino.   What? Fear not to speak your thought.
Words are but holy as the deeds they cover.
A priest who has forsworn the God he serves;
A judge who makes Truth weep at his decree;
A friend who should weave counsel, as I now,
But as the mantle of some selfish guile;
A father who is all a tyrant seems;
Were the profaner for his sacred name.
    Giacomo.   Ask me not what I think! The unwilling brain
Feigns often what it would not; and we trust
Imagination with such fantasies
As the tongue dares not fashion into words;
Which have no words,—their horror makes them dim
To the mind's eye. My heart denies itself
To think what you demand.
    Orsino.   But a friend's bosom
Is as the inmost cave of our own mind,
Where we sit shut from the wide gaze of day,
And from the all-communicating air.
You look what I suspected—

Giacomo. Spare me now.
I am as one lost in a midnight wood,
Who dares not ask some harmless passenger
The path across the wilderness, lest he,
As my thoughts are, should be—a murderer.
I know thou art my friend; and all I dare
Speak to my soul, that will I trust with thee.
But now my heart is heavy, and would take
Lone counsel from a night of sleepless care.
Pardon me that I say farewell—farewell.
I would that to my own suspected self
I could address a word so full of peace.
   Orsino. Farewell!—Be your thoughts better—or more
         bold.   [*Exit* GIACOMO.
I had disposed the Cardinal Camillo
To feed his hope with cold encouragement.
It fortunately serves my close designs
That 'tis a trick of this same family
To analyse their own and other minds.
Such self-anatomy shall teach the will
Dangerous secrets: for it tempts our powers,
Knowing what must be thought and may be done,
Into the depth of darkest purposes.
So Cenci fell into the pit: even I—
Since Beatrice unveiled me to myself,
And made me shrink from what I cannot shun—
Show a poor figure to my own esteem,
To which I grow half reconciled. I'll do
As little mischief as I can; that thought
Shall fee the accuser Conscience.   [*After a pause.*
                    Now what harm
If Cenci should be murdered?—Yet, if murdered,
Wherefore by me? And what if I could take
The profit, yet omit the sin and peril
In such an action? Of all earthly things
I fear a man whose blows outspeed his words;
And such is Cenci: and, while Cenci lives,

His daughter's dowry were a secret grave,
If a priest wins her.—O fair Beatrice!
Would that I loved thee not, or, loving thee,
Could but despise danger, and gold, and all
That frowns between my wish and its effect,
Or smiles beyond it!—There is no escape.
Her bright form kneels beside me at the altar,
And follows me to the resort of men,
And fills my slumber with tumultuous dreams,—
So when I wake my blood seems liquid fire;
And, if I strike my damp and dizzy head,
My hot palm scorches it: her very name,
But spoken by a stranger, makes my heart
Sicken and pant; and thus unprofitably
I clasp the phantom of unfelt delights,
Till weak imagination half possesses
The self-created shadow.   Yet much longer
Will I not nurse this life of feverous hours:
From the unravelled hopes of Giacomo
I must work out my own dear purposes.
I see, as from a tower, the end of all:—
Her father dead; her brother bound to me
By a dark secret, surer than the grave;
Her mother scared and unexpostulating
From the dread manner of her wish achieved:
And she!—Once more take courage, my faint heart
What dares a friendless maiden matched with thee?
I have such foresight as assures success.
Some unbeheld divinity doth ever,
When dread events are near, stir up men's minds
To black suggestions; and he prospers best,
Not who becomes the instrument of ill,
But who can flatter the dark spirit that makes
Its empire and its prey of other hearts,
Till it become his slave—as I will do.
                                                                [*Exit.*

ACT III.

Scene I.—*An Apartment in the Cenci Palace.*
Lucretia; *to her enter* Beatrice (*she enters staggering, and speaks wildly*).

Beatrice. Reach me that handkerchief!—My brain is hurt,
My eyes are full of blood; just wipe them for me—
I see but indistinctly.—
    Lucretia.   My sweet child,
You have no wound; 'tis only a cold dew
That starts from your dear brow.—Alas! Alas!
What has befallen?
    Beatrice.   How comes this hair undone?
Its wandering strings must be what blind me so,
And yet I tied it fast.—Oh horrible!
The pavement sinks under my feet! the walls
Spin round! I see a woman weeping there,
And standing calm and motionless, whilst I
Slide giddily as the world reels!—My God!
The beautiful blue heaven is flecked with blood!
The sunshine on the floor is black! the air
Is changed to vapours such as the dead breathe
In charnel-pits! Pah! I am choked! There creeps
A clinging, black, contaminating mist
About me—'tis substantial, heavy, thick;
I cannot pluck it from me, for it glues
My fingers and my limbs to one another,
And eats into my sinews, and dissolves
My flesh to a pollution, poisoning
The subtle, pure, and inmost spirit of life!
My God! I never knew what the mad felt
Before; for I am mad beyond all doubt!   [*More wildly.*
No, I am dead! These putrefying limbs
Shut round and sepulchre the panting soul
Which would burst forth into the wandering air!   [*A pause.*
What hideous thought was that I had even now?

'Tis gone; and yet its burthen remains here,
O'er these dull eyes—upon this weary heart!
Oh world! Oh life! Oh day! Oh misery!
   Lucretia. What ails thee, my poor child? She answers not.
Her spirit apprehends the sense of pain,
But not its cause; suffering has dried away
The source from which it sprung.
   Beatrice (frantically).   Like Parricide,
Misery has killed its father: yet its father
Never like mine—O God! What thing am I?
   Lucretia. My dearest child, what has your father done?
   Beatrice (doubtfully). Who art thou, questioner? I have no
      father.
(*Aside.*) She is the madhouse nurse who tends on me;
It is a piteous office.   [*To* LUCRETIA, *in a slow subdued voice.*
               Do you know,
I thought I was that wretched Beatrice
Men speak of, whom her father sometimes hales
From hall to hall by the entangled hair;
At others, pens up naked in damp cells
Where scaly reptiles crawl, and starves her there
Till she will eat strange flesh. This woful story
So did I overact in my sick dreams
That I imagined—no, it cannot be!
Horrible things have been in this wild world,
Prodigious mixtures, and confusions strange
Of good and ill; and worse have been conceived
Than ever there was found a heart to do.
But never fancy imaged such a deed
As—   [*Pauses, suddenly recollecting herself.*
     Who art thou? Swear to me, ere I die
With fearful expectation, that indeed
Thou art not what thou seemest—Mother!
   Lucretia. Oh! my sweet child, know you—
   Beatrice.   Yet speak it not:
For then, if this be truth, that other too
Must be a truth, a firm enduring truth,

Linked with each lasting circumstance of life,
Never to change, never to pass away.
Why, so it is. This is the Cenci Palace;
Thou art Lucretia; I am Beatrice.
I have talked some wild words, but will no more.
Mother, come near me: from this point of time,
I am— [*Her voice dies away faintly.*

Lucretia. Alas! what has befallen thee, child?
What has thy father done?

Beatrice. What have I done?
Am I not innocent? Is it my crime
That one with white hair and imperious brow,
Who tortured me from my forgotten years
As parents only dare, should call himself
My father, yet should be!—Oh! what am I?
What name, what place, what memory, shall be mine?
What retrospects, outliving even despair?

Lucretia. He is a violent tyrant, surely, child:
We know that death alone can make us free,—
His death or ours. But what can he have done
Of deadlier outrage or worse injury?
Thou art unlike thyself; thine eyes shoot forth
A wandering and strange spirit. Speak to me,—
Unlock those pallid hands whose fingers twine
With one another.

Beatrice. 'Tis the restless life
Tortured within them. If I try to speak,
I shall go mad. Ay, something must be done;
What, yet I know not—something which shall make
The thing that I have suffered but a shadow
In the dread lightning which avenges it;
Brief, rapid, irreversible, destroying
The consequence of what it cannot cure.
Some such thing is to be endured or done:
When I know what, I shall be still and calm,
And never anything will move me more.
But now!—O blood, which art my father's blood,

Circling through these contaminated veins,
If thou, poured forth on the polluted earth,
Couldst wash away the crime, and punishment
By which I suffer—no, that cannot be!
Many might doubt there were a God above,
Who sees and permits evil, and so die:
That faith no agony shall obscure in me.
 Lucretia. It must indeed have been some bitter wrong:
Yet what I dare not guess! Oh! my lost child,
Hide not in proud impenetrable grief
Thy sufferings from my fear.
 Beatrice.   I hide them not.
What are the words which you would have me speak?
I, who can feign no image in my mind
Of that which has transformed me—I, whose thought
Is like a ghost shrouded and folded up
In its own formless horror! Of all words
That minister to mortal intercourse,
Which wouldst thou hear? for there is none to tell
My misery. If another ever knew
Aught like to it, she died as I will die,
And left it, as I must, without a name.
Death! Death! our law and our religion call thee
A punishment and a reward. Oh, which
Have I deserved?
 Lucretia.   The peace of innocence,
Till in your season you be called to heaven.
Whate'er you may have suffered, you have done
No evil. Death must be the punishment
Of crime, or the reward of trampling down
The thorns which God has strewed upon the path
Which leads to immortality.
 Beatrice.   Ay, death
The punishment of crime. I pray thee, God,
Let me not be bewildered while I judge.
If I must live day after day, and keep
These limbs, the unworthy temple of thy Spirit,

As a foul den from which what thou abhorrest
May mock thee, unavenged—it shall not be!
Self-murder—no: that might be no escape,
For thy decree yawns like a hell between
Our will and it.—Oh! in this mortal world
There is no vindication and no law
Which can adjudge and execute the doom
Of that through which I suffer!

Enter ORSINO.

(*She approaches him solemnly.*) Welcome, friend!
I have to tell you that, since last we met,
I have endured a wrong so great and strange
That neither life nor death can give me rest.
Ask me not what it is, for there are deeds
Which have no form, sufferings which have no tongue.
   Orsino. And what is he who has thus injured you?
   Beatrice. The man they call my father: a dread name.
   Orsino. It cannot be—
   Beatrice. What it can be, or not,
Forbear to think. It is, and it has been;
Advise me how it shall not be again.
I thought to die; but a religious awe
Restrains me, and the dread lest death itself
Might be no refuge from the consciousness
Of what is yet unexpiated. Oh speak!
   Orsino. Accuse him of the deed, and let the law
Avenge thee.
   Beatrice. O ice-hearted counsellor!
If I could find a word that might make known
The crime of my destroyer; and, that done,
My tongue should like a knife tear out the secret
Which cankers my heart's core,—ay, lay all bare,
So that my unpolluted fame should be
With vilest gossips a stale-mouthèd story,
A mock, a by-word, an astonishment:—
If this were done, which never shall be done,

Think of the offender's gold, his dreaded hate,
And the strange horror of the accuser's tale,
Baffling belief and overpowering speech;
Scarce whispered, unimaginable, wrapped
In hideous hints.—Oh! most assured redress!

 Orsino. You will endure it then?
 Beatrice.   Endure!—Orsino
It seems your counsel is small profit.
      [*Turns from him and speaks half to herself.*
        Ay,
All must be suddenly resolved and done.
What is this undistinguishable mist
Of thoughts which rise, like shadow after shadow,
Darkening each other?
 Orsino.   Should the offender live?
Triumph in his misdeed? and make by use
His crime, whate'er it is (dreadful, no doubt)
Thine element? until thou mayst become
Utterly lost, subdued even to the hue
Of that which thou permittest.
 Beatrice (to herself).   Mighty death!
Thou double-visaged shadow! only judge!
Rightfullest arbiter! [*She retires, absorbed in thought.*
 Lucretia. If the lightning
Of God has e'er descended to avenge—
 Orsino. Blaspheme not! His high providence commits
Its glory on this earth, and their own wrongs,
Into the hands of men; if they neglect
To punish crime—
 Lucretia.   But if one, like this wretch,
Should mock with gold opinion, law, and power?
If there be no appeal to that which makes
The guiltiest tremble? If, because our wrongs,
For that they are unnatural, strange, and monstrous,
Exceed all measure of belief.... O God!
If, for the very reasons which should make

Redress most swift and sure, our injurer triumphs?
And we, the victims, bear worse punishment
Than that appointed for their torturer?
 Orsino.   Think not
But that there is redress where there is wrong,
So we be bold enough to seize it.
 Lucretia.   How?
If there were any way to make all sure,
I know not—but I think it might be good
To—
 Orsino. Why, his late outrage to Beatrice;
For it is such, as I but faintly guess
As makes remorse dishonour, and leaves her
Only one duty, how she may avenge;
You, but one refuge from ills ill endured;
Me, but one counsel—
 Lucretia.   For we cannot hope
That aid or retribution or resource
Will arise thence where every other one
Might find them with less need. [BEATRICE *advances.*
 Orsino.   Then—
 Beatrice.   Peace, Orsino!
And, honoured lady, while I speak, I pray
That you put off, as garments overworn,
Forbearance and respect, remorse and fear,
And all the fit restraints of daily life,
Which have been borne from childhood, but which now
Would be a mockery to my holier plea.
As I have said, I have endured a wrong
Which, though it be expressionless, is such
As asks atonement, both for what is past,
And lest I be reserved, day after day,
To load with crimes an overburthened soul,
And be—what ye can dream not. I have prayed
To God, and I have talked with my own heart,
And have unravelled my entangled will,
And have at length determined what is right.

Art thou my friend, Orsino? False or true?
Pledge thy salvation ere I speak.
    Orsino.   I swear
To dedicate my cunning and my strength,
My silence, and whatever else is mine,
To thy commands.
    Lucretia.   You think we should devise
His death?
    Beatrice. And execute what is devised,
And suddenly. We must be brief and bold.
    Orsino. And yet most cautious.
    Lucretia.   For the jealous laws
Would punish us with death and infamy
For that which it became themselves to do.
    Beatrice. Be cautious as ye may, but prompt. Orsino,
What are the means?
    Orsino.   I know two dull fierce outlaws,
Who think man's spirit as a worm's, and they
Would trample out, for any slight caprice,
The meanest or the noblest life. This mood
Is marketable here in Rome. They sell
What we now want.
    Lucretia.   To-morrow, before dawn,
Cenci will take us to that lonely rock,
Petrella, in the Apulian Apennines.
If he arrive there—
    Beatrice.   He must not arrive.
    Orsino. Will it be dark before you reach the tower?
    Lucretia. The sun will scarce be set.
    Beatrice.   But I remember,
Two miles on this side of the fort, the road
Crosses a deep ravine; 'tis rough and narrow,
And winds with short turns down the precipice.
And in its depth there is a mighty rock,
Which has, from unimaginable years,
Sustained itself with terror and with toil
Over a gulf, and with the agony

With which it clings seems slowly coming down;
Even as a wretched soul hour after hour
Clings to the mass of life; yet, clinging, leans;
And, leaning, makes more dark the dread abyss
In which it fears to fall.   Beneath this crag,
Huge as despair, as if in weariness
The melancholy mountain yawns.   Below,
You hear but see not an impetuous torrent
Raging among the caverns, and a bridge
Crosses the chasm; and high above there grow,
With intersecting trunks, from crag to crag,
Cedars and yews and pines, whose tangled hair
Is matted in one solid roof of shade
By the dark ivy's twine.   At noonday here
'Tis twilight, and at sunset blackest night.
 Orsino. Before you reach that bridge, make some excuse
For spurring on your mules, or loitering
Until—
 Beatrice. What sound is that?
 Lucretia.   Hark! No, it cannot be a servant's step;
It must be Cenci, unexpectedly
Returned.—Make some excuse for being here.
 Beatrice (*to* ORSINO *as she goes out*).   That step we hear
  approach must never pass
The bridge of which we spoke.
      [*Exeunt* LUCRETIA *and* BEATRICE.
 Orsino.   What shall I do?
Cenci must find me here, and I must bear
The imperious inquisition of his looks
As to what brought me hither! Let me mask
Mine own in some inane and vacant smile.

   Enter GIACOMO, *in a hurried manner.*

How! Have you ventured thither? know you then
That Cenci is from home?
 Giacomo.   I sought him here:
And now must wait till he returns.

Orsino.   Great God!
Weigh you the danger of this rashness?
    Giacomo.   Ay!
Does my destroyer know his danger? We
Are now no more, as once, parent and child,
But man to man; the oppressor to the oppressed;
The slanderer to the slandered; foe to foe.
He has cast Nature off which was his shield,
And Nature casts him off who is her shame;
And I spurn both. Is it a father's throat
Which I will shake? and say, "I ask not gold;
I ask not happy years; nor memories
Of tranquil childhood; nor home-sheltered love;
Though all these hast thou torn from me, and more;—
But only my fair fame; only one hoard
Of peace, which I thought hidden from thy hate,
Under the penury heaped on me by thee;
Or I will" . . . God can understand and pardon,
Why should I speak with man?
    Orsino.   Be calm, dear friend.
    Giacomo. Well, I will calmly tell you what he did.
This old Francesco Cenci, as you know,
Borrowed the dowry of my wife from me,
And then denied the loan; and left me so
In poverty, the which I sought to mend
By holding a poor office in the state.
It had been promised to me, and already
I bought new clothing for my ragged babes,—
And my wife smiled, and my heart knew repose;
When Cenci's intercession, as I found,
Conferred this office on a wretch whom thus
He paid for vilest service. I returned
With this ill news, and we sate sad together,
Solacing our despondency with tears
Of such affection and unbroken faith
As temper life's worst bitterness; when he,
As he is wont, came to upbraid and curse,

Mocking our poverty, and telling us
Such was God's scourge for disobedient sons.
And then, that I might strike him dumb with shame,
I spoke of my wife's dowry; but he coined
A brief yet specious tale, how I had wasted
The sum in secret riot; and he saw
My wife was touched, and he went smiling forth.
And, when I knew the impression he had made,
And felt my wife insult with silent scorn
My ardent truth, and look averse and cold,
I went forth too: but soon returned again.
Yet not so soon but that my wife had taught
My children her harsh thoughts; and they all cried,
"Give us clothes, father! Give us better food!
What you in one night squander were enough
For months!" I looked, and saw that home was hell.
And to that hell will I return no more,
Until mine enemy has rendered up
Atonement, or, as he gave life to me,
I will, reversing Nature's law—
   Orsino.   Trust me
The compensation which thou seekest here
Will be denied.
   Giacomo.   Then—Are you not my friend?
Did you not hint at the alternative
Upon the brink of which you see I stand,
The other day when we conversed together?
My wrongs were then less. That word "Parricide,"
Although I am resolved, haunts me like fear.
   Orsino.   It must be fear itself, for the bare word
Is hollow mockery. Mark how wisest God
Draws to one point the threads of a just doom,
So sanctifying it: what you devise
Is, as it were, accomplished.'
   Giacomo.   Is he dead?
   Orsino.   His grave is ready. Know that, since we met,
Cenci has done an outrage to his daughter.

Giacomo. What outrage!
Orsino.   That she speaks not, but you may
Conceive such half conjectures as I do,
From her fixed paleness, and the lofty grief
Of her stern brow bent on the idle air,
And her severe unmodulated voice,
Drowning both tenderness and dread; and last
From this:—That whilst her stepmother and I,
Bewildered in our horror, talked together
With obscure hints (both self-misunderstood,
And darkly guessing, stumbling in our talk
Over the truth, and yet to its revenge),
She interrupted us, and with a look
Which told, before she spoke it, "He must die"—
Giacomo. It is enough. My doubts are well appeased.
There is a higher reason for the act
Than mine; there is a holier judge than me,
A more unblamed avenger. Beatrice,
Who in the gentleness of thy sweet youth
Hast never trodden on a worm, or bruised
A living flower, but thou hast pitied it
With needless tears! fair sister, thou in whom
Men wondered how such loveliness and wisdom
Did not destroy each other! is there made
Ravage of thee? O heart, I ask no more
Justification!—Shall I wait, Orsino,
Till he return, and stab him at the door?
Orsino. Not so; some accident might interpose
To rescue him from what is now most sure;
And you are unprovided where to fly,
How to excuse or to conceal. Nay, listen:
All is contrived; success is so assured
That—

Enter BEATRICE.

Beatrice. 'Tis my brother's voice! You know me not?
Giacomo. My sister, my lost sister!
Beatrice.   Lost indeed!

I see Orsino has talked with you, and
That you conjecture things too horrible
To speak, yet far less than the truth. Now, stay not,—
He might return. Yet kiss me; I shall know
That then thou hast consented to his death.
Farewell, farewell! Let piety to God,
Brotherly love, justice and clemency,
And all things that make tender hardest hearts,
Make thine hard, brother! Answer not—farewell.
         [Exeunt severally.

  Scene II.—*A mean Apartment in* Giacomo's *House.*
     Giacomo *alone.*

Giacomo. 'Tis midnight, and Orsino comes not yet.
     [Thunder, and the sound of a storm.
What! can the everlasting elements
Feel with a worm like man? If so, the shaft
Of mercy-winged lightning would not fall
On stones and trees. My wife and children sleep:
They are now living in unmeaning dreams:
But I must wake, still doubting if that deed
Be just which was most necessary. Oh!
Thou unreplenished lamp, whose narrow fire
Is shaken by the wind, and on whose edge
Devouring darkness hovers! thou small flame,
Which, as a dying pulse rises and falls,
Still flickerest up and down! how very soon,
Did I not feed thee, wouldst thou fail, and be
As thou hadst never been! So wastes and sinks,
Even now perhaps, the life that kindled mine:
But that no power can fill with vital oil
That broken lamp of flesh. Ha! 'tis the blood
Which fed these veins that ebbs till all is cold:
It is the form that moulded mine that sinks
Into the white and yellow spasms of death:
It is the soul by which mine was arrayed

In God's immortal likeness which now stands
Naked before Heaven's judgment-seat!   [*A bell strikes.*
                      One! Two!
The hours crawl on; and, when my hairs are white,
My son will then perhaps be waiting thus,
Tortured between just hate and vain remorse;
Chiding the tardy messenger of news
Like those which I expect. I almost wish
He be not dead, although my wrongs are great;
Yet—'Tis Orsino's step.

               Enter ORSINO.
             Speak!
  Orsino.   I am come
To say he has escaped.
  Giacomo.   Escaped!
  Orsino.   And safe
Within Petrella. He passed by the spot
Appointed for the deed, an hour too soon.
  Giacomo. Are we the fools of such contingencies?
And do we waste in blind misgiving thus
The hours when we should act? Then wind and thunder,
Which seemed to howl his knell, is the loud laughter
With which Heaven mocks our weakness! I henceforth
Will ne'er repent of aught designed or done,
But my repentance.
  Orsino.   See, the lamp is out.
  Giacomo. If no remorse is ours when the dim air
Has drank this innocent flame, why should we quail
When Cenci's life, that light by which ill spirits
See the worst deeds they prompt, shall sink for ever?
No, I am hardened.
  Orsino.   Why, what need of this?
Who feared the pale intrusion of remorse
In a just deed? Although our first plan failed,
Doubt not but he will soon be laid to rest.
But light the lamp; let us not talk i' the dark.

Giacomo (lighting the lamp). And yet, once quenched, I
    cannot thus relume
My father's life: do you not think his ghost
Might plead that argument with God?
    Orsino.   Once gone,
You cannot now recall your sister's peace;
Your own extinguished years of youth and hope;
Nor your wife's bitter words; nor all the taunts
Which from the prosperous weak misfortune takes;
Nor your dead mother; nor—
    Giacomo.   Oh speak no more!
I am resolved, although this very hand
Must quench the life that animated it.
    Orsino. There is no need of that. Listen. You know
Olimpio, the castellan of Petrella
In old Colonna's time,—him whom your father
Degraded from his post? and Marzio,
That desperate wretch whom he deprived last year
Of a reward of blood well earned and due?
    Giacomo. I knew Olimpio; and they say he hated
Old Cenci so that in his silent rage
His lips grew white only to see him pass.
Of Marzio I know nothing.
    Orsino.   Marzio's hate
Matches Olimpio's. I have sent these men—
But in your name, and as at your request—
To talk with Beatrice and Lucretia.
    Giacomo. Only to talk?
    Orsino.   The moments which even now
Pass onward to to-morrow's midnight hour
May memorize their flight with death. Ere then
They must have talked, and may perhaps have done,
And made an end.
    Giacomo.   Listen! What sound is that?
    Orsino. The house-dog moans, and the beams crack:
    nought else.
    Giacomo. It is my wife complaining in her sleep.

I doubt not she is saying bitter things
Of me; and all my children round her dreaming
That I deny them sustenance.
   Orsino.   Whilst he
Who truly took it from them, and who fills
Their hungry rest with bitterness, now sleeps
Lapped in bad pleasures, and triumphantly
Mocks thee in visions of successful hate
Too like the truth of day.
   Giacomo.   If e'er he wakes
Again, I will not trust to hireling hands—
   Orsino. Why, that were well. I must be gone; good night!
When next we meet . .
   Giacomo.   May all be done,—and all
Forgotten! Oh that I had never been!   [*Exeunt.*

ACT IV.

SCENE I.—*An Apartment in the Castle of Petrella. Enter* CENCI.

   Cenci. She comes not; yet I left her even now
Vanquished and faint. She knows the penalty
Of her delay. Yet what if threats are vain?
Am I not now within Petrella's moat?
Or fear I still the eyes and ears of Rome?
Might I not drag her by the golden hair?
Stamp on her! keep her sleepless till her brain
Be overworn? tame her with chains and famine?
Less would suffice. Yet so to leave undone
What I most seek! No, 'tis her stubborn will
Which, by its own consent, shall stoop as low
As that which drags it down.

                    Enter LUCRETIA.
                           Thou loathed wretch!
Hide thee from my abhorrence; fly, begone!
Yet stay—Bid Beatrice come hither.

Lucretia. O
Husband! I pray, for thine own wretched sake,
Heed what thou dost. A man who walks like thee
Through crimes, and through the danger of his crimes,
Each hour may stumble o'er a sudden grave.
And thou art old; thy hairs are hoary grey.
As thou wouldst save thyself from death and hell,
Pity thy daughter; give her to some friend
In marriage; so that she may tempt thee not
To hatred,—or worse thoughts, if worse there be.
  Cenci. What! like her sister, who has found a home
To mock my hate from with prosperity?
Strange ruin shall destroy both her and thee,
And all that yet remain. My death may be
Rapid; her destiny outspeeds it. Go,
Bid her come hither, and before my mood
Be changed, lest I should drag her by the hair.
  Lucretia. She sent me to thee, husband. At thy presence
She fell, as thou dost know, into a trance;
And in that trance she heard a voice which said,
"Cenci must die! Let him confess himself!
Even now the accusing angel waits to hear
If God, to punish his enormous crimes,
Harden his dying heart!"
  Cenci.   Why—such things are:
No doubt divine revealings may be made.
'Tis plain I have been favoured from above,
For, when I cursed my sons, they died.—Ay—so—
As to the right or wrong, that's talk!—Repentance—
Repentance is an easy moment's work,
And more depends on God than me. Well—well—
I must give up the greater point, which was
To poison and corrupt her soul.   [*A pause;* LUCRETIA
    approaches anxiously, and then shrinks back as he speaks.
                One, two;
Ay—Rocco and Cristofano my curse
Strangled: and Giacomo, I think, will find

Life a worse hell than that beyond the grave:
Beatrice shall, if there be skill in hate,
Die in despair, blaspheming: to Bernardo,
He is so innocent, I will bequeath
The memory of these deeds, and make his youth
The sepulchre of hope, where evil thoughts
Shall grow like weeds on a neglected tomb.
When all is done, out in the wide Campagna
I will pile up my silver and my gold;
My costly robes, paintings, and tapestries;
My parchments, and all records of my wealth;
And make a bonfire in my joy, and leave
Of my possessions nothing but my name,—
Which shall be an inheritance to strip
Its wearer bare as infamy.   That done,
My soul, which is a scourge, will I resign
Into the hands of him who wielded it;
Be it for its own punishment or theirs,
He will not ask it of me till the lash
Be broken in its last and deepest wound,—
Until its hate be all inflicted.   Yet,
Lest death outspeed my purpose, let me make
Short work and sure.

   Lucretia (*stops him*).   Oh stay!   It was a feint:
She had no vision, and she heard no voice.
I said it but to awe thee.

   Cenci.   That is well.
Vile palterer with the sacred truth of God,
Be thy soul choked with that blaspheming lie!
For Beatrice, worse terrors are in store
To bend her to my will.

   Lucretia.   Oh! to what will?
What cruel sufferings, more than she has known,
Canst thou inflict?

   Cenci,   Andrea! go, call my daughter;
And, if she comes not, tell her that I come.—
What sufferings?   I will drag her, step by step,

Through infamies unheard of among men;
She shall stand shelterless in the broad noon
Of public scorn, for acts blazoned abroad,
One among which shall be—what? Canst thou guess?
She shall become (for what she most abhors
Shall have a fascination to entrap
Her loathing will), to her own conscious self
All she appears to others; and, when dead,
As she shall die unshrived and unforgiven,
A rebel to her father and her God,
Her corpse shall be abandoned to the hounds;
Her name shall be the terror of the earth;
Her spirit shall approach the throne of God
Plague-spotted with my curses. I will make
Body and soul a monstrous lump of ruin.

Enter ANDREA.

Andrea. The Lady Beatrice—
Cenci. Speak, pale slave! What said she?
Andrea. My lord, 'twas what she looked. She said:
"Go tell my father that I see the gulf
Of hell betwen us two, which he may pass;
I will not." [*Exit* ANDREA.
Cenci. Go thou quick, Lucretia,—
Tell her to come; yet let her understand
Her coming is consent: and say moreover
That, if she come not, I will curse her. [*Exit* LUCRETIA.
Ha!
With what but with a father's curse doth God
Panic-strike armed Victory, and make pale
Cities in their prosperity? The world's Father
Must grant a parent's prayer against his child,
Be he who asks even what men call me.
Will not the deaths of her rebellious brothers
Awe her before I speak? for I on them
Did imprecate quick ruin, and it came. [*Enter* LUCRETIA.
Well, what? Speak, wretch!

Lucretia. She said, "I cannot come
Go tell my father that I see a torrent
Of his own blood raging between us."
    Cenci (kneeling). God!
Hear me! If this most specious mass of flesh
Which thou hast made my daughter; this my blood,
This particle of my divided being;
Or rather, this my bane and my disease,
Whose sight infects and poisons me; this devil
Which sprung from me as from a hell,—was meant
To aught good use; if her bright loveliness
Was kindled to illumine this dark world;
If, nursed by thy selectest dew of love,
Such virtues blossom in her as should make
The peace of life; I pray thee for my sake,
As thou the common God and Father art
Of her and me and all, reverse that doom!
Earth, in the name of God, let her food be
Poison, until she be encrusted round
With leprous stains! Heaven, rain upon her head
The blistering drops of the Maremma's dew,
Till she be speckled like a toad; parch up
Those love-enkindled lips, warp those fine limbs
To loathed lameness! All-beholding sun,
Strike in thine envy those life-darting eyes
With thine own blinding beams!
    Lucretia. Peace! peace!
For thine own sake unsay those dreadful words!
When high God grants, he punishes such prayers.
    Cenci (leaping up, and throwing his right hand towards Heaven).
           He does his will, I mine! This in addition:
That, if she have a child——
    Lucretia. Horrible thought!
    Cenci. That, if she ever have a child,—and thou,
Quick Nature! I adjure thee by thy God
That thou be fruitful in her, and increase
And multiply, fulfilling his command

And my deep imprecation,—may it be
A hideous likeness of herself! that, as
From a distorting mirror, she may see
Her image mixed with what she most abhors,
Smiling upon her from her nursing breast.
And that the child may from its infancy
Grow day by day more wicked and deformed,
Turning her mother's-love to misery:
And that both she and it may live, until
It shall repay her care and pain with hate,
Or what may else be more unnatural—
So he may hunt her through the clamorous scoffs
Of the loud world to a dishonoured grave!
Shall I revoke this curse? Go, bid her come
Before my words are chronicled in heaven. [*Exit* LUCRETIA.
I do not feel as if I were a man,
But like a fiend appointed to chastise
The offences of some unremembered world.
My blood is running up and down my veins;
A fearful pleasure makes it prick and tingle:
I feel a giddy sickness of strange awe;
My heart is beating with an expectation
Of horrid joy. [*Enter* LUCRETIA.
        What! Speak!
  Lucretia.   She bids thee curse;
And, if thy curses, as they cannot do,
Could kill her soul—
  Cenci.   She would not come. 'Tis well.
I can do both: first take what I demand,
And then extort concession. To thy chamber!
Fly ere I spurn thee: and beware this night
That thou cross not my footsteps. It were safer
To come between the tiger and his prey. [*Exit* LUCRETIA.
It must be late; mine eyes grow weary dim
With unaccustomed heaviness of sleep.
Conscience! O thou most insolent of lies!
They say that sleep, that healing dew of heaven,

Steeps not in balm the foldings of the brain
Which thinks thee an impostor. I will go,
First to belie thee with an hour of rest,
Which will be deep and calm, I feel; and then—
O multitudinous hell, the fiends will shake
Thine arches with the laughter of their joy!
There shall be lamentation heard in heaven
As o'er an angel fallen; and upon earth
All good shall droop and sicken, and ill things
Shall with a spirit of unnatural life
Stir and be quickened—even as I am now! [*Exit.*

SCENE II.—*Before the Castle of Petrella.*

Enter BEATRICE *and* LUCRETIA *above on the ramparts.*

Beatrice. They come not yet.
Lucretia. 'Tis scarce midnight.
Beatrice. How slow
Behind the course of thought, even sick with speed,
Lags leaden-footed Time!
Lucretia. The minutes pass—
If he should wake before the deed is done?
Beatrice. Oh mother! he must never wake again.
What thou hast said persuades me that our act
Will but dislodge a spirit of deep hell
Out of a human form.
Lucretia. 'Tis true he spoke
Of death and judgment with strange confidence
For one so wicked; as a man believing
In God, yet recking not of good or ill.
And yet to die without confession!—
Beatrice. Oh!
Believe that Heaven is merciful and just,
And will not add our dread necessity,
To the amount of his offences.

Enter OLIMPIO *and* MARZIO, *below.*

Lucretia. See,
They come.

Beatrice. All mortal things must hasten thus
To their dark end. Let us go down.
[*Exeunt* LUCRETIA *and* BEATRICE *from above.*

Olimpio. How feel you to this work?

Marzio. As one who thinks
A thousand crowns excellent market-price
For an old murderer's life. Your cheeks are pale.

Olimpio. It is the white reflection of your own
Which you call pale.

Marzio. Is that their natural hue?

Olimpio. Or 'tis my hate, and the deferred desire
To wreak it, which extinguishes their blood.

Marzio. You are inclined then to this business?

Olimpio. Ay:
If one should bribe me with a thousand crowns
To kill a serpent which had stung my child,
I could not be more willing.

Enter BEATRICE *and* LUCRETIA *below.*

Noble ladies!

Beatrice. Are ye resolved?

Olimpio. Is he asleep?

Marzio. Is all
Quiet?

Lucretia. I mixed an opiate with his drink:
He sleeps so soundly—

Beatrice. That his death will be
But as a change of sin-chastising dreams,
A dark continuance of the hell within him,
Which God extinguish! But ye are resolved?
Ye know it is a high and holy deed?

Olimpio. We are resolved.

Marzio. As to the how this act
Be warranted, it rests with you.

Beatrice. Well, follow.
Olimpio. Hush! Hark! What noise is that?
Marzio. Ha! some one comes!
Beatrice. Ye conscience-stricken cravens, rock to rest
Your baby hearts. It is the iron gate,
Which ye left open, swinging to the wind,
That enters whistling as in scorn. Come, follow:
And be your steps like mine, light, quick, and bold. [*Exeunt.*

SCENE III.—*An Apartment in the Castle.*

Enter BEATRICE *and* LUCRETIA.

Lucretia. They are about it now.
Beatrice. Nay, it is done.
Lucretia. I have not heard him groan.
Beatrice. He will not groan.
Lucretia. What sound is that?
Beatrice. List! 'tis the tread of feet
About his bed.
Lucretia. My God!
If he be now a cold stiff corpse—
Beatrice. Oh fear not
What may be done, but what is left undone:
The act seals all.

Enter OLIMPIO *and* MARZIO.
Is it accomplished?
Marzio. What?
Olimpio. Did you not call?
Beatrice. When?
Olimpio. Now.
Beatrice. I ask if all is over.
Olimpio. We dare not kill an old and sleeping man.
His thin grey hair, his stern and reverent brow
His veined hands crossed on his heaving breast,
And the calm innocent sleep in which he lay,
Quelled me. Indeed, indeed, I cannot do it.

Marzio. But I was bolder; for I chid Olimpio,
And bade him bear his wrongs to his own grave,
And leave me the reward. And now my knife
Touched the loose wrinkled throat, when the old man
Stirred in his sleep, and said, "God! hear, oh hear,
A father's curse! What, art thou not our father?"
And then he laughed. I knew it was the ghost
Of my dead father speaking through his lips,
And could not kill him.
 Beatrice.   Miserable slaves!
Where, if ye dare not kill a sleeping man,
Found ye the boldness to return to me
With such a deed undone? Base palterers!
Cowards and traitors! Why, the very conscience
Which ye would sell for gold and for revenge
Is an equivocation: it sleeps over
A thousand daily acts disgracing men;
And, when a deed where mercy insults Heaven——
Why do I talk?
   [*Snatching a dagger from one of them, and raising it.*
   Hadst thou a tongue to say
"She murdered her own father," I must do it!—
But never dream ye shall outlive him long!
 Olimpio. Stop, for God's sake!
 Marzio.   I will go back and kill him.
 Olimpio. Give me the weapon; we must do thy will.
 Beatrice. Take it! Depart! Return!
      [*Exeunt* OLIMPIO *and* MARZIO.
       How pale thou art!
We do but that which 'twere a deadly crime
To leave undone.
 Lucretia. Would it were done!
 Beatrice.   Even whilst
That doubt is passing through your mind, the world
Is conscious of a change. Darkness and hell
Have swallowed up the vapour they sent forth
To blacken the sweet light of life. My breath

Comes, methinks, lighter, and the gelid blood
Runs freely through my veins. Hark!
Enter OLIMPIO *and* MARZIO.
                                                He is—
  Olimpio.   Dead!
  Marzio. We strangled him, that there might be no blood;
And then we threw his heavy corpse i' the garden
Under the balcony; 'twill seem it fell.
  Beatrice (*giving them a bag of coin*). Here, take this gold,
              and hasten to your homes.
And, Marzio, because thou wast only awed
By that which made me tremble, wear thou this!
                      [*Clothes him in a rich mantle.*
It was the mantle which my grandfather
Wore in his high prosperity, and men
Envied his state: so may they envy thine!
Thou wert a weapon in the hand of God
To a just use. Live long and thrive! And mark,
If thou hast crimes, repent: this deed is none.
                          [*A horn is sounded.*
  Lucretia. Hark, 'tis the castle horn: my God! it sounds
Like the last trump!
  Beatrice.   Some tedious guest is coming.
  Lucretia. The drawbridge is let down; there is a tramp
Of horses in the court! Fly, hide yourselves!
                    [*Exeunt* OLIMPIO *and* MARZIO.
  Beatrice. Let us retire to counterfeit deep rest.
I scarcely need to counterfeit it now;
The spirit which doth reign within these limbs
Seems strangely undisturbed: I could even sleep
Fearless and calm. All ill is surely past.   [*Exeunt.*

      SCENE IV.—*Another Apartment in the Castle.*
Enter on one side the Legate SAVELLA, *introduced by a Servant, and
          on the other* LUCRETIA *and* BERNARDO.
  Savella. Lady, my duty to his Holiness
Be my excuse that thus unseasonably

I break upon your rest. I must speak with
Count Cenci; doth he sleep?
    Lucretia (in a hurried and confused manner.) I think he sleeps.
Yet wake him not, I pray; spare me awhile.
He is a wicked and a wrathful man;
Should he be roused out of his sleep to-night,
Which is, I know, a hell of angry dreams,
It were not well; indeed it were not well.
Wait till daybreak.— *(Aside.)* Oh! I am deadly sick!
    Savella. I grieve thus to distress you, but the Count
Must answer charges of the gravest import,
And suddenly; such my commission is.
    Lucretia (with increased agitation.) I dare not rouse him, I
        know none who dare;
'Twere perilous;—you might as safely waken
A serpent, or a corpse in which some fiend
Were laid to sleep.
    Savella.   Lady, my moments here
Are counted. I must rouse him from his sleep,
Since none else dare.
    Lucretia (aside.)   Oh terror! Oh despair!
(*To* BERNARDO.) Bernardo, conduct you the Lord Legate to
Your father's chamber. [*Exeunt* SAVELLA *and* BERNARDO.
        Enter BEATRICE.
    Beatrice.   'Tis a messenger
Come to arrest the culprit who now stands
Before the throne of unappealable God.
Both Earth and Heaven, consenting arbiters,
Acquit our deed.
    Lucretia.   Oh agony of fear!
Would that he yet might live! Even now I heard
The legate's followers whisper as they passed
They had a warrant for his instant death.
All was prepared, by unforbidden means,
Which we must pay so dearly, having done.
Even now they search the tower, and find the body;
Now they suspect the truth; now they consult,

Before they come to tax us with the fact;
Oh horrible, 'tis all discovered!
 Beatrice.   Mother,
What is done wisely is done well. Be bold
As thou art just. 'Tis like a truant child
To fear that others know what thou hast done,
Even from thine own strong consciousness; and thus
Write on unsteady eyes and altered cheeks
All thou wouldst hide. Be faithful to thyself,
And fear no other witness but thy fear.
For, if, as cannot be, some circumstance
Should rise in accusation, we can blind
Suspicion with such cheap astonishment,
Or overbear it with such guiltless pride,
As murderers cannot feign. The deed is done,
And what may follow now regards not me.
I am as universal as the light;
Free as the earth-surrounding air; as firm
As the world's centre. Consequence, to me,
Is as the wind which strikes the solid rock,
But shakes is not.   [*A cry within and tumult.*
 Voices.   Murder! Murder! Murder!

   Enter BERNARDO *and* SAVELLA.

 Savella (*to his followers.*) Go search the castle round; sound
   the alarm;
Look to the gates, that none escape!
 Beatrice.   What now?
 Bernardo. I know not what to say—My father's dead.
 Beatrice. How, dead! he only sleeps; you mistake, brother.
His sleep is very calm, very like death;
'Tis wonderful how well a tyrant sleeps.
He is not dead.
 Bernardo.   Dead, murdered!
 Lucretia (*with extreme agitation.*) Oh no, no!
He is not murdered, though he may be dead;
I have alone the keys of those apartments.

Savella. Ha! Is it so?
Beatrice. My lord, I pray excuse us;
We will retire; my mother is not well;
She seems quite overcome with this strange horror.
                    [*Exeunt* LUCRETIA *and* BEATRICE.
Savella. Can you suspect who may have murdered him?
Bernardo. I know not what to think.
Savella. Can you name any
Who had an interest in his death?
Bernardo. Alas!
I can name none who had not, and those most
Who most lament that such a deed is done;
My mother, and my sister, and myself.
Savella. 'Tis strange! There were clear marks of violence.
I found the old man's body in the moonlight,
Hanging beneath the window of his chamber
Among the branches of a pine: he could not
Have fallen there, for all his limbs lay heaped
And effortless; 'tis true there was no blood.—
Favour me, sir—it much imports your house
That all should be made clear—to tell the ladies
That I request their presence. [*Exit* BERNARDO.

Enter Guards, bringing in MARZIO.

Guard. We have one.
Officer. My lord, we found this ruffian and another
Lurking among the rocks; there is no doubt
But that they are the murderers of Count Cenci.
Each had a bag of coin. This fellow wore
A gold-inwoven robe, which, shining bright
Under the dark rocks to the glimmering moon,
Betrayed them to our notice. The other fell
Desperately fighting.
Savella. What does he confess?
Officer. He keeps firm silence; but these lines found on him
May speak.
Savella. Their language is at least sincere. [*Reads.*

> "To the Lady Beatrice.
>
> "That the atonement of what my nature sickens to conjecture may soon arrive, I send thee, at thy brother's desire, those who will speak and do more than I dare write.
>
> > "Thy devoted servant,
> > > "Orsino."

Enter Lucretia, Beatrice, *and* Bernardo.

Know'st thou this writing, lady?
   Beatrice.   No.
   Savella.   Nor thou?
   Lucretia (her conduct throughout the scene is marked by extreme agitation).
Where was it found? What is it? It should be
Orsino's hand! It speaks of that strange horror
Which never yet found utterance, but which made
Between that hapless child and her dead father
A gulf of obscure hatred.
   Savella.   Is it so?
Is it true, lady, that thy father did
Such outrages as to awaken in thee
Unfilial hate?
   Beatrice.   Not hate, 'twas more than hate:
This is most true, yet wherefore question me?
   Savella.   There is a deed demanding question done;
Thou hast a secret which will answer not.
   Beatrice. What say'st? My lord, your words are bold and rash.
   Savella.   I do arrest all present in the name
Of the Pope's Holiness. You must to Rome.
   Lucretia. Oh not to Rome! Indeed we are not guilty.
   Beatrice. Guilty! Who dares talk of guilt? My lord,
I am more innocent of parricide
Than is a child born fatherless. Dear mother,
Your gentleness and patience are no shield
For this keen-judging world, this two-edged lie,
Which seems, but is not. What! will human laws—

Rather, will ye who are their ministers—
Bar all access to retribution first?
And then, when Heaven doth interpose to do
What ye neglect, arming familiar things
To the redress of an unwonted crime,
Make ye the victims who demanded it
Culprits? 'Tis ye are culprits! That poor wretch
Who stands so pale and trembling and amazed,
If it be true he murdered Cenci, was
A sword in the right hand of justest God.
Wherefore should I have wielded it? unless
The crimes which mortal tongue dare never name
God therefore scruples to avenge.
   Savella.   You own
That you desired his death?
   Beatrice.   It would have been
A crime no less than his if for one moment
That fierce desire had faded in my heart.
'Tis true I did believe, and hope and pray,
Ay, I even knew—for God is wise and just—
That some strange sudden death hung over him.
'Tis true that this did happen, and most true
There was no other rest for me on earth,
No other hope in heaven;—now what of this?
   Savella. Strange thoughts beget strange deeds; and here
          are both.
I judge thee not.
   Beatrice.   And yet, if you arrest me,
You are the judge and executioner
Of that which is the life of life: the breath
Of accusation kills an innocent name,
And leaves for lame acquittal the poor life
Which is a mask without it. 'Tis most false
That I am guilty of foul parricide;
Although I must rejoice, for justest cause,
That other hands have sent my father's soul
To ask the mercy he denied to me.

Now leave us free: stain not a noble house
With vague surmises of rejected crime;
Add to our sufferings and your own neglect
No heavier sum; let them have been enough.
Leave us the wreck we have.
  Savella.   I dare not, lady.
I pray that you prepare yourselves for Rome:
There the Pope's further pleasure will be known.
  Lucretia. Oh not to Rome! Oh take us not to Rome!
  Beatrice. Why not to Rome, dear mother? There, as here,
Our innocence is an armed heel
To trample accusation. God is there
As here, and with his shadow ever clothes
The innocent, the injured, and the weak;
And such are we. Cheer up, dear lady! lean
On me; collect your wandering thoughts. My lord,
As soon as you have taken some refreshment,
And had all such examinations made
Upon the spot as may be necessary
To the full understanding of this matter,
We shall be ready. Mother, will you come?
  Lucretia. Ha! they will bind us to the rack, and wrest
Self-accusation from our agony!
Will Giacomo be there? Orsino? Marzio?
All present; all confronted; all demanding,
Each from the other's countenance, the thing
Which is in every heart! Oh misery!
          [*She faints, and is borne out.*
  Savella. She faints; an ill appearance this.
  Beatrice.   My lord,
She knows not yet the uses of the world.
She fears that Power is as a beast which grasps
And loosens not: a snake whose look transmutes
All things to guilt, which is its nutriment.
She cannot know how well the supine slaves
Of blind authority read the truth of things
When written on a brow of guilelessness:

She sees not yet triumphant Innocence
Stand at the judgment-seat of mortal man,
A judge and an accuser of the wrong
Which drags it there.—Prepare yourself, my lord;
Our suite will join yours in the court below. [*Exeunt.*

ACT V.

SCENE I.—*An Apartment in* ORSINO'S *Palace.*

Enter ORSINO *and* GIACOMO.

Giacomo. Do evil deeds thus quickly come to end?
Oh that the vain remorse which must chastise
Crimes done had but as loud a voice to warn
As its keen sting is mortal to avenge!
Oh that the hour when present had cast off
The mantle of its mystery, and shown
The ghastly form with which it now returns,
When its scared game is roused, cheering the hounds
Of conscience to their prey! Alas, alas!
It was a wicked thought, a piteous deed,
To kill an old and hoary-headed father!
   Orsino. It has turned out unluckily, in truth.
   Giacomo. To violate the sacred doors of sleep;
To cheat kind Nature of the placid death
Which she prepares for overwearied age;
To drag from heaven an unrepentant soul,
Which might have quenched in reconciling prayers
A life of burning crimes—
   Orsino. You cannot say
I urged you to the deed.
   Giacomo. Oh! had I never
Found in thy smooth and ready countenance
The mirror of my darkest thoughts; hadst thou
Never with hints and questions made me look
Upon the monster of my thought, until
It grew familiar to desire—

Orsino.   'Tis thus
Men cast the blame of their unprosperous acts
Upon the abettors of their own resolve,
Or anything but their weak guilty selves.
And yet, confess the truth, it is the peril
In which you stand that gives you this pale sickness
Of penitence; confess, 'tis fear, disguised
From its own shame, that takes the mantle now
Of thin remorse. What if we yet were safe?
    Giacomo. How can that be? Already Beatrice,
Lucretia, and the murderer, are in prison.
I doubt not, officers are, whilst we speak,
Sent to arrest us.
    Orsino.   I have all prepared
For instant flight. We can escape even now,
So we take fleet occasion by the hair.
    Giacomo. Rather expire in tortures, as I may!
What! will you cast by self-accusing flight
Assured conviction upon Beatrice?
She who alone, in this unnatural work,
Stands like God's angel ministered upon
By fiends; avenging such a nameless wrong
As turns black parricide to piety;
Whilst we for basest ends . . . I fear, Orsino,
While I consider all your words and looks,
Comparing them with your proposal now,
That you must be a villain. For what end
Could you engage in such a perilous crime,
Training me on with hints and signs and smiles
Even to this gulf? Thou art no liar? No,
Thou art a lie! Traitor and murderer!
Coward and slave! But no—defend thyself;   [*Drawing.*
Let the sword speak what the indignant tongue
Disdains to brand thee with!
    Orsino.   Put up your weapon.
Is it the desperation of your fear
Makes you thus rash and sudden with a friend

Now ruined for your sake? If honest anger
Have moved you, know that what I just proposed
Was but to try you. As for me, I think
Thankless affection led me to this point;
From which, if my firm temper could repent,
I cannot now recede. Even whilst we speak,
The ministers of justice wait below:
They grant me these brief moments. Now, if you
Have any word of melancholy comfort
To speak to your pale wife, 'twere best to pass
Out at the postern, and avoid them so.
   Giacomo. O generous friend! How canst thou pardon me?
Would that my life could purchase thine!
   Orsino.   That wish
Now comes a day too late. Haste; fare thee well!
Hear'st thou not steps along the corridor? [*Exit* GIACOMO.
I'm sorry for it; but the guards are waiting
At his own gate, and such was my contrivance
That I might rid me both of him and them.
I thought to act a solemn comedy
Upon the painted scene of this new world,
And to attain my own peculiar ends
By some such plot of mingled good and ill
As others weave; but there arose a Power
Which grasped and snapped the threads of my device,
And turned it to a net of ruin—Ha!   [*A shout is heard.*
Is that my name I hear proclaimed abroad?
But I will pass, wrapped in a vile disguise,
Rags on my back, and a false innocence
Upon my face, through the misdeeming crowd
Which judges by what seems. 'Tis easy then,
For a new name and for a country new,
And a new life fashioned on old desires,
To change the honours of abandoned Rome:
And these must be the masks of that within,
Which must remain unaltered.—Oh! I fear
That what is past will never let me rest!

Why, when none else is conscious, but myself,
Of my misdeeds, should my own heart's contempt
Trouble me? have I not the power to fly
My own reproaches? shall I be the slave
Of—what? A word! which those of this false world
Employ against each other, not themselves;
As men wear daggers not for self-offence.
But, if I am mistaken, where shall I
Find the disguise to hide me from myself,
As now I skulk from every other eye? [*Exit.*

SCENE II.—*A Hall of Justice.*

CAMILLO, JUDGES, &c., *are discovered seated;* MARZIO *is led in.*

First Judge. Accused, do you persist in your denial?
I ask you, are you innocent or guilty?
I demand who were the participators
In your offence? Speak truth, and the whole truth.
   Marzio. My God! I did not kill him; I know nothing;
Olimpio sold the robe to me from which
You would infer my guilt.
   Second Judge.   Away with him!
   First Judge. Dare you, with lips yet white from the rack's kiss,
Speak false? Is it so soft a questioner
That you would bandy lover's talk with it,
Till it wind out your life and soul? Away!
   Marzio. Spare me! Oh spare! I will confess.
   First Judge.   Then speak.
   Marzio. I strangled him in his sleep.
   First Judge.   Who urged you to it?
   Marzio. His own son Giacomo, and the young prelate
Orsino, sent me to Petrella; there
The ladies Beatrice and Lucretia
Tempted me with a thousand crowns, and I
And my companion forthwith murdered him.
Now let me die.

THE CENCI.   237

First Judge.   This sounds as bad as truth.
Guards there, lead forth the prisoners.
    Enter LUCRETIA, BEATRICE, *and* GIACOMO, *guarded.*
                                    Look upon
This man.   When did you see him last?
    Beatrice.   We never
Saw him.
    Marzio.   You know me too well, Lady Beatrice.
    Beatrice.   I know thee! How! where? when?
    Marzio.   You know 'twas I
Whom you did urge with menaces and bribes
To kill your father.   When the thing was done,
You clothed me in a robe of woven gold,
And bade me thrive: how I have thriven you see.
You, my Lord Giacomo, Lady Lucretia,
You know that what I speak is true.
    [BEATRICE *advances towards him; he covers his face, and
        shrinks back.*
                                    Oh! dart
The terrible resentment of those eyes
On the dead earth!   Turn them away from me—
They wound!   'Twas torture forced the truth.   My lords,
Having said this, let me be led to death.
    Beatrice.   Poor wretch, I pity thee: yet stay awhile.
    Camillo.   Guards, lead him not away.
    Beatrice.   Cardinal Camillo,
You have a good repute for gentleness
And wisdom: can it be that you sit here
To countenance a wicked farce like this?
When some obscure and trembling slave is dragged
From sufferings which might shake the sternest heart,
And bade to answer, not as he believes,
But as those may suspect or do desire
Whose questions thence suggest their own reply,—
And that in peril of such hideous torments
As merciful God spares even the damned!   Speak now
The thing you surely know, which is that you,

If your fine frame were stretched upon that wheel,
And you were told, "Confess that you did poison
Your little nephew, that fair blue-eyed child
Who was the lodestar of your life;"—and though
All see, since his most swift and piteous death,
That day and night, and heaven and earth, and time,
And all the things hoped for or done therein,
Are changed to you, through your exceeding grief;—
Yet you would say, "I confess anything,"
And beg from your tormentors, like that slave,
The refuge of dishonourable death.
I pray you, Cardinal, that you assert
My innocence.

 Camillo (*much moved*). What shall we think, my lords?
Shame on these tears! I thought the heart was frozen
Which is their fountain. I would pledge my soul
That she is guiltless.

 Judge.   Yet she must be tortured.

 Camillo. I would as soon have tortured mine own nephew
(If he now lived, he would be just her age;
His hair, too, was her colour, and his eyes
Like hers in shape, but blue and not so deep)
As that most perfect image of God's love
That ever came sorrowing upon the earth.
She is as pure as speechless infancy!

 Judge. Well, be her purity on your head, my lord,
If you forbid the rack. His Holiness
Enjoined us to pursue this monstrous crime
By the severest forms of law; nay, even
To stretch a point against the criminals.
The prisoners stand accused of parricide,
Upon such evidence as justifies
Torture.

 Beatrice. What evidence? This man's?
 Judge.   Even so.
 Beatrice (*to* MARZIO). Come near. And who art thou thus
   chosen forth

Out of the multitude of living men
To kill the innocent?
   Marzio.   I am Marzio,
Thy father's vassal.
   Beatrice.   Fix thine eyes on mine;
Answer to what I ask.   *[Turning to the Judges.*
                  I prithee mark
His countenance: unlike bold calumny
Which sometimes dares not speak the thing it looks,
He dares not look the thing he speaks, but bends
His gaze on the blind earth.
           (*To* MARZIO.)   What! wilt thou say
That I did murder my own father?
   Marzio.   Oh!
Spare me! My brain swims round—I cannot speak—
It was that horrid torture forced the truth.
Take me away! Let her not look on me!
I am a guilty miserable wretch!
I have said all I know; now, let me die!
   Beatrice.   My lords, if by my nature I had been
So stern as to have planned the crime alleged
(Which your suspicions dictate to this slave,
And the rack makes him utter), do you think
I should have left this two-edged instrument
Of my misdeed, this man, this bloody knife
With my own name engraven on the heft,
Lying unsheathed amid a world of foes,
For my own death? that, with such horrible need
For deepest silence, I should have neglected
So trivial a precaution as the making
His tomb the keeper of a secret written
On a thief's memory? What is his poor life?
What are a thousand lives? A parricide
Had trampled them like dust; and see, he lives!
                       [Turning to MARZIO.
And thou—
   Marzio.   Oh spare me! Speak to me no more!

That stern yet piteous look, those solemn tones,
Wound worse than torture.
    (*To the Judges.*) I have told it all;
For pity's sake lead me away to death!
  Camillo. Guards, lead him nearer the Lady Beatrice.
He shrinks from her regard like autumn's leaf
From the keen breath of the serenest north.
  Beatrice. O thou who tremblest on the giddy verge
Of life and death, pause ere thou answerest me;
So mayst thou answer God with less dismay.
What evil have we done thee? I, alas!
Have lived but on this earth a few sad years;
And so my lot was ordered that a father
First turned the moments of awakening life
To drops each poisoning youth's sweet hope; and then
Stabbed with one blow my everlasting soul,
And my untainted fame, and even that peace
Which sleeps within the core of the heart's heart.
But the wound was not mortal; so my hate
Became the only worship I could lift
To our great Father, who in pity and love
Armed thee, as thou dost say, to cut him off;
And thus his wrong becomes my accusation!
And art thou the accuser? If thou hopest
Mercy in heaven, show justice upon earth:
Worse than a bloody hand is a hard heart.
If thou hast done murders, made thy life's path
Over the trampled laws of God and man,
Rush not before thy Judge, and say: "My Maker,
I have done this, and more; for there was one
Who was most pure and innocent on earth;
And, because she endured what never any,
Guilty or innocent, endured before,
Because her wrongs could not be told nor thought,
Because thy hand at length did rescue her,
I with my words killed her and all her kin."
Think, I adjure thee, what it is to slay

The reverence living in the minds of men
Towards our ancient house and stainless fame!
Think what it is to strangle infant pity,
Cradled in the belief of guileless looks,—
Till it become a crime to suffer. Think
What 'tis to blot with infamy and blood
All that which shows like innocence, and is—
Hear me, great God!—I swear, most innocent;
So that the world lose all discrimination
Between the sly, fierce, wild regard of guilt,
And that which now compels thee to reply
To what I ask: Am I, or am I not
A parricide?

 Marzio.   Thou art not!
 Judge.   What is this?
 Marzio. I here declare those whom I did accuse
Are innocent. 'Tis I alone am guilty.
 Judge. Drag him away to torments; let them be
Subtle and long drawn out, to tear the folds
Of the heart's inmost cell. Unbind him not
Till he confess.
 Marzio.   Torture me as ye will:
A keener pain has wrung a higher truth
From my last breath. She is most innocent.
Bloodhounds, not men, glut yourselves well with me!
I will not give you that fine piece of nature
To rend and ruin.   [*Exit* MARZIO, *guarded.*
 Camillo.   What say ye now, my lords?
 Judge. Let tortures strain the truth till it be white
As snow thrice sifted by the frozen wind.
 Camillo. Yet stained with blood.
 Judge (*to* BEATRICE).   Know you this paper, lady?
 Beatrice. Entrap me not with questions. Who stands here
As my accuser? Ha! wilt thou be he,
Who art my judge? Accuser, witness, judge,
What, all in one? Here is Orsino's name;
Where is Orsino? Let his eye meet mine.

What means this scrawl? Alas! ye know not what;
And therefore, on the chance that it may be
Some evil, will ye kill us!

Enter an Officer.

Officer.   Marzio's dead.
Judge. What did he say?
Officer.   Nothing. As soon as we
Had bound him on the wheel, he smiled on us,
As one who baffles a deep adversary;
And, holding his breath, died.
Judge.   There remains nothing
But to apply the question to those prisoners
Who yet remain stubborn.
Camillo.   I overrule
Further proceedings, and in the behalf
Of these most innocent and noble persons
Will use my interest with the Holy Father.
Judge. Let the Pope's pleasure then be done. Meanwhile
Conduct these culprits each to separate cells.
And be the engines ready: for this night—
If the Pope's resolution be as grave,
Pious, and just, as once—I'll wring the truth
Out of those nerves and sinews, groan by groan.   [*Exeunt.*

Scene III.—*The Cell of a Prison.* Beatrice *is discovered asleep on a couch.*

Enter Bernardo.

Bernardo. How gently slumber rests upon her face,
Like the last thoughts of some day sweetly spent,
Closing in night and dreams, and so prolonged!
After such torments as she bore last night,
How light and soft her breathing comes! Ah me!
Methinks that I shall never sleep again.
But I must shake the heavenly dew of rest
From this sweet folded flower, thus—wake! awake!
What, sister, canst thou sleep?

Beatrice (awaking). I was just dreaming
That we were all in paradise. Thou knowest
This cell seems like a kind of paradise
After our father's presence.
  Bernardo.   Dear, dear sister,
Would that thy dream were not a dream! O God!
How shall I tell?
  Beatrice.   What wouldst thou tell, sweet brother?
  Bernardo. Look not so calm and happy, or, even whilst
I stand considering what I have to say,
My heart will break!
  Beatrice.   See now, thou mak'st me weep.
How very friendless thou wouldst be, dear child,
If I were dead. Say what thou hast to say.
  Bernardo. They have confessed; they could endure no
      more
The tortures—
  Beatrice.   Ha! What was there to confess?
They must have told some weak and wicked lie
To flatter their tormentors. Have they said
That they were guilty? O white Innocence,
That thou shouldst wear the mask of guilt to hide
Thine awful and serenest countenance
From those who know thee not!

  Enter JUDGE, *with* LUCRETIA *and* GIACOMO, *guarded.*
        Ignoble hearts!
For some brief spasms of pain, which are at least
As mortal as the limbs through which they pass,
Are centuries of high splendour laid in dust?
And that eternal honour which should live
Sunlike above the reek of mortal fame
Changed to a mockery and a by-word? What!
Will you give up these bodies to be dragged
At horses' heels, so that our hair should sweep
The footsteps of the vain and senseless crowd,
Who, that they may make our calamity

Their worship and their spectacle, will leave
The churches and the theatres as void
As their own hearts? Shall the light multitude
Fling, at their choice, curses or faded pity,
Sad funeral flowers to deck a living corpse,
Upon us as we pass, to pass away,
And leave—what memory of our having been?
Infamy, blood, terror, despair! O thou
Who wert a mother to the parentless,
Kill not thy child! Let not her wrongs kill thee!
Brother, lie down with me upon the rack,
And let us each be silent as a corpse;
It soon will be as soft as any grave.
'Tis but the falsehood it can wring from fear
Makes the rack cruel.
    Giacomo.   They will tear the truth
Even from thee at last, those cruel pains:
For pity's sake, say thou art guilty now.
    Lucretia. Oh speak the truth! Let us all quickly die:
And after death God is our judge, not they;
He will have mercy on us.
    Bernardo.   If indeed
It can be true, say so, dear sister mine;
And then the Pope will surely pardon you,
And all be well.
    Judge.   Confess, or I will warp
Your limbs with such keen tortures—
    Beatrice.   Tortures! Turn
The rack henceforth into a spinning-wheel!
Torture your dog, that he may tell when last
He lapped the blood his master shed—not me!
My pangs are of the mind and of the heart
And of the soul: ay, of the inmost soul,
Which weeps within tears as of burning gall
To see, in this ill world where none are true,
My kindred false to their deserted selves;
And with considering all the wretched life

Which I have lived, and its now wretched end;
And the small justice shown by Heaven and Earth
To me or mine; and what a tyrant thou art,
And what slaves these; and what a world we make,
The oppressor and the oppressed—Such pangs compel
My answer. What is it thou wouldst with me?

Judge. Art thou not guilty of thy father's death?

Beatrice. Or wilt thou rather tax high-judging God
That he permitted such an act as that
Which I have suffered, and which he beheld;
Made it unutterable, and took from it
All refuge, all revenge, all consequence,
But that which thou hast called my father's death?
Which is or is not what men call a crime,
Which either I have done, or have not done;
Say what ye will. I shall deny no more.
If ye desire it thus, thus let it be—
And so an end of all. Now do your will;
No other pains shall force another word.

Judge. She is convicted, but has not confessed.
Be it enough. Until their final sentence,
Let none have converse with them. You, young lord,
Linger not here.

Beatrice. Oh tear him not away!

Judge. Guards! do your duty.

Bernardo (embracing BEATRICE). Oh! would ye divide
Body from soul?

Officer. That is the headsman's business.

[*Exeunt all but* LUCRETIA, BEATRICE, *and* GIACOMO.

Giacomo. Have I confessed? Is it all over now?
No hope? no refuge? O weak wicked tongue
Which has destroyed me, would that thou hadst been
Cut out and thrown to dogs first! To have killed
My father first, and then betrayed my sister—
Ay, thee! the one thing innocent and pure
In this black guilty world—to that which I

So well deserve! My wife! my little ones!
Destitute, helpless; and I—Father! God!
Canst thou forgive even the unforgiving,
When their full hearts break thus, thus?—
[*Covers his face and weeps*
Lucretia. Oh my child!
To what a dreadful end are we all come!
Why did I yield? Why did I not sustain
Those torments? Oh that I were all dissolved
Into these fast and unavailing tears,
Which flow and feel not!
Beatrice. What 'twas weak to do
'Tis weaker to lament, once being done.
Take cheer! The God who knew my wrong, and made
Our speedy act the angel of his wrath,
Seems, and but seems, to have abandoned us.
Let us not think that we shall die for this.
Brother, sit near me; give me your firm hand,
You had a manly heart. Bear up! bear up!
Oh! dearest lady, put your gentle head
Upon my lap, and try to sleep awhile:
Your eyes look pale, hollow, and overworn,
With heaviness of watching and slow grief.
Come, I will sing you some low sleepy tune,
Not cheerful nor yet sad; some dull old thing,
Some outworn and unused monotony,
Such as our country gossips sing and spin,
Till they almost forget they live. Lie down!
So; that will do. Have I forgot the words?
Faith! they are sadder than I thought they were.

    ♪ 'False friend, wilt thou smile or weep
    When my life is laid asleep?
    Little cares for a smile or a tear
    The clay-cold corpse upon the bier.
      Farewell! Heigh ho!
    What is this whispers low?
    There is a snake in thy smile, my dear,
    And bitter poison within thy tear.

"Sweet sleep! were death like to thee,
Or if thou couldst mortal be,
I would close these eyes of pain,
When to wake? Never again.
  O world! farewell!
  Listen to the passing bell!
It says, thou and I must part,
With a light and a heavy heart."

[*The scene closes.*

SCENE IV.—*A Hall of the Prison.*

Enter CAMILLO *and* BERNARDO.

Camillo. The Pope is stern; not to be moved or bent.
He looked as calm and keen as is the engine
Which tortures and which kills, exempt itself
From aught that it inflicts; a marble form,
A rite, a law, a custom; not a man.
He frowned, as if to frown had been the trick
Of his machinery, on the advocates
Presenting the defences, which he tore
And threw behind, muttering with hoarse harsh voice:
"Which among ye defended their old father
Killed in his sleep?" Then to another: "Thou
Dost this in virtue of thy place; 'tis well."
He turned to me then looking deprecation,
And said these three words coldly: "They must die."
  Bernardo. And yet you left him not!
  Camillo.   I urged him still
Pleading, as I could guess, the devilish wrong
Which prompted your unnatural parent's death.
And he replied; "Paolo Santa Croce
Murdered his mother yester evening,
And he is fled. Parricide grows so rife
That soon, for some just cause no doubt, the young
Will strangle us all, dozing in our chairs.
Authority and power and hoary hair
Are grown crimes capital. You are my nephew,—
You come to ask their pardon. Stay a moment;

Here is their sentence; never see me more,
Till to the letter it be all fulfilled."
    Bernardo.   O God, not so! I did believe indeed
That all you said was but sad preparation
For happy news. Oh there are words and looks
To bend the sternest purpose! Once I knew them;
Now I forget them at my dearest need.
What think you if I seek him out, and bathe
His feet and robe with hot and bitter tears?
Importune him with prayers, vexing his brain
With my perpetual cries, until in rage
He strike me with his pastoral cross, and trample
Upon my prostrate head so that my blood
May stain the senseless dust on which he treads,
And remorse waken mercy? I will do it!
Oh wait till I return!   [*Rushes out.*
    Camillo.   Alas! poor boy!
A wreck-devoted seaman thus might pray
To the deaf sea.

    Enter LUCRETIA, BEATRICE, *and* GIACOMO, *guarded.*

    Beatrice.   I hardly dare to fear
That thou bring'st other news than a just pardon.
    Camillo.   May God in heaven be less inexorable
To the Pope's prayers than he has been to mine!
Here is the sentence and the warrant.
    Beatrice (*wildly*).   Oh
My God! Can it be possible I have
To die so suddenly? so young to go
Under the obscure, cold, rotting, wormy ground?
To be nailed down into a narrow place;
To see no more sweet sunshine; hear no more
Blithe voice of living thing; muse not again
Upon familiar thoughts,—sad, yet thus lost
How fearful! To be nothing! or to be—
What? Oh where am I? Let me not go mad!
Sweet Heaven, forgive weak thoughts! If there should be

No God, no heaven, no earth, in the void world,
The wide, grey, lampless, deep, unpeopled world!
If all things then should be my father's spirit,
His eye, his voice, his touch, surrounding me,
The atmosphere and breath of my dead life!
If sometimes, as a shape more like himself,
Even the form which tortured me on earth,
Masked in grey hairs and wrinkles, he should come,
And wind me in his hellish arms, and fix
His eyes on mine, and drag me down, down, down!
For was he not alone omnipotent
On earth, and ever present? Even though dead
Does not his spirit live in all that breathe,
And work for me and mine still the same ruin,
Scorn, pain, despair? Who ever yet returned
To teach the laws of death's untrodden realm?
Unjust perhaps as those which drive us now,
Oh whither, whither?
  Lucretia.   Trust in God's sweet love,
The tender promises of Christ: ere night
Think we shall be in Paradise.
  Beatrice.   ... 'Tis past!
Whatever comes, my heart shall sink no more.
And yet, I know not why, your words strike chill.
How tedious, false, and cold, seem all things! I
Have met with much injustice in this world;
No difference has been made by God or man,
Or any power moulding my wretched lot,
'Twixt good or evil, as regarded me.
I am cut off from the only world I know,
From light and life and love, in youth's sweet prime.
You do well telling me to trust in God;
I hope I do trust in him: in whom else
Can any trust? And yet my heart is cold.
  [*During the latter speeches* GIACOMO *has retired conversing
   with* CAMILLO, *who now goes out;* GIACOMO *advances.*
  Giacomo. Know you not, mother—sister, know you not?

Bernardo even now is gone to implore
The Pope to grant our pardon.
  Lucretia.   Child, perhaps
It will be granted! We may all then live
To make these woes a tale for distant years.
Oh what a thought! It gushes to my heart
Like the warm blood.
  Beatrice.   Yet both will soon be cold.
Oh trample out that thought! Worse than despair,
Worse than the bitterness of death, is hope:
It is the only ill which can find place
Upon the giddy, sharp, and narrow hour
Tottering beneath us. Plead with the swift frost
That it should spare the eldest flower of Spring:
Plead with awakening earthquake, o'er whose couch
Even now a city stands, strong, fair, and free—
Now stench and blackness yawn, like death: oh plead
With famine or wind-walking pestilence,
Blind lightning or the deaf sea;—not with man!
Cruel, cold, formal man; righteous in words,
In deeds a Cain! No, mother, we must die:
Since such is the reward of innocent lives,
Such the alleviation of worst wrongs.
And, whilst our murderers live, and hard cold men,
Smiling and slow, walk through a world of tears
To death as to life's sleep, 'twere just the grave
Were some strange joy for us. Come, obscure Death,
And wind me in thine all-embracing arms!
Like a fond mother hide me in thy bosom,
And rock me to the sleep from which none wake!
Live, ye who live, subject to one another,
As we were once, who now—
      BERNARDO *rushes in.*
  Bernardo.   Oh horrible!
That tears, that looks, that hope poured forth in prayer
Even till the heart is vacant and despairs,
Should all be vain! The ministers of death

Are waiting round the doors. I thought I saw
Blood on the face of one.—What if 'twere fancy?
Soon the heart's blood of all I love on earth
Will sprinkle him, and he will wipe it off
As if 'twere only rain. O life! O world!
Cover me! let me be no more! To see
That perfect mirror of pure innocence,
Wherein I gazed, and grew happy and good,
Shivered to dust! To see thee, Beatrice,
Who mad'st all lovely thou didst look upon—
Thee, light of life—dead, dark! while I say "Sister,"
To hear I have no sister! And thou, mother,
Whose love was as a bond to all our loves—
Dead—the sweet bond broken!

Enter CAMILLO *and Guards.*

                      They come! Let me
Kiss those warm lips before their crimson leaves
Are blighted—white—cold. Say farewell, before
Death chokes that gentle voice! Oh let me hear
You speak!

   Beatrice. Farewell, my tender brother. Think
Of our sad fate with gentleness, as now:
And let mild pitying thoughts lighten for thee
Thy sorrow's load. Err not in harsh despair,
But tears and patience. One thing more, my child:
For thine own sake be constant to the love
Thou bearest us; and to the faith that I,
Though wrapped in a strange cloud of crime and shame,
Lived ever holy and unstained. And, though
Ill tongues shall wound me, and our common name
Be as a mark stamped on thine innocent brow
For men to point at as they pass, do thou
Forbear, and never think a thought unkind
Of those who perhaps love thee in their graves.
So mayst thou die as I do, fear and pain
Being subdued. Farewell! farewell! farewell!

Bernardo. I cannot say farewell!
Camillo.   Oh Lady Beatrice
Beatrice.   Give yourself no unnecessary pain,
My dear Lord Cardinal.—Here, mother, tie
My girdle for me, and bind up this hair
In any simple knot: ay, that does well.
And yours, I see, is coming down. How often
Have we done this for one another! now
We shall not do it any more. My lord,
We are quite ready. Well, 'tis very well.

JULIAN AND MADDALO.

A CONVERSATION.

   COUNT MADDALO is a Venetian nobleman of ancient family and of great fortune, who, without mixing much in the society of his countrymen, resides chiefly at his magnificent palace in that city. He is a person of the most consummate genius, and capable, if he would direct his energies to such an end, of becoming the redeemer of his degraded country. But it is his weakness to be proud: he derives, from a comparison of his own extraordinary mind with the dwarfish intellects that surround him, an intense apprehension of the nothingness of human life. His passions and his powers are incomparably greater than those of other men; and, instead of the latter having been employed in curbing the former, they have mutually lent each other strength. His ambition preys upon itself, for want of objects which it can consider worthy of exertion. I say that Maddalo is proud, because I can find no other word to express the concentred and impatient feelings which consume him; but it is on his own hopes and affections only that he seems to trample, for in social life no human being can be more gentle, patient, and unassuming, than Maddalo. He is cheerful, frank, and witty. His more serious conversation is a sort of intoxication; men are held by it as by a spell. He has travelled much, and there is an inexpressible charm in his relation of his adventures in different countries.
   Julian is an Englishman of good family; passionately attached to those philosophical notions which assert the power of man over his own mind, and the immense improvements of which, by the extinction of certain moral superstitions, human society may yet be susceptible. Without concealing the evil in the world, he is for ever speculating how good may be made superior. He is a complete infidel, and a scoffer at all things reputed holy; and Maddalo takes a wicked pleasure in drawing out his taunts against religion. What Maddalo thinks on these matters is not exactly known. Julian, in spite of his heterodox opinions, is conjectured by his friends to possess some good qualities. How far this is possible the pious reader will determine. Julian is rather serious.
   Of the Maniac I can give no information. He seems, by his own account, to have been disappointed in love. He was evidently a very cultivated and amiable person when in his right senses. His story, told at length, might be like many other stories of the same kind: the unconnected exclamations of his agony will perhaps be found a sufficient comment for the text of every heart.

> The meadows with fresh streams, the bees with thyme,
> The goats with the green leaves of budding Spring,
> Are saturated not—nor Love with tears.—VIRGIL'S GALLUS.

I RODE one evening with Count Maddalo
Upon the bank of land which breaks the flow
Of Adria towards Venice. A bare strand
Of hillocks heaped from ever-shifting sand,
Matted with thistles and amphibious weeds
Such as from earth's embrace the salt ooze breeds,
Is this; an uninhabited sea-side,
Which the lone fisher, when his nets are dried,
Abandons. And no other object breaks
The waste, but one dwarf tree, and some few stakes
Broken and unrepaired; and the tide makes
A narrow space of level sand thereon,—
Where 'twas our wont to ride while day went down.
This ride was my delight. I love all waste
And solitary places; where we taste
The pleasure of believing what we see
Is boundless, as we wish our souls to be:
And such was this wide ocean, and this shore
More barren than its billows. And, yet more
Than all, with a remembered friend I love
To ride as then I rode;—for the winds drove
The living spray along the sunny air
Into our faces; the blue heavens were bare,
Stripped to their depths by the awakening north;
And from the waves sound like delight broke forth,
Harmonizing with solitude, and sent
Into our hearts aërial merriment.

So, as we rode, we talked; and the swift thought,
Winging itself with laughter, lingered not,
But flew from brain to brain. Such glee was ours,
Charged with light memories of remembered hours,
None slow enough for sadness: till we came
Homeward, which always makes the spirit tame.
This day had been cheerful but cold, and now
The sun was sinking, and the wind also.

Our talk grew somewhat serious, as may be
Talk interrupted with such raillery
As mocks itself, because it cannot scorn
The thoughts it would extinguish:—'twas forlorn,
Yet pleasing; such as once, so poets tell,
The devils held within the vales of hell,
Concerning God, freewill, and destiny.
Of all that Earth has been, or yet may be;
All that vain men imagine or believe,
Or hope can paint or suffering can achieve,
We descanted; and I (for ever still
Is it not wise to make the best of ill?)
Argued against despondency; but pride
Made my companion take the darker side.
The sense that he was greater than his kind
Had struck, methinks, his eagle spirit blind
By gazing on its own exceeding light.

Meanwhile the sun paused ere it should alight
Over the horizon of the mountains.—Oh!
How beautiful is sunset, when the glow
Of heaven descends upon a land like thee,
Thou paradise of exiles, Italy,
Thy mountains, seas, and vineyards, and the towers
Of cities they encirle!—It was ours
To stand on thee, beholding it: and then,
Just where we had dismounted, the Count's men
Were waiting for us with the gondola.
As those who pause on some delightful way,
Though bent on pleasant pilgrimage, we stood
Looking upon the evening, and the flood
Which lay between the city and the shore,
Paved with the image of the sky. The hoar
And airy Alps, towards the north, appeared
Through mist—an heaven-sustaining bulwark reared
Between the east and west; and half the sky
Was roofed with clouds of rich emblazonry,

Dark purple at the zenith, which still grew
Down the steep west into a wondrous hue
Brighter than burning gold, even to the rent
Where the swift sun yet paused in his descent
Among the many-folded hills. They were
Those famous Euganean hills, which bear,
As seen from Lido through the harbour piles,
The likeness of a clump of peaked isles.
And then, as if the earth and sea had been
Dissolved into one lake of fire, were seen
Those mountains towering, as from waves of flame,
Around the vaporous sun; from which there came
The inmost purple spirit of light, and made
Their very peaks transparent.
                              "Ere it fade,"
Said my companion, "I will show you soon
A better station."
                  So, o'er the lagune
We glided; and from that funereal bark
I leaned, and saw the city, and could mark
How from their many isles, in evening's gleam,
Its temples and its palaces did seem
Like fabrics of enchantment piled to heaven.
I was about to speak, when—
                              "We are even
Now at the point I meant," said Maddalo,—
And bade the gondolieri cease to row.
"Look, Julian, on the west, and listen well
If you hear not a deep and heavy bell."

I looked, and saw between us and the sun
A building on an island, such an one
As age to age might add, for uses vile,—
A windowless, deformed, and dreary pile;
And on the top an open tower, where hung
A bell which in the radiance swayed and swung,—
We could just hear its hoarse and iron tongue;

The broad sun sank behind it, and it tolled
In strong and black relief.—
                    "What we behold
Shall be the madhouse and its belfry tower,"—
Said Maddalo; "and ever at this hour
Those who may cross the water hear that bell,
Which calls the maniacs, each one from his cell,
To vespers."
            "As much skill as need to pray
In thanks or hope for their dark lot have they
To their stern maker," I replied.
                        "Oho!
You talk as in years past," said Maddalo.
"'Tis strange men change not. You were ever still
Among Christ's flock a perilous infidel,
A wolf for the meek lambs. If you can't swim,
Beware of providence!" I looked on him,
But the gay smile had faded from his eye.
"And such," he cried, "is our mortality!
And this must be the emblem and the sign
Of what should be eternal and divine;
And, like that black and dreary bell, the soul,
Hung in an heaven-illumined tower, must toll
Our thoughts and our desires to meet below
Round the rent heart, and pray—as madmen do;
For what! they know not, till the night of death,
As sunset that strange vision, severeth
Our memory from itself, and us from all
We sought, and yet were baffled."—
                        I recall
The sense of what he said, although I mar
The force of his expressions. The broad star
Of day meanwhile had sunk behind the hill;
And the black bell became invisible;
And the red tower looked grey; and, all between,
The churches, ships, and palaces, were seen
Huddled in gloom; into the purple sea

The orange hues of heaven sunk silently.
We hardly spoke, and soon the gondola
Conveyed me to my lodging by the way.

The following morn was rainy, cold, and dim.
Ere Maddalo arose, I called on him;
And, whilst I waited, with his child I played.
A lovelier toy sweet Nature never made;
A serious, subtle, wild, yet gentle being;
Graceful without design, and unforeseeing;
With eyes—oh speak not of her eyes! which seem
Twin mirrors of Italian heaven, yet gleam
With such deep meaning as we never see
But in the human countenance.   With me
She was a special favourite: I had nursed
Her fine and feeble limbs when she came first
To this bleak world; and she yet seemed to know
On second sight her ancient playfellow,
Less changed than she was by six months or so
For, after her first shyness was worn out,
We sate there, rolling billiard balls about,—
When the Count entered.   Salutations passed:
"The words you spoke last night might well have cast
A darkness on my spirit.   If man be
The passive thing you say, I should not see
Much harm in the religions and old saws
(Though *I* may never own such leaden laws)
Which break a teachless nature to the yoke:
Mine is another faith."—Thus much I spoke,
And, noting he replied not, added—"See
This lovely child; blithe, innocent, and free:
She spends a happy time, with little care;
While we to such sick thoughts subjected are
As came on you last night.   It is our will
Which thus enchains us to permitted ill.
We might be otherwise; we might be all

We dream of, happy, high, majestical.
Where is the beauty, love, and truth, we seek,
But in our minds? And, if we were not weak,
Should we be less in deed than in desire?"—

"Ay, if we were not weak,—and we aspire,
How vainly! to be strong," said Maddalo:
"You talk Utopia."
                "It remains to know,"
I then rejoined; "and those who try may find
How strong the chains are which our spirit bind:
Brittle perchance as straw. We are assured
Much may be conquered, much may be endured,
Of what degrades and crushes us. We know
That we have power over ourselves to do
And suffer—*what*, we know not till we try,
But something nobler than to live and die.
So taught the kings of old philosophy
Who reigned before religion made men blind;
And those who suffer with their suffering kind
Yet feel this faith, Religion."
                       "My dear friend,"
Said Maddalo, "my judgment will not bend
To your opinion, though I think you might
Make such a system refutation-tight,
As far as words go. I knew one like you,
Who to this city came some months ago,
With whom I argued in this sort,—and he
Is now gone mad—and so he answered me,
Poor fellow!—But, if you would like to go,
We'll visit him, and his wild talk will show
How vain are such aspiring theories."

"I hope to prove the induction otherwise,
And that a want of that true theory still
Which seeks a soul of goodness in things ill,
Or in himself or others, has thus bowed
His being. There are some by nature proud

Who, patient in all else, demand but this—
To love and be beloved with gentleness:
And, being scorned, what wonder if they die
Some living death? This is not destiny,
But man's own wilful ill."
       As thus I spoke,
Servants announced the gondola, and we
Through the fast-falling rain and high-wrought sea
Sailed to the island where the Madhouse stands.
We disembarked. The clap of tortured hands,
Fierce yells, and howlings, and lamentings keen,
And laughter where complaint had merrier been,
Accosted us. We climbed the oozy stairs
Into an old courtyard. I heard on high
Then fragments of most touching melody;
But, looking up, saw not the singer there.
Through the black bars, in the tempestuous air,
I saw, like weeds on a wrecked palace growing,
Long tangled locks, flung wildly forth and flowing,
Of those who on a sudden were beguiled
Into strange silence, and looked forth and smiled,
Hearing sweet sounds. Then I:—
       "Methinks there were
A cure of these with patience and kind care,
If music can thus move. But what is he
Whom we seek here?"
      "Of his sad history
I know but this," said Maddalo. "He came
To Venice a dejected man, and fame
Said he was wealthy, or he had been so:
Some thought the loss of fortune wrought him woe.
But he was ever talking in such sort
As you do,—but more sadly; he seemed hurt,
Even as a man with his peculiar wrong,
To hear but of the oppression of the strong,
Or those absurd deceits (I think with you
In some respects, you know) which carry through

The excellent impostors of this earth,
When they outface detection. He had worth,
Poor fellow, but a humourist in his way."

"Alas! what drove him mad?"
                              "I cannot say:
A lady came with him from France; and, when
She left him and returned, he wandered then
About yon lonely isles of desert sand,
Till he grew wild. He had no cash or land
Remaining. The police had brought him here:
Some fancy took him, and he would not bear
Removal. So I fitted up for him
Those rooms beside the sea, to please his whim;
And sent him busts, and books, and urns for flowers,
Which had adorned his life in happier hours,
And instruments of music. You may guess
A stranger could do little more, or less,
For one so gentle and unfortunate:
And those are his sweet strains which charm the weight
From madmen's chains, and make this hell appear
A heaven of sacred silence hushed to hear."

"Nay, this was kind of you,—he had no claim,
As the world says."
                    "None but the very same
Which I on all mankind, were I, as he,
Fallen to such deep reverse. His melody
Is interrupted now: we hear the din
Of madmen, shriek on shriek, again begin;
Let us now visit him: after this strain,
He ever communes with himself again,
And sees and hears not any."
                            Having said
These words, we called the keeper, and he led
To an apartment opening on the sea.
There the poor wretch was sitting mournfully
Near a piano, his pale fingers twined

One with the other; and the ooze and wind
Rushed through an open casement, and did sway
His hair, and starred it with the brackish spray.
His head was leaning on a music-book,
And he was muttering, and his lean limbs shook.
His lips were pressed against a folded leaf,
In hue too beautiful for health, and grief
Smiled in their motions as they lay apart,
As one who wrought from his own fervid heart
The eloquence of passion. Soon he raised
His sad meek face, and eyes lustrous and glazed,
And spoke,—sometimes as one who wrote, and thought
His words might move some heart that heeded not,
If sent to distant lands; and then as one
Reproaching deeds never to be undone,
With wondering self-compassion. Then his speech
Was lost in grief, and then his words came each
Unmodulated and expressionless,—
But that from one jarred accent you might guess
It was despair made them so uniform:
And all the while the loud and gusty storm
Hissed through the window;—and we stood behind,
Stealing his accents from the envious wind,
Unseen. I yet remember what he said
Distinctly, such impression his words made.

"Month after month," he cried, "to bear this load!
And, as a jade urged by the whip and goad,
To drag life on—which like a heavy chain
Lengthens behind with many a link of pain!
And not to speak my grief—Oh not to dare
To give a human voice to my despair!
But live, and move, and, wretched thing! smile on,
As if I never went aside to groan,—
And wear this mask of falsehood even to those
Who are most dear; not for my own repose,—
Alas! no scorn or pain or hate could be

So heavy as that falsehood is to me—
But that I cannot bear more altered faces
Than needs must be, more changed and cold embraces,
More misery, disappointment, and mistrust,
To own me for their father. Would the dust
Were covered in upon my body now—
That the life ceased to toil within my brow!
And then these thoughts would at the last be fled:
Let us not fear such pain can vex the dead.

"What power delights to torture us? I know
That to myself I do not wholly owe
What now I suffer, though in part I may.
Alas! none strewed fresh flowers upon the way
Where, wandering heedlessly, I met pale Pain,
My shadow, which will leave me not again.
If I have erred, there was no joy in error,
But pain and insult and unrest and terror.
I have not, as some do, bought penitence
With pleasure and a dark yet sweet offence;
For then, if love and tenderness and truth
Had overlived hope's momentary youth,
My creed should have redeemed me from repenting.
But loathed scorn and outrage unrelenting
Met love, excited by far other seeming,
Until the end was gained:—as one from dreaming
Of sweetest peace, I woke, and found my state
Such as it is—
    "O thou, my spirit's mate!
Who, for thou art compassionate and wise,
Wouldst pity me from thy most gentle eyes
If this sad writing thou shouldst ever see,
My secret groans must be unheard by thee;
Thou wouldst weep tears bitter as blood, to know
Thy lost friend's incommunicable woe.
Ye few by whom my nature has been weighed
In friendship, let me not that name degrade

By placing on your hearts the secret load
Which crushes mine to dust.   There is one road
To peace,—and that is truth, which follow ye:
Love sometimes leads astray to misery.
Yet think not, though subdued (and I may well
Say that I am subdued), that the full hell
Within me would infect the untainted breast
Of sacred nature with its own unrest;
As some perverted beings think to find
In scorn or hate a medicine for the mind
Which scorn or hate hath wounded:—oh how vain!
The dagger heals not, but may rend again.
Believe that I am ever still the same
In creed as in resolve; and what may tame
My heart must leave the understanding free,
Or all would sink under this agony.
Nor dream that I will join the vulgar lie,
Or with my silence sanction tyranny;
Or seek a moment's shelter from my pain
In any madness which the world calls gain,
Ambition, or revenge, or thoughts as stern
As those which make me what I am; or turn
To avarice or misanthropy or lust.
Heap on me soon, O grave, thy welcome dust!
Till then the dungeon may demand its prey;
And Poverty and Shame may meet and say,
Halting beside me in the public way,
'That love-devoted youth is ours: let's sit
Beside him: he may live some six months yet.'
Or the red scaffold, as our country bends,
May ask some willing victim; or ye, friends,
May fall under some sorrow, which this heart
Or hand may share or vanquish or avert.
I am prepared,—in truth, with no proud joy,—
To do or suffer aught; as when, a boy,
I did devote to justice and to love
My nature, worthless now.

"I must remove
A veil from my pent mind. 'Tis torn aside!
Oh pallid as Death's dedicated bride,
Thou mockery which art sitting by my side,
Am I not wan like thee? At the grave's call
I haste, invited to thy wedding-ball,
To meet the ghastly paramour for whom
Thou hast deserted me, and made the tomb
Thy bridal bed. But I beside thy feet
Will lie, and watch ye from my winding-sheet
Thus—wide awake though dead.—Yet stay, oh stay!
Go not so soon!—I know not what I say—
Hear but my reasons!—I am mad, I fear,
My fancy is o'erwrought.—Thou art not here;
Pale art thou, 'tis most true——But thou art gone—
Thy work is finished; I am left alone.
* * * * * *

"Nay, was it I who wooed thee to this breast,
Which like a serpent thou envenomest
As in repayment of the warmth it lent?
Didst thou not seek me for thine own content?
Did not thy love awaken mine? I thought
That thou wert she who said, ' You kiss me not
Ever; I fear you do not love me now.'
In truth I love even to my overthrow
Her who would fain forget these words,—but they
Cling to her mind, and cannot pass away.
* * * * * *

"You say that I am proud; that, when I speak,
My lip is tortured with the wrongs which break
The spirit it expresses.—Never one
Humbled himself before as I have done.
Even the instinctive worm on which we tread
Turns, though it wound not—then with postrate head
Sinks in the dust, and writhes like me—and dies:
——No, wears a living death of agonies.

As the slow shadows of the pointed grass
Mark the eternal periods, its pangs pass,
Slow, ever-moving, making moments be
As mine seem—each an immortality!

"That you had never seen me! never heard
My voice! and more than all had ne'er endured
The deep pollution of my loathed embrace!
That your eyes ne'er had lied love in my face!
That, like some maniac monk, I had torn out
The nerves of manhood by their bleeding root
With mine own quivering fingers, so that ne'er
Our hearts had for a moment mingled there,
To disunite in horror! These were not,
With thee, like some suppressed and hideous thought,
Which flits athwart our musings, but can find
No rest within a pure and gentle mind:
Thou sealedst them with many a bare broad word,
And searedst my memory o'er them,—for I heard
And can forget not;—they were ministered
One after one, those curses. Mix them up
Like self-destroying poisons in one cup;
And they will make one blessing which thou ne'er
Didst imprecate for on me——death!

        "It were
A cruel punishment for one most cruel,
If such can love, to make that love the fuel
Of the mind's hell—hate, scorn, remorse, despair.
But *me*, whose heart a stranger's tear might wear
As water-drops the sandy fountain-stone;
Who loved and pitied all things, and could moan
For woes which others hear not, and could see
The absent with a glass of fantasy,
And near the poor and trampled sit and weep,
Following the captive to his dungeon deep;
Me, who am as a nerve o'er which do creep
The else-unfelt oppressions of this earth,

And was to thee the flame upon thy hearth
When all beside was cold:—that thou on me
Shouldst rain these plagues of blistering agony!
Such curses are, from lips once eloquent
With love's too partial praise. Let none relent,
Who intend deeds too dreadful for a name,
Henceforth, if an example for the same
They seek:—for thou on me lookedst so and so,
And didst speak thus and thus! I live to show
How much men bear, and die not.
* * * * * *
         "Thou wilt tell,
With the grimace of hate, how horrible
It was to meet my love when thine grew less;
Thou wilt admire how I could e'er address
Such features to love's work. This taunt, though true,
(For indeed Nature nor in form nor hue
Bestowed on me her choicest workmanship)
Shall not be thy defence: for, since thy lip
Met mine first, years long past—since thine eye kindled
With soft fire under mine,—I have not dwindled,
Nor changed in mind or body, or in aught,
But as love changes what it loveth not
After long years and many trials.
* * * * * *
        "How vain
Are words! I thought never to speak again,
Not even in secret, not to my own heart—
But from my lips the unwilling accents start,
And from my pen the words flow as I write,
Dazzling my eyes with scalding tears. My sight
Is dim to see that charactered in vain
On this unfeeling leaf which burns the brain
And eats into it, blotting all things fair
And wise and good which time had written there.
Those who inflict must suffer; for they see
The work of their own hearts, and that must be

Our chastisement or recompense.—O child!
I would that thine were like to be more mild,
For both our wretched sakes,—for thine the most,
Who feel'st already all that thou hast lost,
Without the power to wish it thine again.
And, as slow years pass, a funereal train,
Each with the ghost of some lost hope or friend
Following it like its shadow, wilt thou bend
No thought on my dead memory?

   * * * * * *

           "Alas, love!
Fear me not: against thee I'd not move
A finger in despite. Do I not live
That thou mayst have less bitter cause to grieve?
I give thee tears for scorn, and love for hate;
And, that thy lot may be less desolate
Than his on whom thou tramplest, I refrain
From that sweet sleep which medicines all pain.
Then—when thou speakest of me—never say
'He could forgive not.'—Here I cast away
All human passions, all revenge, all pride;
I think, speak, act, no ill; I do but hide
Under these words, like embers, every spark
Of that which has consumed me. Quick and dark
The grave is yawning:—as its roof shall cover
My limbs with dust and worms, under and over,
So let oblivion hide this grief.—The air
Closes upon my accents, as despair
Upon my heart—let death upon despair!"

He ceased, and overcome leant back awhile;
Then rising, with a melancholy smile,
Went to a sofa, and lay down, and slept
A heavy sleep; and in his dreams he wept,
And muttered some familiar name, and we
Wept without shame in his society.
I think I never was impressed so much:

The man who were not must have lacked a touch
Of human nature.—
             Then we lingered not,
Although our argument was quite forgot;
But, calling the attendants, went to dine
At Maddalo's. Yet neither cheer nor wine
Could give us spirits, for we talked of him,
And nothing else, till daylight made stars dim.
And we agreed it was some dreadful ill
Wrought on him boldly, yet unspeakable,
By a dear friend; some deadly change in love
Of one vowed deeply (which he dreamed not of),
For whose sake he, it seemed, had fixed a blot
Of falsehood in his mind, which flourished not
But in the light of all-beholding truth;
And, having stamped this canker on his youth,
She had abandoned him. And how much more
Might be his woe we guessed not. He had store
Of friends and fortune once, as we could guess
From his nice habits and his gentleness:
These now were lost— it were a grief indeed
If he had changed one unsustaining reed
For all that such a man might else adorn.
The colours of his mind seemed yet unworn;
For the wild language of his grief was high—
Such as in measure were called poetry.
And I remember one remark which then
Maddalo made: he said—"Most wretched men
Are cradled into poetry by wrong:
They learn in suffering what they teach in song."

If I had been an unconnected man,
I, from this moment, should have formed some plan
Never to leave sweet Venice. For to me
It was delight to ride by the lone sea:
And then the town is silent—one may write
Or read in gondolas, by day or night,

Having the little brazen lamp alight,
Unseen, uninterrupted. Books are there,
Pictures, and casts from all those statues fair
Which were twin-born with poetry, and all
We seek in towns, with little to recall
Regret for the green country. I might sit
In Maddalo's great palace, and his wit
And subtle talk would cheer the winter night,
And make me know myself: and the fire-light
Would flash upon our faces, till the day
Might dawn, and make me wonder at my stay.
But I had friends in London too. The chief
Attraction here was that I sought relief
From the deep tenderness that maniac wrought
Within me. . . . 'Twas perhaps an idle thought,
But I imagined that—if day by day
I watched him, and seldom went away,
And studied all the beatings of his heart
With zeal (as men study some stubborn art
For their own good), and could by patience find
An entrance to the caverns of his mind—
I might reclaim him from his dark estate.
In friendships I had been most fortunate;
Yet never saw I one whom I would call
More willingly my friend.—And this was all
Accomplished not. Such dreams of baseless good
Oft come and go, in crowds or solitude,
And leave no trace: but what I now designed
Made, for long years, impression on my mind.—
The following morning, urged by my affairs,
I left bright Venice.
     After many years
And many changes, I returned. The name
Of Venice, and its aspect, was the same.
But Maddalo was travelling, far away,
Among the mountains of Armenia:
His dog was dead; his child had now become

A woman, such as it has been my doom
To meet with few; a wonder of this earth,
Where there is little of transcendent worth,—
Like one of Shakspeare's women. Kindly she,
And with a manner beyond courtesy,
Received her father's friend; and, when I asked
Of the lorn maniac, she her memory tasked,
And told, as she had heard, the mournful tale:
That the poor sufferer's health began to fail
Two years from my departure; but that then
The lady who had left him came again.
"Her mien had been imperious, but she now
Looked meek; perhaps remorse had brought her low.
Her coming made him better; and they stayed
Together at my father's—(for I played,
As I remember, with the lady's shawl;
I might be six years old).—But, after all,
She left him."
                    "Why, her heart must have been tough!
How did it end?"
                    "And was not this enough?
They met, they parted."
                    "Child, is there no more?"

"Something within that interval which bore
The stamp of *why* they parted, *how* they met.—
Yet, if thine aged eyes disdain to wet
Those wrinkled cheeks with youth's remembered tears,
Ask me no more; but let the silent years
Be closed and cered over their memory,—
As yon mute marble where their corpses lie."

I urged and questioned still. She told me how
All happened—But the cold world shall not know.

THE WITCH OF ATLAS.

TO MARY

(ON HER OBJECTING TO THE FOLLOWING POEM, UPON THE SCORE OF ITS CONTAINING NO HUMAN INTEREST.)

I.

How, my dear Mary, are you critic-bitten,
  (For vipers kill, though dead) by some review,—
That you condemn these verses I have written,
  Because they tell no story, false or true?
What though no mice are caught by a young kitten?
  May it not leap and play as grown cats do,
Till its claws come? Prithee, for this one time,
Content thee with a visionary rhyme.

II.

What hand would crush the silken-winged fly,
  The youngest of inconstant April's minions,
Because it cannot climb the purest sky,
  Where the swan sings amid the sun's dominions?
Not thine. Thou knowest 'tis its doom to die
  When Day shall hide within her twilight pinions
The lucent eyes and the eternal smile,
Serene as thine, which lent it life awhile.

III.

To thy fair feet a winged Vision came,
  Whose date should have been longer than a day,
And o'er thy head did beat its wings for fame,
  And in thy sight its fading plumes display;
The watery bow burned in the evening flame;
  But the shower fell, the swift Sun went his way—

And that is dead.—Oh let me not believe
That any thing of mine is fit to live!

IV.

Wordsworth informs us he was nineteen years
  Considering and re-touching Peter Bell;
Watering his laurels with the killing tears
  Of slow dull care, so that their roots to hell
Might pierce, and their wide branches blot the spheres
  Of heaven, with dewy leaves and flowers: this well
May be, for heaven and earth conspire to foil
The over-busy gardener's blundering toil.

V.

My Witch indeed is not so sweet a creature
  As Ruth or Lucy, whom his graceful praise
Clothes for our grandsons—but she matches Peter,
  Though he took nineteen years, and she three days,
In dressing. Light the vest of flowing metre
  She wears: he, proud as dandy with his stays,
Has hung upon his wiry limbs a dress
Like King Lear's looped and windowed raggedness.

VI.

If you strip Peter, you will see a fellow
  Scorched by hell's hyperequatorial climate
Into a kind of a sulphureous yellow;
  A lean mark, hardly fit to fling a rhyme at:
In shape a Scaramouch, in hue Othello.
  If you unveil my Witch, no priest nor primate
Can shrive you of that sin,—if sin there be
In love when it becomes idolatry.

THE WITCH OF ATLAS.

I.

BEFORE those cruel twins whom at one birth
  Incestuous Change bore to her father Time,
Error and Truth, had hunted from the earth
  All those bright natures which adorned its prime,

And left us nothing to believe in, worth
   The pains of putting into learned rhyme,
A Lady Witch there lived on Atlas mountain
Within a cavern by a secret fountain.

II.

Her mother was one of the Atlantides.
   The all-beholding Sun had ne'er beholden
In his wide voyage o'er continents and seas
   So fair a creature, as she lay enfolden
In the warm shadow of her loveliness;
   He kissed her with his beams, and made all golden
The chamber of grey rock in which she lay—
She, in that dream of joy, dissolved away.

III.

'Tis said she was first changed into a vapour,
   And then into a cloud,—such clouds as flit
(Like splendour-winged moths about a taper)
   Round the red west when the Sun dies in it;
And then into a meteor, such as caper
   On hill-tops when the Moon is in a fit;
Then into one of those mysterious stars
Which hide themselves between the Earth and Mars.

IV.

Ten times the Mother of the Months had bent
   Her bow beside the folding-star, and bidden
With that bright sign the billows to indent
   The sea-deserted sand—(like children chidden,
At her command they ever came and went)—
   Since in that cave a dewy splendour hidden
Took shape and motion. With the living form
Of this embodied Power the cave grew warm.

V.

A lovely Lady garmented in light
   From her own beauty—deep her eyes, as are

Two openings of unfathomable night
  Seen through a tempest's cloven roof;—her hair
Dark—the dim brain whirls dizzy with delight,
  Picturing her form;—her soft smiles shone afar;
And her low voice was heard like love, and drew
All living things towards this wonder new.

VI.

And first the spotted camelopard came;
  And then the wise and fearless elephant;
Then the sly serpent, in the golden flame
  Of his own volumes intervolved. All gaunt
And sanguine beasts her gentle looks made tame,—
  They drank before her at her sacred fount;
And every beast of beating heart grew bold,
Such gentleness and power even to behold.

VII.

The brinded lioness led forth her young,
  That she might teach them how they should forego
Their inborn thirst of death; the pard unstrung
  His sinews at her feet, and sought to know,
With looks whose motions spoke without a tongue,
  How he might be as gentle as the doe.
The magic circle of her voice and eyes
All savage natures did imparadise.

VIII.

And old Silenus, shaking a green stick
  Of lilies, and the Wood-gods in a crew,
Came, blithe, as in the olive copses thick
  Cicadæ are, drunk with the noonday dew;
And Dryope and Faunus followed quick,
  Teazing the God to sing them something new;
Till in this cave they found the Lady lone,
Sitting upon a seat of emerald stone.

IX.

And universal Pan, 'tis said, was there.
　　And, though none saw him,—through the adamant
Of the deep mountains, through the trackless air,
　　And through those living spirits, like a want,
He passed out of his everlasting lair
　　Where the quick heart of the great world doth pant,
And felt that wondrous Lady all alone,—
And she felt him upon her emerald throne.

X.

And every Nymph of stream and spreading tree,
　　And every Shepherdess of Ocean's flocks
Who drives her white waves over the green sea,
　　And Ocean with the brine on his grey locks,
And quaint Priapus with his company,—
　　All came, much wondering how the enwombed rocks
Could have brought forth so beautiful a birth:
Her love subdued their wonder and their mirth.

XI.

The herdsmen and the mountain maidens came,
　　And the rude kings of pastoral Garamant—
Their spirits shook within them, as a flame
　　Stirred by the air under a cavern gaunt:
Pygmies and Polyphemes, by many a name,
　　Centaurs and Satyrs, and such shapes as haunt
Wet clefts,—and lumps neither alive nor dead,
Dog-headed, bosom-eyed, and bird-footed.

XII.

For she was beautiful. Her beauty made
　　The bright world dim, and everything beside
Seemed like the fleeting image of a shade.
　　No thought of living spirit could abide
(Which to her looks had ever been betrayed)
　　On any object in the world so wide,
On any hope within the circling skies,—
But on her form, and in her inmost eyes.

XIII.

Which when the Lady knew, she took her spindle,
  And twined three threads of fleecy mist, and three
Long lines of light, such as the dawn may kindle
  The clouds and waves and mountains with, and she
As many starbeams, ere their lamps could dwindle
  In the belated moon, wound skilfully;
And with these threads a subtle veil she wove—
A shadow for the splendour of her love.

XIV.

The deep recesses of her odorous dwelling
  Were stored with magic treasures:—sounds of air
Which had the power all spirits of compelling,
  Folded in cells of crystal silence there;
Such as we hear in youth, and think the feeling
  Will never die—yet, ere we are aware,
The feeling and the sound are fled and gone,
And the regret they leave remains alone.

XV.

And there lay visions swift and sweet and quaint,
  Each in its thin sheath like a chrysalis;—
Some eager to burst forth; some weak and faint
  With the soft burthen of intensest bliss
It is their work to bear to many a saint
  Whose heart adores the shrine which holiest is,
Even Love's—and others, white, green, grey, and black,
And of all shapes:—and each was at her beck.

XVI.

And odours in a kind of aviary
  Of ever-blooming Eden-trees she kept,
Clipped in a floating net a love-sick Fairy
  Had woven from dew-beams while the moon yet slept;
As bats at the wired window of a dairy,
  They beat their vans; and each was an adept—
When loosed and missioned, making wings of winds—
To stir sweet thoughts or sad in destined minds.

XVII.

And liquors clear and sweet, whose healthful might
   Could medicine the sick soul to happy sleep,
And change eternal death into a night
   Of glorious dreams—or, if eyes needs must weep,
Could make their tears all wonder and delight—
   She in her crystal phials did closely keep:
If men could drink of those clear phials, 'tis said
The living were not envied of the dead.

XVIII.

Her cave was stored with scrolls of strange device,
   The works of some Saturnian Archimage,
Which taught the expiations at whose price
   Men from the Gods might win that happy age
Too lightly lost, redeeming native vice,—
   And which might quench the earth-consuming rage
Of gold and blood, till men should live and move
Harmonious as the sacred stars above:—

XIX.

And how all things that seem untameable,
   Not to be checked and not to be confined,
Obey the spells of Wisdom's wizard skill;
   Time, Earth, and Fire, the Ocean, and the Wind,
And all their shapes, and man's imperial will;—
   And other scrolls whose writings did unbind
The inmost lore of Love—let the profane
Tremble to ask what secrets they contain.

XX.

And wondrous works of substances unknown,
   To which the enchantment of her Father's power
Had changed those rugged blocks of savage stone,
   Were heaped in the recesses of her bower;
Carved lamps and chalices, and phials which shone
   In their own golden beams—each like a flower
Out of whose depth a firefly shakes his light,
Under a cypress in a starless night.

XXI.

At first she lived alone in this wild home,
  And her own thoughts were each a minister,
Clothing themselves or with the ocean foam,
  Or with the wind, or with the speed of fire,
To work whatever purposes might come
  Into her mind: such power her mighty Sire
Had girt them with, whether to fly or run
Through all the regions which he shines upon.

XXII.

The Ocean-nymphs and Hamadryades,
  Oreads and Naiads with long weedy locks,
Offered to do her bidding through the seas,
  Under the earth, and in the hollow rocks,
And far beneath the matted roots of trees,
  And in the gnarled heart of stubborn oaks;
So they might live for ever in the light
Of her sweet presence—each a satellite.

XXIII.

"This may not be," the Wizard Maid replied;
  "The fountains where the Naiades bedew
Their shining hair at length are drained and dried;
  The solid oaks forget their strength, and strew
Their latest leaf upon the mountains wide;
  The boundless ocean like a drop of dew
Will be consumed; the stubborn centre must
Be scattered like a cloud of summer dust.

XXIV.

"And ye, with them, will perish one by one.
  If I must sigh to think that this shall be,
If I must weep when the surviving Sun
  Shall smile on your decay—oh ask not me
To love you till your little race is run;
  I cannot die as ye must—over me
Your leaves shall glance—the streams in which ye dwell
Shall be my paths henceforth, and so farewell!"

XXV.

She spoke and wept. The dark and azure well
  Sparkled beneath the shower of her bright tears,
And every little circlet where they fell
  Flung to the cavern-roof inconstant spheres
And intertangled lines of light. A knell
  Of sobbing voices came upon her ears
From those departing Forms, o'er the serene
Of the white streams and of the forest green.

XXVI.

All day the Wizard Lady sat aloof;
  Spelling out scrolls of dread antiquity
Under the cavern's fountain-lighted roof;
  Or broidering the pictured poesy
Of some high tale upon her growing woof,
  Which the sweet splendour of her smiles could dye
In hues outshining heaven—and ever she
Added some grace to the wrought poesy:—

XXVII.

While on her hearth lay blazing many a piece
  Of sandal wood, rare gums, and cinnamon.
Men scarcely know how beautiful fire is;
  Each flame of it is as a precious stone
Dissolved in ever-moving light, and this
  Belongs to each and all who gaze thereon.
The Witch beheld it not, for in her hand
She held a woof that dimmed the burning brand.

XXVIII.

This Lady never slept, but lay in trance
  All night within the fountain—as in sleep.
Its emerald crags glowed in her beauty's glance:
  Through the green splendour of the water deep
She saw the constellations reel and dance
  Like fireflies—and withal did ever keep
The tenour of her contemplations calm,
With open eyes, closed feet, and folded palm.

XXIX.

And, when the whirlwinds and the clouds descended
  From the white pinnacles of that cold hill,
She passed at dewfall to a space extended,
  Where, in a lawn of flowering asphodel
Amid a wood of pines and cedars blended,
  There yawned an inextinguishable well
Of crimson fire, full even to the brim,
And overflowing all the margin trim:—

XXX.

Within the which she lay when the fierce war
  Of wintry winds shook that innocuous liquor,
In many a mimic moon and bearded star,
  O'er woods and lawns. The serpent heard it flicker
In sleep, and, dreaming still, he crept afar.
  And, when the windless snow descended thicker
Than autumn leaves, she watched it as it came
Melt on the surface of the level flame.

XXXI.

She had a Boat which some say Vulcan wrought
  For Venus, as the chariot of her star;
But it was found too feeble to be fraught
  With all the ardours in that sphere which are,
And so she sold it, and Apollo bought
  And gave it to this daughter: from a car,
Changed to the fairest and the lightest boat
Which ever upon mortal stream did float.

XXXII.

And others say that, when but three hours old,
  The firstborn Love out of his cradle leapt,
And clove dun chaos with his wings of gold,
  And, like a horticultural adept,
Stole a strange seed, and wrapped it up in mould,
  And sowed it in his mother's star, and kept
Watering it all the summer with sweet dew,
And with his wings fanning it as it grew.

XXXIII.

The plant grew strong and green—the snowy flower
   Fell, and the long and gourd-like fruit began
To turn the light and dew by inward power
   To its own substance: woven tracery ran
Of light firm texture, ribbed and branching, o'er
   The solid rind, like a leaf's veined fan,—
Of which Love scooped this boat, and with soft motion
Piloted it round the circumfluous ocean.

XXXIV.

This boat she moored upon her fount, and lit
   A living spirit within all its frame,
Breathing the soul of swiftness into it.
   Couched on the fountain—like a panther tame
One of the twain at Evan's feet that sit;
   Or as on Vesta's sceptre a swift flame,
Or on blind Homer's heart a winged thought—
In joyous expectation lay the boat.

XXXV.

Then by strange art she kneaded fire and snow
   Together, tempering the repugnant mass
With liquid love—all things together grow
   Through which the harmony of love can pass;
And a fair Shape out of her hands did flow—
   A living Image which did far surpass
In beauty that bright shape of vital stone
Which drew the heart out of Pygmalion.

XXXVI.

A sexless thing it was, and in its growth
   It seemed to have developed no defect
Of either sex, yet all the grace of both.
   In gentleness and strength its limbs were decked;
The bosom lightly swelled with its full youth;
   The countenance was such as might select
Some artist that his skill should never die,
Imaging forth such perfect purity.

XXXVII.

From its smooth shoulders hung two rapid wings
   Fit to have borne it to the seventh sphere,
Tipped with the speed of liquid lightenings,
   Dyed in the ardours of the atmosphere.
She led her creature to the boiling springs.
   Where the light boat was moored, and said "Sit here,"
And pointed to the prow, and took her seat
Beside the rudder with opposing feet.

XXXVIII.

And down the streams which clove those mountains vast,
   Around their inland islets, and amid
The panther-peopled forests, whose shade cast
   Darkness and odours, and a pleasure hid
In melancholy gloom, the pinnace passed;
   By many a star-surrounded pyramid
Of icy crag cleaving the purple sky,
And caverns yawning round unfathomably.

XXXIX.

The silver noon into that winding dell,
   With slanted gleam athwart the forest tops,
Tempered like golden evening, feebly fell;
   A green and glowing light, like that which drops
From folded lilies in which glow-worms dwell,
   When earth over her face night's mantle wraps;
Between the severed mountains lay on high,
Over the stream, a narrow rift of sky.

XL.

And, ever as she went, the Image lay
   With folded wings and unawakened eyes;
And o'er its gentle countenance did play
   The busy dreams, as thick as summer flies,
Chasing the rapid smiles that would not stay,
   And drinking the warm tears, and the sweet sighs
Inhaling, which with busy murmur vain
They had aroused from that full heart and brain.

XLI.

And ever down the prone vale, like a cloud
  Upon a stream of wind, the pinnace went:
Now lingering on the pools, in which abode
  The calm and darkness of the deep content
In which they paused; now o'er the shallow road
  Of white and dancing waters, all besprent
With sand and polished pebbles:—mortal boat
In such a shallow rapid could not float.

XLII.

And down the earthquaking cataracts, which shiver
  Their snow-like waters into golden air,
Or under chasms unfathomable ever
  Sepulchre them, till in their rage they tear
A subterranean portal for the river,
  It fled. The circling sunbows did upbear
Its fall down the hoar precipice of spray,
Lighting it far upon its lampless way.

XLIII.

And, when the Wizard Lady would ascend
  The labyrinths of some many-winding vale
Which to the inmost mountain upward tend,
  She called "Hermaphroditus!"—and the pale
And heavy hue which slumber could extend
  Over its lips and eyes, as on the gale
A rapid shadow from a slope of grass,
Into the darkness of the stream did pass.

XLIV.

And it unfurled its heaven-coloured pinions;
  With stars of fire spotting the stream below,
And from above into the Sun's dominions
  Flinging a glory like the golden glow
In which Spring clothes her emerald-winged minions,
  All interwoven with fine feathery snow,
And moonlight splendour of intensest rime
With which frost paints the pines in winter time.

XLV.

And then it winnowed the Elysian air
  Which ever hung about that Lady bright,
With its etherial vans: and, speeding there,
  Like a star up the torrent of the night,
Or a swift eagle in the morning glare
  Breasting the whirlwind with impetuous flight,
The pinnace, oared by those enchanted wings,
Clove the fierce streams towards their upper springs.

XLVI.

The water flashed like sunlight, by the prow
  Of a noon-wandering meteor flung to heaven;
The still air seemed as if its waves did flow
  In tempest down the mountains; loosely driven,
The Lady's radiant hair streamed to and fro;
  Beneath, the billows, having vainly striven
Indignant and impetuous, roared to feel
The swift and steady motion of the keel.

XLVII.

Or, when the weary moon was in the wane,
  Or in the noon of interlunar night
The Lady Witch in visions could not chain
  Her spirit; but sailed forth under the light
Of shooting stars, and bade extend amain
  His storm-outspeeding wings the Hermaphrodite;
She to the Austral waters took her way,
Beyond the fabulous Thamondocana.

XLVIII.

Where, like a meadow which no scythe has shaven,
  Which rain could never bend or whirlblast shake,
With the Antarctic constellations paven,
  Canopus and his crew, lay the Austral lake—
There she would build herself a windless haven,
  Out of the clouds whose moving turrets make
The bastions of the storm, when through the sky
The spirits of the tempest thundered by:—

XLIX.

A haven beneath whose translucent floor
  The tremulous stars sparkled unfathomably;
And around which the solid vapours hoar,
  Based on the level waters, to the sky
Lifted their dreadful crags, and, like a shore
  Of wintry mountains, inaccessibly
Hemmed in with rifts and precipices grey,
And hanging crags, many a cove and bay.

L.

And whilst the outer lake beneath the lash
  Of the wind's scourge foamed like a wounded thing,
And the incessant hail with stony clash
  Ploughed up the waters, and the flagging wing
Of the roused cormorant in the lightning flash
  Looked like the wreck of some wind-wandering
Fragment of inky thunder-smoke—this haven
Was as a gem to copy heaven engraven.

LI.

On which that Lady played her many pranks,
  Circling the image of a shooting star
(Even as a tiger on Hydaspes' banks
  Outspeeds the antelopes which speediest are)
In her light boat; and many quips and cranks
  She played upon the water; till the car
Of the late moon, like a sick matron wan,
To journey from the misty east began.

LII.

And then she called out of the hollow turrets
  Of those high clouds, white, golden, and vermilion,
The armies of her ministering spirits.
  In mighty legions million after million
They came, each troop emblazoning its merits
  On meteor flags; and many a proud pavilion
Of the intertexture of the atmosphere
They pitched upon the plain of the calm mere.

LIII.

They framed the imperial tent of their great Queen
  Of woven exhalations, underlaid
With lambent lightning-fire, as may be seen
  A dome of thin and open ivory inlaid
With crimson silk. Cressets from the serene
  Hung there, and on the water for her tread
A tapestry of fleece-like mist was strewn,
Dyed in the beams of the ascending moon.

LIV.

And on a throne o'erlaid with starlight, caught
  Upon those wandering isles of airy dew
Which highest shoals of mountain shipwreck not,
  She sate, and heard all that had happened new
Between the earth and moon since they had brought
  The last intelligence: and now she grew
Pale as that moon lost in the watery night,
And now she wept, and now she laughed outright.

LV.

These were tame pleasures.—She would often climb
  The steepest ladder of the crudded rack
Up to some beaked cape of cloud sublime,
  And like Arion on the dolphin's back
Ride singing through the shoreless air. Oft-time,
  Following the serpent lightning's winding track,
She ran upon the platforms of the wind,
And laughed to hear the fireballs roar behind.

LVI.

And sometimes to those streams of upper air
  Which whirl the earth in its diurnal round
She would ascend, and win the Spirits there
  To let her join their chorus. Mortals found
That on those days the sky was calm and fair,
  And mystic snatches of harmonious sound
Wandered upon the earth where'er she passed,
And happy thoughts of hope, too sweet to last.

LVII.

But her choice sport was, in the hours of sleep,
  To glide adown old Nilus, when he threads
Egypt and Ethiopia from the steep
  Of utmost Axumé until he spreads,
Like a calm flock of silver-fleeced sheep,
  His waters on the plain,—and crested heads
Of cities and proud temples gleam amid,
And many a vapour-belted pyramid:—

LVIII.

By Mœris and the Mareotid lakes,
  Strewn with faint blooms like bridal-chamber floors,
Where naked boys bridling tame water-snakes,
  Or charioteering ghastly alligators,
Had left on the sweet waters mighty wakes
  Of those huge forms;—within the brazen doors
Of the Great Labyrinth slept both boy and beast,
Tired with the pomp of their Osirian feast.

LIX.

And where within the surface of the river
  The shadows of the massy temples lie,
And never are erased, but tremble ever
  Like things which every cloud can doom to die,—
Through lotus-paven canals, and wheresoever
  The works of man pierced that serenest sky
With tombs and towers and fanes,—'twas her delight
To wander in the shadow of the night.

LX.

With motion like the spirit of that wind
  Whose soft step deepens slumber, her light feet
Passed through the peopled haunts of humankind,
  Scattering sweet visions from her presence sweet,—
Through fane and palace-court and labyrinth mined
  With many a dark and subterranean street
Under the Nile; through chambers high and deep
She passed, observing mortals in their sleep.

LXI.

A pleasure sweet doubtless it was to see
  Mortals subdued in all the shapes of sleep.
Here lay two sister-twins in infancy;
  There a lone youth who in his dreams did weep;
Within, two lovers linked innocently
  In their loose locks which over both did creep
Like ivy from one stem; and there lay calm
Old age with snow-bright hair and folded palm.

LXII.

But other troubled forms of sleep she saw,
  Not to be mirrored in a holy song,—
Distortions foul of supernatural awe,
  And pale imaginings of visioned wrong,
And all the code of Custom's lawless law
  Written upon the brows of old and young.
"This," said the Wizard Maiden, "is the strife
Which stirs the liquid surface of man's life."

LXIII.

And little did the sight disturb her soul.
  We, the weak mariners of that wide lake,
Where'er its shores extend or billows roll,
  Our course unpiloted and starless make
O'er its wild surface to an unknown goal;
  But she in the calm depths her way could take,
Where in bright bowers immortal forms abide
Beneath the weltering of the restless tide.

LXIV.

And she saw princes couched under the glow
  Of sunlike gems; and round each temple-court
In dormitories ranged, row after row,
  She saw the priests asleep,—all of one sort,
For all were educated to be so.
  The peasants in their huts, and in the port
The sailors she saw cradled on the waves,
And the dead lulled within their dreamless graves.

LXV.

And all the forms in which those spirits lay.
  Were to her sight like the diaphanous
Veils in which those sweet ladies oft array
  Their delicate limbs who would conceal from us
Only their scorn of all concealment: they
  Move in the light of their own beauty thus.
But these and all now lay with sleep upon them,
And little thought a Witch was looking on them.

LXVI.

She all those human figures breathing there
  Beheld as living spirits—to her eyes
The naked beauty of the soul lay bare,
  And often through a rude and worn disguise
She saw the innner form most bright and fair:
  And then she had a charm of strange device,
Which, murmured on mute lips with tender tone,
Could make that spirit mingle with her own.

LXVII.

Alas, Aurora! what wouldst thou have given
  For such a charm, when Tithon became grey?
Or how much, Venus, of thy silver heaven
  Wouldst thou have yielded, ere Proserpina
Had half (oh! why not all?) the debt forgiven
  Which dear Adonis had been doomed to pay,
To any witch who would have taught you it?
The Heliad doth not know its value yet.

LXVIII.

'Tis said in after times her spirit free
  Knew what love was, and felt itself alone:
But holy Dian could not chaster be
  Before she stooped to kiss Endymion
Than now this Lady. Like a sexless bee,
  Tasting all blossoms and confined to none,
Among those mortal forms the Wizard Maiden
Passed with an eye serene and heart unladen.

LXIX.
To those she saw most beautiful she gave
   Strange panacea in a crystal bowl.
They drank in their deep sleep of that sweet wave,
   And lived thenceforward as if some control,
Mightier than life, were in them; and the grave
   Of such, when death oppressed the weary soul,
Was as a green and overarching bower
Lit by the gems of many a starry flower.

LXX.
For, on the night that they were buried, she
   Restored the embalmer's ruining, and shook
The light out of the funeral lamps, to be
   A mimic day within that deathy nook;
And she unwound the woven imagery
   Of second childhood's swaddling bands, and took
The coffin, its last cradle, from its niche,
And threw it with contempt into a ditch.

LXXI.
And there the body lay, age after age,
   Mute, breathing, beating, warm, and undecaying,
Like one asleep in a green hermitage,—
   With gentle sleep about its eyelids playing,
And living in its dreams beyond the rage
   Of death or life; while they were still arraying
In liveries ever new the rapid, blind,
And fleeting generations of mankind.

LXXII.
And she would write strange dreams upon the brain
   Of those who were less beautiful, and make
All harsh and crooked purposes more vain
   Than in the desert is the serpent's wake
Which the sand covers;—all his evil gain
   The miser, in such dreams, would rise and shake
Into a beggar's lap;—the lying scribe
Would his own lies betray without a bribe.

LXXIII.

The priests would write an explanation full,
   Translating hieroglyphics into Greek,
How the god Apis really was a bull,
   And nothing more; and bid the herald stick
The same against the temple doors, and pull
   The old cant down: they licensed all to speak
Whate'er they thought of hawks and cats and geese,
By pastoral letters to each diocese.

LXXIV.

The king would dress an ape up in his crown
   And robes, and seat him on his glorious seat,
And on the right hand of the sunlike throne
   Would place a gaudy mockbird to repeat
The chatterings of the monkey. Every one
   Of the prone courtiers crawled to kiss the feet
Of their great emperor when the morning came;
And kissed—alas, how many kiss the same!

LXXV.

The soldiers dreamed that they were blacksmiths, and
   Walked out of quarters in somnambulism;
Round the red anvils you might see them stand
   Like Cyclopses in Vulcan's sooty abysm,
Beating their swords to ploughshares:—in a band
   The gaolers sent those of the liberal schism
Free through the streets of Memphis—much, I wis,
To the annoyance of king Amasis.

LXXVI.

And timid lovers, who had been so coy
   They hardly knew whether they loved or not,
Would rise out of their rest, and take sweet joy,
   To the fulfilment of their inmost thought;
And, when next day the maiden and the boy
   Met one another, both, like sinners caught,
Blushed at the thing which each believed was done
Only in fancy—till the tenth moon shone;

LXXVII.

And then the Witch would let them take no ill:
    Of many thousand schemes which lovers find,
The Witch found one,—and so they took their fill
    Of happiness in marriage warm and kind.
Friends who, by practice of some envious skill,
    Were torn apart, a wide wound, mind from mind!
She did unite again with visions clear
Of deep affection and of truth sincere.

LXXVIII.

These were the pranks she played among the cities
    Of mortal men. And what she did to Sprites
And Gods, entangling them in her sweet ditties,
    To do her will, and show their subtle sleights,
I will declare another time; for it is
    A tale more fit for the weird winter nights
Than for these garish summer days, when we
Scarcely believe much more than we can see.

EPIPSYCHIDION:

VERSES ADDRESSED TO THE NOBLE AND UNFORTUNATE LADY

EMILIA VIVIANI,

NOW IMPRISONED IN THE CONVENT OF ST ANNE, PISA.

L'anima amante si alancia fuori del creato, e si crea nell' infinito un mondo tutto per essa, diverso assai da questo oscuro e pauroso baratro.—*Her own words.*

> My Song, I fear that thou wilt find but few
> Who fitly shall conceive thy reasoning,
> Of such hard matter dost thou entertain;
> Whence, if by misadventure chance should bring
> Thee to base company (as chance may do)
> Quite unaware of what thou dost contain
> I prithee comfort thy sweet self again,
> My last delight: tell them that they are dull,
> And bid them own that thou art beautiful.

ADVERTISEMENT.

THE writer of the following lines died at Florence, as he was preparing for a voyage to one of the wildest of the Sporades, which he had bought, and where he had fitted up the ruins of an old building; and where it was his hope to have realized a scheme of life suited perhaps to that happier and better world of which he is now an inhabitant, but hardly practicable in this. His life was singular; less on account of the romantic vicissitudes which diversified it than the ideal tinge which it received from his own character and feelings. The present poem, like the *Vita Nova* of Dante, is sufficiently intelligible to a certain class of readers without a matter-of-fact history of the circumstances to which it relates; and to a certain other class it must ever remain incomprehensible, from a defect of a common organ of perception for the ideas of which it treats. Not but that "*gran vergogna sarebbe a colui che rimasse cosa sotto veste di figura o di colore rettorico, e domandato non sapesse denudare le sue parole da cotal veste, in guisa che avessero verace intendimento.*"

The present poem appears to have been intended by the writer as the dedication to some longer one. The stanza on the preceding page is almost a literal translation from Dante's famous canzone

Voi che intendendo il terzo ciel movete, &c.

The presumptuous application of the concluding lines to his own composition will raise a smile at the expense of my unfortunate friend: be it a smile not of contempt, but pity.

S.

EPIPSYCHIDION.

SWEET Spirit! Sister of that orphan one
Whose empire is the name thou weepest on,
In my heart's temple I suspend to thee
These votive wreaths of withered memory.
Poor captive bird! who, from thy narrow cage,
Pourest such music, that it might assuage
The rugged hearts of those who prisoned thee,
Were they not deaf to all sweet melody,—
This song shall be thy rose: its petals pale
Are dead, indeed, my adored Nightingale!
But soft and fragrant is the faded blossom,
And it has no thorn left to wound thy bosom.

High spirit-winged Heart! who dost for ever
Beat thine unfeeling bars with vain endeavour,
Till those bright plumes of thought, in which arrayed
It oversoared this low and worldly shade,
Lie shattered, and thy panting wounded breast
Stains with dear blood its unmaternal nest!
I weep vain tears: blood would less bitter be,
Yet poured forth gladlier could it profit thee.

Seraph of Heaven! too gentle to be human,
Veiling beneath that radiant form of Woman
All that is insupportable in thee
Of light, and love, and immortality!

Sweet Benediction in the eternal Curse!
Veiled Glory of this lampless Universe!
Thou Moon beyond the clouds! Thou living Form
Among the Dead! Thou Star above the Storm!
Thou Wonder, and thou Beauty, and thou Terror!
Thou Harmony of Nature's art! thou Mirror
In whom, as in the splendour of the Sun,
All shapes look glorious which thou gazest on!
Ay, even the dim words which obscure thee now
Flash, lightning-like, with unaccustomed glow!
I pray thee that thou blot from this sad song
All of its much mortality and wrong,
With those clear drops, which start like sacred dew
From the twin lights thy sweet soul darkens through,
Weeping till sorrow becomes ecstacy:
Then smile on it, so that it may not die.

I never thought before my death to see
Youth's vision thus made perfect: Emily,
I love thee,—though the world by no thin name
Will hide that love from its unvalued shame.
Would we two had been twins of the same mother!
Or, that the name my heart lent to another
Could be a sister's bond for her and thee,
Blending two beams of one eternity!
Yet were one lawful and the other true,
These names, though dear, could paint not as is due
How beyond refuge I am thine. Ah me!
I am not thine—I am a part of *thee!*

Sweet lamp! my moth-like Muse has burnt its wings;
Or, like a dying swan who soars and sings,
Young Love should teach Time, in his own grey style,
All that thou art. Art thou not void of guile,
A lovely soul formed to be blessed and bless?
A well of sealed and secret happiness,
Whose waters like blithe light and music are,
Vanquishing dissonance and gloom? A Star

Which moves not in the moving Heavens, alone?
A smile amid dark frowns? a gentle tone
Amid rude voices? a beloved light?
A Solitude, a Refuge, a Delight?
A lute, which those whom Love has taught to play
Make music on to soothe the roughest day,
And lull fond grief asleep? a buried treasure?
A cradle of young thoughts of wingless pleasure?
A violet-shrouded grave of woe?—I measure
The world of fancies, seeking one like thee,
And find—alas! mine own infirmity.

She met me, Stranger, upon life's rough way,
And lured me towards sweet death; as Night by Day,
Winter by Spring, or Sorrow by swift Hope,
Led into light, life, peace. An antelope
In the suspended impulse of its lightness
Were less etherially light. The brightness
Of her divinest presence trembles through
Her limbs, as underneath a cloud of dew
Embodied in the windless heaven of June,
Amid the splendour-winged stars, the Moon
Burns inextinguishably beautiful:
And from her lips, as from a hyacinth full
Of honey-dew, a liquid murmur drops,
Killing the sense with passion, sweet as stops
Of planetary music heard in trance.
In her mild lights the starry spirits dance,
The sunbeams of those wells which ever leap
Under the lightnings of the soul—too deep
For the brief fathom-line of thought or sense.
The glory of her being, issuing thence,
Stains the dead, blank, cold air with a warm shade
Of unentangled intermixture, made,
By Love, of light and motion; one intense
Diffusion, one serene Omnipresence,
Whose flowing outlines mingle in their flowing

Around her cheeks and utmost fingers glowing
With the unintermitted blood, which there
Quivers (as in a fleece of snow-like air
The crimson pulse of living Morn may quiver),
Continuously prolonged and ending never,
Till they are lost, and in that Beauty furled
Which penetrates and clasps and fills the world;
Scarce visible from extreme loveliness.
Warm fragrance seems to fall from her light dress,
And her loose hair; and, where some heavy tress
The air of her own speed has disentwined,
The sweetness seems to satiate the faint wind;
And in the soul a wild odour is felt,
Beyond the sense, like fiery dews that melt
Into the bosom of a frozen bud.
See where she stands! a mortal shape indued
With love and life and light and deity,
And motion which may change but cannot die;
An image of some bright Eternity;
A shadow of some golden dream; a Splendour
Leaving the third sphere pilotless; a tender
Reflection of the eternal Moon of Love
Under whose motions life's dull billows move;
A Metaphor of Spring and Youth and Morning;
A vision like incarnate April, warning
With smiles and tears Frost the anatomy
Into his summer grave.

      Ah! woe is me!
What have I dared? where am I lifted? how
Shall I descend, and perish not? I know
That love makes all things equal: I have heard
By mine own heart this joyous truth averred,—
The spirit of the worm beneath the sod,
In love and worship, blends itself with God.

Spouse! Sister! Angel! Pilot of the fate
Whose course has been so starless! O too late

Beloved, O too soon adored, by me!
For in the fields of immortality
My spirit should at first have worshipped thine,
A divine presence in a place divine;
Or should have moved beside it on this earth,
A shadow of that substance, from its birth:
But not as now.—I love thee; yes, I feel
That on the fountain of my heart a seal
Is set, to keep its waters pure and bright
For thee, since in those tears thou hast delight.
We—are we not formed, as notes of music are,
For one another, though dissimilar?
Such difference without discord as can make
Those sweetest sounds in which all spirits shake,
As trembling leaves in a continuous air.

Thy wisdom speaks in me, and bids me dare
Beacon the rocks on which high hearts are wrecked.
I never was attached to that great sect
Whose doctrine is that each one should select
Out of the crowd a mistress or a friend,
And all the rest, though fair and wise, commend
To cold oblivion; though it is in the code
Of modern morals, and the beaten road
Which those poor slaves with weary footsteps tread
Who travel to their home among the dead
By the broad highway of the world, and so
With one chained friend, perhaps a jealous foe,
The dreariest and the longest journey go.

True Love in this differs from gold and clay,
That to divide is not to take away.
Love is like understanding, that grows bright,
Gazing on many truths; 'tis like thy light,
Imagination! which from earth and sky,
And from the depths of human phantasy,
As from a thousand prisms and mirrors, fills
The Universe with glorious beams, and kills

Error the worm with many a sunlike arrow
Of its reverberated lightning. Narrow
The heart that loves, the brain that contemplates,
The life that wears, the spirit that creates,
One object and one form, and builds thereby
A sepulchre for its eternity!

Mind from its object differs most in this:
Evil from good; misery from happiness;
The baser from the nobler; the impure
And frail from what is clear and must endure.
If you divide suffering or dross, you may
Diminish till it is consumed away;
If you divide pleasure and love and thought,
Each part exceeds the whole; and we know not
How much, while any yet remains unshared,
Of pleasure may be gained, of sorrow spared.
This truth is that deep well whence sages draw
The unenvied light of hope; the eternal law
By which those live to whom this world of life
Is as a garden ravaged, and whose strife
Tills for the promise of a later birth
The wilderness of this Elysian earth.

There was a Being whom my spirit oft
Met on its visioned wanderings, far aloft,
In the clear golden prime of my youth's dawn,
Upon the fairy isles of sunny lawn,
Amid the enchanted mountains, and the caves
Of divine sleep, and on the air-like waves
Of wonder-level dream, whose tremulous floor
Paved her light steps;—on an imagined shore,
Under the grey beak of some promontory,
She met me, robed in such exceeding glory
That I beheld her not. In solitudes
Her voice came to me through the whispering woods,
And from the fountains, and the odours deep
Of flowers, which, like lips murmuring in their sleep

Of the sweet kisses which had lulled them there,
Breathed but of her to the enamoured air;
And from the breezes whether low or loud,
And from the rain of every passing cloud,
And from the singing of the summer birds,
And from all sounds, all silence. In the words
Of antique verse and high romance—in form,
Sound, colour—in whatever checks that storm
Which with the shattered present chokes the past—
And in that best philosophy whose taste
Makes this cold common hell, our life, a doom
As glorious as a fiery martyrdom—
Her Spirit was the harmony of truth.

Then from the caverns of my dreamy youth
I sprang, as one sandalled with plumes of fire,
And towards the lodestar of my one desire
I flitted, like a dizzy moth whose flight
Is as a dead leaf's in the owlet light,
When it would seek in Hesper's setting sphere
A radiant death, a fiery sepulchre,
As if it were a lamp of earthly flame.
But She, whom prayers or tears then could not tame,
Passed, like a God throned on a winged planet,
Whose burning plumes to tenfold swiftness fan it,
Into the dreary cone of our life's shade.
And, as a man with mighty loss dismayed,
I would have followed, though the grave between
Yawned like a gulf whose spectres are unseen:
When a voice said, "O thou of hearts the weakest,
The phantom is beside thee whom thou seekest."
Then I—"Where?" The world's echo answered "where?"
And in that silence and in my despair
I questioned every tongueless wind that flew
Over my tower of mourning, if it knew
Whither 'twas fled, this soul out of my soul;
And murmured names and spells which have control

Over the sightless tyrants of our fate.
But neither prayer nor verse could dissipate
The night which closed on her; nor uncreate
That world within this Chaos, mine and me,
Of which she was the veiled Divinity—
The world, I say, of thoughts that worshipped her.
And therefore I went forth—with hope and fear
And every gentle passion, sick to death,
Feeding my course with expectation's breath—
Into the wintry forest of our life;
And, struggling through its error with vain strife,
And stumbling in my weakness and my haste,
And half bewildered by new forms, I passed,
Seeking among those untaught foresters
If I could find one form resembling hers
In which she might have masked herself from me.
There,—One, whose voice was venomed melody
Sate by a well, under blue nightshade bowers;
The breath of her false mouth was like faint flowers,
Her touch was as electric poison, flame
Out of her looks into my vitals came,
And from her living cheeks and bosom flew
A killing air which pierced like honey-dew
Into the core of my green heart, and lay
Upon its leaves;—until, as hair grown grey
O'er a young brow, they hid its unblown prime
With ruins of unseasonable time.

In many mortal forms I rashly sought
The shadow of that idol of my thought.
And some were fair—but beauty dies away:
Others were wise—but honeyed words betray:
And One was true—oh! why not true to me?
Then, as a hunted deer that could not flee,
I turned upon my thoughts, and stood at bay,
Wounded, and weak, and panting; the cold day
Trembled for pity of my strife and pain,—

When, like a noonday dawn, there shone again
Deliverance. One stood on my path who seemed
As like the glorious shape which I had dreamed
As is the Moon, whose changes ever run
Into themselves, to the eternal Sun;
The cold chaste Moon, the queen of heaven's bright isles,
Who makes all beautiful on which she smiles—
That wandering shrine of soft yet icy flame
Which ever is transformed yet still the same,
And warms not, but illumines. Young and fair
As the descended Spirit of that sphere,
She bid me, as the Moon may hide the night
From its own darkness, until all was bright
Between the heaven and earth of my calm mind;
And, as a cloud charioted by the wind,
She led me to a cave in that wild place,
And sat beside me, with her downward face
Illumining my slumbers, like the Moon
Waxing and waning o'er Endymion.
And I was laid asleep, spirit and limb,
And all my being became bright or dim
As the Moon's image in a summer sea,
According as she smiled or frowned on me;
And there I lay within a chaste cold bed.
Alas! I then was nor alive nor dead:—
For at her silver voice came Death and Life,
Unmindful each of their accustomed strife,
Masked like twin babes, a sister and a brother,
The wandering hopes of one abandoned mother;
And through the cavern without wings they flew,
And cried, "Away! he is not of our crew."
I wept; and, though it be a dream, I weep.

What storms then shook the ocean of my sleep,
Blotting that Moon whose pale and waning lips
Then shrank as in the sickness of eclipse;
And how my soul was as a lampless sea,

And who was then its tempest; and, when She,
The Planet of that hour, was quenched, what frost
Crept o'er those waters, till from coast to coast
The moving billows of my being fell
Into a death of ice, immovable;
And then—what earthquakes made it gape and split,
The white Moon smiling all the while on it;—
These words conceal. If not, each word would be
The key of staunchless tears. Weep not for me!

At length into the obscure forest came
The vision I had sought through grief and shame.
Athwart that wintry wilderness of thorns
Flashed from her motion splendour like the Morn's,
And from her presence life was radiated
Through the grey earth and branches bare and dead;
So that her way was paved and roofed above
With flowers as soft as thoughts of budding love;
And music from her respiration spread
Like light,—all other sounds were penetrated
By the small, still, sweet spirit of that sound,
So that the savage winds hung mute around;
And odours warm and fresh fell from her hair,
Dissolving the dull cold in the frore air.
Soft as an Incarnation of the Sun,
When light is changed to love, this glorious One
Floated into the cavern where I lay,
And called my spirit; and the dreaming clay
Was lifted by the thing that dreamed below
As smoke by fire, and in her beauty's glow
I stood, and felt the dawn of my long night
Was penetrating me with living light:
I knew it was the Vision veiled from me
So many years—that it was Emily.

Twin spheres of light who rule this passive Earth,
This world of love, this *me;* and into birth

Awaken all its fruits and flowers, and dart
Magnetic might into its central heart;
And lift its billows and its mists, and guide
By everlasting laws each wind and tide
To its fit cloud and its appointed cave;
And lull its storms, each in the craggy grave
Which was its cradle, luring to faint bowers
The armies of the rainbow-winged showers;
And, as those married lights which from the towers
Of heaven look forth, and fold the wandering globe
In liquid sleep and splendour as a robe,
And all their many-mingled influence blend,
If equal yet unlike, to one sweet end;
So ye, bright regents, with alternate sway,
Govern my sphere of being, night and day—
Thou, not disdaining even a borrowed might,
Thou, not eclipsing a remoter light,—
And through the shadow of the seasons three,
From Spring to Autumn's sere maturity,
Light it into the Winter of the tomb,
Where it may ripen to a brighter bloom!—
Thou too, O Comet, beautiful and fierce,
Who drew the heart of this frail universe
Towards thine own; till, wrecked in that convulsion,
Alternating attraction and repulsion,
Thine went astray, and that was rent in twain;
Oh! float into our azure heaven again!
Be there love's folding-star at thy return!
The living Sun will feed thee from its urn
Of golden fire; the Moon will veil her horn
In thy last smiles; adoring Even and Morn
Will worship thee with incense of calm breath
And lights and shadow, as the star of death
And birth is worshiped by those sisters wild
Called Hope and Fear. Upon the heart are piled
Their offerings,—of this sacrifice divine.
A world shall be the altar.

                                        Lady mine,
Scorn not these flowers of thought, the fading birth
Which from its heart of hearts that plant puts forth
Whose fruit, made perfect by thy sunny eyes,
Will be as of the trees of Paradise.
The day is come, and thou wilt fly with me!

To whatsoe'er of dull mortality
Is mine remain a vestal sister still;
To the intense, the deep, the imperishable—
Not mine, but me—henceforth be thou united,
Even as a bride, delighting and delighted.
The hour is come:—the destined Star has risen
Which shall descend upon a vacant prison.
The walls are high, the gates are strong, thick set
The sentinels—but true Love never yet
Was thus constrained. It overleaps all fence:
Like lightning, with invisible violence
Piercing its continents; like heaven's free breath,
Which he who grasps can hold not; liker Death,
Who rides upon a thought, and makes his way
Through temple, tower, and palace, and the array
Of arms. More strength has Love than he or they;
For he can burst *his* charnel, and makes free
The limbs in chains, the heart in agony,
The soul in dust and chaos.
                                        Emily,
A ship is floating in the harbour now,
A wind is hovering o'er the mountain's brow.
There is a path on the sea's azure floor,—
No keel has ever ploughed that path before;
The halcyons brood around the foamless isles;
The treacherous ocean has forsworn its wiles;
The merry mariners are bold and free:
Say, my heart's sister, wilt thou sail with me?
Our bark is as an albatross, whose nest
Is a far Eden of the purple east;

And we between her wings will sit, while Night,
And Day, and Storm, and Calm, pursue their flight,
Our ministers, along the boundless sea,
Treading each other's heels, unheededly.
It is an isle under Ionian skies,
Beautiful as a wreck of Paradise;
And, for the harbours are not safe and good,
This land would have remained a solitude
But for some pastoral people native there,
Who from the Elysian, clear, and golden air
Draw the last spirit of the age of gold,—
Simple and spirited, innocent and bold.
The blue Ægean girds this chosen home,
With ever-changing sound and light and foam,
Kissing the sifted sands and caverns hoar;
And all the winds wandering along the shore
Undulate with the undulating tide.
There are thick woods where sylvan forms abide;
And many a fountain, rivulet, and pond,
As clear as elemental diamond,
Or serene morning air. And far beyond,
The mossy tracks made by the goats and deer
(Which the rough shepherd treads but once a year)
Pierce into glades, caverns, and bowers, and halls
Built round with ivy, which the waterfalls
Illumining, with sound that never fails,
Accompany the noonday nightingales.
And all the place is peopled with sweet airs.
The light clear element which the isle wears
Is heavy with the scent of lemon-flowers,
Which floats like mist laden with unseen showers,
And falls upon the eyelids like faint sleep;
And from the moss violets and jonquils peep,
And dart their arrowy odour through the brain,
Till you might faint with that delicious pain.
And every motion, odour, beam, and tone,
With that deep music is in unison

Which is a soul within the soul: they seem
Like echoes of an antenatal dream.
It is an isle 'twixt Heaven, Air, Earth, and Sea,
Cradled, and hung in clear tranquillity;
Bright as that wandering Eden, Lucifer,
Washed by the soft blue oceans of young air.
It is a favoured place. Famine or blight,
Pestilence, war, and earthquake, never light
Upon its mountain-peaks; blind vultures, they
Sail onward far upon their fatal way.
The wingèd storms, chanting their thunder-psalm
To other lands, leave azure chasms of calm
Over this isle, or weep themselves in dew,
From which its fields and woods ever renew
Their green and golden immortality.
And from the sea there rise, and from the sky
There fall, clear exhalations, soft and bright,
Veil after veil, each hiding some delight:
Which sun or moon or zephyr draws aside,
Till the isle's beauty, like a naked bride
Glowing at once with love and loveliness,
Blushes and trembles at its own excess.
Yet, like a buried lamp, a soul no less
Burns in the heart of this delicious isle,
An atom of the Eternal, whose own smile
Unfolds itself, and may be felt not seen
O'er the grey rocks, blue waves, and forests green,
Filling their bare and void interstices.

But the chief marvel of the wilderness
Is a lone dwelling, built by whom or how
None of the rustic island-people know.
'Tis not a tower of strength, though with its height
It overtops the woods; but, for delight,
Some wise and tender Ocean-king, ere crime
Had been invented, in the world's young prime,
Reared it, a wonder of that simple time,

And envy of the isles—a pleasure-house
Made sacred to his sister and his spouse.
It scarce seems now a wreck of human art,
But, as it were, Titanic; in the heart
Of earth having assumed its form, then grown
Out of the mountains, from the living stone
Lifting itself in caverns light and high:
For all the antique and learned imagery
Has been erased, and in the place of it
The ivy and the wild vine interknit
The volumes of their many-twining stems.
Parasite flowers illume with dewy gems
The lampless halls; and, when they fade, the sky
Peeps through their winter-woof of tracery
With moonlight patches or star atoms keen,
Or fragments of the day's intense serene,
Working mosaic on their Parian floors.
And, day and night, aloof, from the high towers
And terraces, the Earth and Ocean seem
To sleep in one another's arms, and dream
Of waves, flowers, clouds, woods, rocks, and all that we
Read in their smiles, and call reality.

This isle and house are mine, and I have vowed
Thee to be lady of the solitude.
And I have fitted up some chambers there
Looking towards the golden eastern air,
And level with the living winds which flow
Like waves above the living waves below.
I have sent books and music there, and all
Those instruments with which high spirits call
The future from its cradle, and the past
Out of its grave, and make the present last
In thoughts and joys which sleep but cannot die,
Folded within their own eternity.
Our simple life wants little, and true taste
Hires not the pale drudge Luxury to waste

The scene it would adorn; and therefore still
Nature with all her children haunts the hill.
The ringdove, in the embowering ivy, yet
Keeps up her love-lament, and the owls flit
Round the evening tower, and the young stars glance
Between the quick bats in their twilight dance;
The spotted deer bask in the fresh moonlight
Before our gate, and the slow silent night
Is measured by the pants of their calm sleep.
Be this our home in life; and, when years heap
Their withered hours like leaves on our decay,
Let us become the overhanging day,
The living soul, of this Elysian isle—
Conscious, inseparable, one. Meanwhile
We two will rise and sit and walk together
Under the roof of blue Ionian weather,
And wander in the meadows, or ascend
The mossy mountains, where the blue heavens bend
With lightest winds to touch their paramour;
Or linger where the pebble-paven shore
Under the quick faint kisses of the sea
Trembles and sparkles as with ecstacy;—
Possessing and possessed by all that is
Within that calm circumference of bliss,
And by each other, till to love and live
Be one;—or at the noontide hour arrive
Where some old cavern hoar seems yet to keep
The moonlight of the expired Night asleep,
Through which the awakened Day can never peep;
A veil for our seclusion, close as Night's,
Where secure sleep may kill thine innocent lights—
Sleep, the fresh dew of languid love, the rain
Whose drops quench kisses till they burn again.
And we will talk, until thought's melody
Become too sweet for utterance, and it die
In words, to live again in looks, which dart
With thrilling tone into the voiceless heart,

Harmonizing silence without a sound.
Our breath shall intermix, our bosoms bound,
And our veins beat together; and our lips,
With other eloquence than words, eclipse
The soul that burns between them; and the wells
Which boil under our being's inmost cells,
The fountains of our deepest life, shall be
Confused in passion's golden purity,
As mountain-springs under the morning sun.
We shall become the same, we shall be one
Spirit within two frames, oh! wherefore two?
One passion in twin—hearts, which grows and grew
Till, like two meteors of expanding flame,
Those spheres instinct with it become the same,
Touch, mingle, are transfigured; ever still
Burning, yet ever inconsumable;
In one another's substance finding food,
Like flames too pure and light and unimbued
To nourish their bright lives with baser prey,
Which point to heaven and cannot pass away:
One hope within two wills, one will beneath
Two overshadowing minds, one life, one death,
One heaven, one hell, one immortality.
And one annihilation!

    Woe is me!
The winged words on which my soul would pierce
Into the height of Love's rare universe
Are chains of lead around its flight of fire—
I pant, I sink, I tremble, I expire!

Weak verses, go, kneel at your Sovereign's feet,
 And say:—"We are the masters of thy slave;
  What wouldest thou with us and ours and thine?"
 Then call your sisters from Oblivion's cave,

All singing loud: "Love's very pain is sweet;
    But its reward is in the world divine,
   Which, if not here, it builds beyond the grave."
   So shall ye live when I am there. Then haste
Over the hearts of men, until ye meet
   Marina, Vanna, Primus, and the rest,
   And bid them love each other, and be blessed:
And leave the troop which errs and which reproves,
And come and be my guest—for I am Love's.

ADONAIS;

AN ELEGY ON THE DEATH OF JOHN KEATS.

Ἀστὴρ πρὶν μὲν ἔλαμπες ἐνὶ ζώοισιν ἑῷος.
Νῦν δὲ θανὼν λάμπεις ἕσπερος ἐν φθιμένοις.
PLATO.

ADONAIS.

I.

I WEEP for Adonais—he is dead!
  Oh! weep for Adonais, though our tears
Thaw not the frost which binds so dear a head!
  And thou, sad Hour selected from all years
  To mourn our loss, rouse thy obscure compeers,
And teach them thine own sorrow! Say: "With me
  Died Adonais! Till the future dares
Forget the past, his fate and fame shall be
An echo and a light unto eternity."

II.

Where wert thou, mighty Mother, when he lay,
  When thy son lay, pierced by the shaft which flies
In darkness? Where was lorn Urania
  When Adonais died? With veiled eyes,
  'Mid listening Echoes, in her Paradise
She sate, while one, with soft enamoured breath,
  Rekindled all the fading melodies
With which, like flowers that mock the corse beneath,
He had adorned and hid the coming bulk of Death.

III.

Oh! weep for Adonais—he is dead!
  Wake, melancholy Mother, wake and weep!—
Yet wherefore? Quench within their burning bed
  Thy fiery tears, and let thy loud heart keep,
  Like his, a mute and uncomplaining sleep;
For he is gone where all things wise and fair
  Descend. Oh! dream not that the amorous Deep
Will yet restore him to the vital air;
Death feeds on his mute voice, and laughs at our despair.

IV.

Most musical of mourners weep again!
  Lament anew, Urania!—He died
Who was the Sire of an immortal strain,
  Blind, old, and lonely, when his country's pride
  The priest, the slave, and the liberticide,
Trampled and mocked with many a loathed rite
  Of lust and blood. He went unterrified
Into the gulf of death; but his clear sprite
Yet reigns o'er earth, the third among the Sons of Light.

V.

Most musical of mourners, weep anew!
  Not all to that bright station dared to climb:
And happier they their happiness who knew,
  Whose tapers yet burn through that night of time
  In which suns perished. Others more sublime,
Struck by the envious wrath of man or god,
  Have sunk, extinct in their refulgent prime;
And some yet live, treading the thorny road
Which leads, through toil and hate, to Fame's serene abode.

VI.

But now thy youngest, dearest one, has perished,
  The nursling of thy widowhood, who grew,
Like a pale flower by some sad maiden cherished,
  And fed with true-love tears instead of dew.

Most musical of mourners, weep anew!
Thy extreme hope, the loveliest and the last,
　The bloom whose petals, nipped before they blew,
　Died on the promise of the fruit, is waste;
The broken lily lies—the storm is overpassed.

VII.

To that high Capital where kingly Death
　Keeps his pale court in beauty and decay
He came; and bought, with price of purest breath,
　A grave among the eternal.—Come away!
　Haste, while the vault of blue Italian day
Is yet his fitting charnel-roof, while still
　He lies as if in dewy sleep he lay.
Awake him not! surely he takes his fill
Of deep and liquid rest, forgetful of all ill.

VIII.

He will awake no more, oh, never more!
　Within the twilight chamber spreads apace
The shadow of white Death, and at the door
　Invisible Corruption waits to trace
　His extreme way to her dim dwelling-place;
The eternal Hunger sits, but pity and awe
　Soothe her pale rage, nor dares she to deface
So fair a prey, till darkness and the law
Of change, shall o'er his sleep the mortal curtain draw.

IX.

Oh weep for Adonais!—The quick Dreams,
　The passion-winged ministers of thought,
Who were his flocks, whom near the living streams
　Of his young spirit he fed, and whom he taught
　The love which was its music, wander not—
Wander no more from kindling brain to brain,
　But droop there whence they sprung; and mourn their lot
Round the cold heart where, after their sweet pain,
They ne'er will gather strength or find a home again.

X.

And one with trembling hand clasps his cold head,
    And fans him with her moonlight wings, and cries,
"Our love, our hope, our sorrow, is not dead!
    See, on the silken fringe of his faint eyes,
    Like dew upon a sleeping flower, there lies
A tear some Dream has loosened from his brain."
    Lost Angel of a ruined Paradise!
    She knew not 'twas her own,—as with no stain
She faded, like a cloud which had outwept its rain.

XI.

One from a lucid urn of starry dew
    Washed his light limbs, as if embalming them:
Another clipped her profuse locks, and threw
    The wreath upon him, like an anadem
    Which frozen tears instead of pearls begem;
Another in her wilful grief would break
    Her bow and winged reeds, as if to stem
A greater loss with one which was more weak,
And dull the barbed fire against his frozen cheek.

XII.

Another Splendour on his mouth alit,
    That mouth whence it was wont to draw the breath
Which gave it strength to pierce the guarded wit,
    And pass into the panting heart beneath
    With lightning and with music: the damp death
Quenched its caress upon his icy lips;
    And, as a dying meteor stains a wreath
Of moonlight vapour which the cold night clips,
It flushed through his pale limbs, and passed to its eclipse.

XIII.

And others came,—Desires and Adorations,
    Winged Persuasions, and veiled Destinies,
Splendours, and Glooms, and glimmering Incarnations
    Of hopes and fears, and twilight Phantasies;

And Sorrow, with her family of Sighs,
And Pleasure, blind with tears, led by the gleam
　Of her own dying smile instead of eyes,
Came in slow pomp;—the moving pomp might seem
Like pageantry of mist on an autumnal stream.

XIV.

All he had loved, and moulded into thought
　From shape and hue and odour and sweet sound,
Lamented Adonais. Morning sought
　Her eastern watch-tower, and her hair unbound,
　Wet with the tears which should adorn the ground,
Dimmed the aerial eyes that kindle day;
　Afar the melancholy thunder moaned,
Pale Ocean in unquiet slumber lay,
And the wild winds flew round, sobbing in their dismay.

XV.

Lost Echo sits amid the voiceless mountains,
　And feeds her grief with his remembered lay,
And will no more reply to winds or fountains,
　Or amorous birds perched on the young green spray,
　Or herdsman's horn, or bell at closing day;
Since she can mimic not his lips, more dear
　Than those for whose disdain she pined away
Into a shadow of all sounds:—a drear
Murmur between their songs, is all the woodmen hear.

XVI.

Grief made the young Spring wild, and she threw down
　Her kindling buds, as if she Autumn were,
Or they dead leaves; since her delight is flown,
　For whom should she have waked the sullen Year?
　To Phœbus was not Hyacinth so dear,
Nor to himself Narcissus, as to both
　Thou, Adonais; wan they stand and sere
Amid the faint companions of their youth,
With dew all turned to tears,—odour, to sighing ruth.

XVII.

Thy spirit's sister, the lorn nightingale,
  Mourns not her mate with such melodious pain;
Not so the eagle, who like thee could scale
  Heaven, and could nourish in the sun's domain
  Her mighty youth with morning, doth complain,
Soaring and screaming round her empty nest,
  As Albion wails for thee: the curse of Cain
Light on his head who pierced thy innocent breast,
And scared the angel soul that was its earthly guest!

XVIII.

Ah woe is me! Winter is come and gone,
  But grief returns with the revolving year.
The airs and streams renew their joyous tone
  The ants, the bees, the swallows, re-appear;
  Fresh leaves and flowers deck the dead Seasons' bier;
The amorous birds now pair in every brake,
  And build their mossy homes in field and brere;
And the green lizard and the golden snake,
Like unimprisoned flames, out of their trance awake.

XIX.

Through wood and stream and field and hill and ocean,
  A quickening life from the Earth's heart has burst,
As it has ever done, with change and motion,
  From the great morning of the world when first
  God dawned on Chaos; in its steam immersed,
The lamps of heaven flash with a softer light;
  All baser things pant with life's sacred thirst,
Diffuse themselves, and spend in love's delight
The beauty and the joy of their renewed might.

XX.

The leprous corpse, touched by this spirit tender,
  Exhales itself in flowers of gentle breath;
Like incarnations of the stars, when splendour
  Is changed to fragrance, they illumine death,

And mock the merry worm that wakes beneath.
Nought we know dies: shall that alone which knows
  Be as a sword consumed before the sheath
By sightless lightning? The intense atom glows
A moment, then is quenched in a most cold repose.

XXI.

Alas that all we loved of him should be,
  But for our grief, as if it had not been,
And grief itself be mortal! Woe is me!
  Whence are we, and why are we? of what scene
  The actors or spectators? Great and mean
Meet massed in death, who lends what life must borrow.
  As long as skies are blue and fields are green,
Evening must usher night, night urge the morrow,
Month follow month with woe, and year wake year to sorrow.

XXII.

He will awake no more, oh, never more!
  "Wake thou," cried Misery, "childless Mother! Rise
Out of thy sleep, and slake in thy heart's core
  A wound more fierce than his, with tears and sighs."
  And all the Dreams that watched Urania's eyes,
And all the Echoes whom their Sister's song
  Had held in holy silence, cried "Arise!"
Swift as a thought by the snake Memory stung,
From her ambrosial rest the fading Splendour sprung.

XXIII.

She rose like an autumnal Night, that springs
  Out of the East, and follows wild and drear
The golden Day, which, on eternal wings,
  Even as a ghost abandoning a bier,
  Had left the Earth a corpse. Sorrow and fear
So struck, so roused, so rapt, Urania;
  So saddened round her like an atmosphere
Of stormy mist; so swept her on her way,
Even to the mournful place where Adonais lay.

XXIV.

Out of her secret Paradise she sped,
   Through camps and cities rough with stone, and steel,
And human hearts, which, to her airy tread
   Yielding not, wounded the invisible
Palms of her tender feet where'er they fell:
And barbed tongues, and thoughts more sharp than they,
   Rent the soft form they never could repel,
Whose sacred blood, like the young tears of May,
Paved with eternal flowers that undeserving way.

XXV.

In the death-chamber for a moment Death,
   Shamed by the presence of that living might,
Blushed to annihilation, and the breath
   Revisited those lips, and life's pale light
Flashed through those limbs so late her dear delight.
"Leave me not wild and drear and comfortless,
   As silent lightning leaves the starless night!
Leave me not!" cried Urania. Her distress
Roused Death: Death rose and smiled, and met her vain caress.

XXVI.

"Stay yet awhile! speak to me once again!
   Kiss me, so long but as a kiss may live!
And in my heartless breast and burning brain
   That word, that kiss, shall all thoughts else survive,
   With food of saddest memory kept alive,
Now thou art dead, as if it were a part
   Of thee, my Adonais! I would give
All that I am, to be as thou now art:—
But I am chained to Time, and cannot thence depart.

XXVII.

"O gentle child, beautiful as thou wert,
   Why didst thou leave the trodden paths of men
Too soon, and with weak hands though mighty heart
   Dare the unpastured dragon in his den?

Defenceless as thou wert, oh! where was then
Wisdom the mirrored shield, or scorn the spear?—
Or, hadst thou waited the full cycle when
Thy spirit should have filled its crescent sphere,
The monsters of life's waste had fled from thee like deer.

XXVIII.

"The herded wolves bold only to pursue,
The obscene ravens clamorous o'er the dead,
The vultures to the conqueror's banner true,
Who feed where desolation first has fed,
And whose wings rain contagion,—how they fled,
When, like Apollo from his golden bow,
The Pythian of the age one arrow sped,
And smiled!—The spoilers tempt no second blow,
They fawn on the proud feet that spurn them lying low.

XXIX.

"The sun comes forth, and many reptiles spawn;
He sets, and each ephemeral insect then
Is gathered into death without a dawn,
And the immortal stars awake again.
So is it in the world of living men:
A godlike mind soars forth, in its delight
Making earth bare and veiling heaven; and when
It sinks, the swarms that dimmed or shared its light
Leave to its kindred lamps the spirit's awful night."

XXX.

Thus ceased she: and the Mountain Shepherds came,
Their garlands sere, their magic mantles rent.
The Pilgrim of Eternity, whose fame
Over his living head like heaven is bent,
An early but enduring monument,
Came, veiling all the lightnings of his song
In sorrow. From her wilds Ierne sent
The sweetest lyrist of her saddest wrong,
And love taught grief to fall like music from his tongue.

XXXI.

'Midst others of less note came one frail form,
    A phantom among men, companionless
As the last cloud of an expiring storm
    Whose thunder is its knell. He, as I guess,
    Had gazed on Nature's naked loveliness
Actæon-like; and now he fled astray
    With feeble steps o'er the world's wilderness,
And his own thoughts along that rugged way
Pursued like raging hounds their father and their prey.

XXXII.

A pard-like Spirit beautiful and swift—
    A love in desolation masked—a power
Girt round with weakness; it can scarce uplift
    The weight of the superincumbent hour;
    It is a dying lamp, a falling shower,
A breaking billow;—even whilst we speak
    Is it not broken? On the withering flower
The killing sun smiles brightly: on a cheek
The life can burn in blood even while the heart may break.

XXXIII.

His head was bound with pansies overblown,
    And faded violets, white and pied and blue;
And a light spear topped with a cypress cone,
    Round whose rude shaft dark ivy-tresses grew
    Yet dripping with the forest's noonday dew,
Vibrated, as the ever-beating heart
    Shook the weak hand that grasped it. Of that crew
He came the last, neglected and apart;
A herd-abandoned deer struck by the hunter's dart.

XXXIV.

All stood aloof, and at his partial moan
    Smiled through their tears. Well knew that gentle band
Who in another's fate now wept his own.
    As in the accents of an unknown land

He sang new sorrow, sad Urania scanned
The Stranger's mien, and murmured "Who art thou?"
He answered not, but with a sudden hand
Made bare his branded and ensanguined brow,
Which was like Cain's or Christ's—Oh! that it should be so!

XXXV.

What softer voice is hushed over the dead?
Athwart what brow is that dark mantle thrown?
What form leans sadly o'er the white death-bed,
In mockery of monumental stone,
The heavy heart heaving without a moan?
If it be he who, gentlest of the wise,
Taught, soothed, loved, honoured, the departed one,
Let me not vex with inharmonious sighs
The silence of that heart's accepted sacrifice.

XXXVI.

Our Adonais has drunk poison—oh!
What deaf and viperous murderer could crown
Life's early cup with such a draught of woe?
The nameless worm would now itself disown;
It felt, yet could escape, the magic tone
Whose prelude held all envy, hate, and wrong,
But what was howling in one breast alone,
Silent with expectation of the song
Whose master's hand is cold, whose silver lyre unstrung.

XXXVII.

Live thou, whose infamy is not thy fame!
Live! fear no heavier chastisement from me,
Thou noteless blot on a remembered name!
But be thyself, and know thyself to be!
And ever at thy season be thou free
To spill the venom when thy fangs o'erflow:
Remorse and self-contempt shall cling to thee,
Hot shame shall burn upon thy secret brow,
And like a beaten hound tremble thou shalt—as now.

XXXVIII.

Nor let us weep that our delight is fled
   Far from these carrion-kites that scream below;
He wakes or sleeps with the enduring dead;
   Thou canst not soar where he is sitting now.
Dust to the dust: but the pure spirit shall flow
Back to the burning fountain whence it came,
   A portion of the Eternal, which must glow
Through time and change, unquenchably the same,
Whilst thy cold embers choke the sordid hearth of shame.

XXXIX.

Peace, peace! he is not dead, he doth not sleep—
   He hath awakened from the dream of life—
'Tis we who, lost in stormy visions, keep
   With phantoms an unprofitable strife,
   And in mad trance strike with our spirit's knife
Invulnerable nothings—*We* decay
   Like corpses in a charnel; fear and grief
Convulse us and consume us day by day,
And cold hopes swarm like worms within our living clay.

XL.

He has outsoared the shadow of our night;
   Envy and calumny and hate and pain,
And that unrest which men miscall delight,
   Can touch him not and torture not again.
   From the contagion of the world's slow stain
He is secure; and now can never mourn
   A heart grown cold, a head grown grey in vain;
Nor, when the spirit's self has ceased to burn,
With sparkless ashes load an unlamented urn.

XLI.

He lives, he wakes—'tis Death is dead, not he;
   Mourn not for Adonais.—Thou young Dawn,
Turn all thy dew to splendour, for from thee
   The spirit thou lamentest is not gone!

Ye caverns and ye forests, cease to moan!
Cease, ye faint flowers and fountains, and thou Air,
  Which like a mourning veil thy scarf hadst thrown
O'er the abandoned Earth, now leave it bare
Even to the joyous stars which smile on its despair!

XLII.

He is made one with Nature: there is heard
  His voice in all her music, from the moan
Of thunder to the song of night's sweet bird;
  He is a presence to be felt and known
  In darkness and in light, from herb and stone,
Spreading itself where'er that Power may move
  Which has withdrawn his being to its own;
Which wields the world with never-wearied love,
Sustains it from beneath, and kindles it above.

XLIII.

He is a portion of the loveliness
  Which once he made more lovely: he doth bear
His part, while the one Spirit's plastic stress
  Sweeps through the dull dense world, compelling there
  All new successions to the forms they wear;
Torturing the unwilling dross, that checks its flight
  To its own likeness, as each mass may bear;
And bursting in its beauty and its might
From trees and beasts and men into the Heaven's light.

XLIV.

The splendours of the firmament of time
  May be eclipsed, but are extinguished not:
Like stars to their appointed height they climb,
  And death is a low mist which cannot blot
  The brightness it may veil. When lofty thought
Lifts a young heart above its mortal lair,
  And love and life contend in it, for what
Shall be its earthly doom, the dead live there,
And move like winds of light on dark and stormy air.

XLV.

The inheritors of unfulfilled renown
   Rose from their thrones, built beyond mortal thought
Far in the unapparent. Chatterton
   Rose pale, his solemn agony had not
   Yet faded from him; Sidney, as he fought,
And as he fell, and as he lived and loved,
   Sublimely mild, a Spirit without spot,
   Arose; and Lucan, by his death approved;—
Oblivion as they rose shrank like a thing reproved.

XLVI.

And many more, whose names on earth are dark,
   But whose transmitted effluence cannot die
So long as fire outlives the parent spark,
   Rose, robed in dazzling immortality.
   "Thou art become as one of us," they cry;
"It was for thee yon kingless sphere has long
   Swung blind in unascended majesty,
Silent alone amid an heaven of song.
Assume thy winged throne, thou Vesper of our throng!"

XLVII.

Who mourns for Adonais? Oh! come forth,
   Fond wretch, and know thyself and him aright.
Clasp with thy panting soul the pendulous Earth;
   As from a centre, dart thy spirit's light
   Beyond all worlds, until its spacious might
Satiate the void circumference: then shrink
   Even to a point within our day and night;
   And keep thy heart light, lest it make thee sink,
When hope has kindled hope, and lured thee to the brink

XLVIII.

Or go to Rome, which is the sepulchre,
   Oh not of him, but of our joy. 'Tis nought

That ages, empires, and religions, there
  Lie buried in the ravage they have wrought;
  For such as he can lend—they borrow not
Glory from those who made the world their prey;
  And he is gathered to the kings of thought
Who waged contention with their time's decay,
And of the past are all that cannot pass away.

XLIX.

Go thou to Rome,—at once the Paradise,
  The grave, the city, and the wilderness;
  And where its wrecks like shattered mountains rise,
  And flowering weeds and fragrant copses dress
  The bones of Desolation's nakedness,
Pass, till the Spirit of the spot shall lead
  Thy footsteps to a slope of green access,
Where, like an infant's smile, over the dead
A light of laughing flowers along the grass is spread.

L.

And grey walls moulder round, on which dull Time
  Feeds, like slow fire upon a hoary brand;
And one keen pyramid with wedge sublime,
  Pavilioning the dust of him who planned
  This refuge for his memory, doth stand
Like flame transformed to marble; and beneath
  A field is spread, on which a newer band
Have pitched in Heaven's smile their camp of death,
Welcoming him we lose with scarce extinguished breath.

LI.

Here pause: these graves are all too young as yet
  To have outgrown the sorrow which consigned
  Its charge to each; and, if the seal is set
  Here on one fountain of a mourning mind,
  Break it not thou! too surely shalt thou find

Thine own well full, if thou returnest home,
  Of tears and gall. From the world's bitter wind
Seek shelter in the shadow of the tomb.
What Adonais, is why fear we to become?

LII.

The One remains, the many change and pass;
  Heaven's light for ever shines, earth's shadows fly;
Life, like a dome of many-coloured glass,
  Stains the white radiance of Eternity,
  Until Death tramples it to fragments.—Die,
If thou wouldst be with that which thou dost seek
  Follow where all is fled!—Rome's azure sky,
Flowers, ruins, statues, music, words are weak
The glory they transfuse with fitting truth to speak.

LIII.

Why linger, why turn back, why shrink, my Heart?
  Thy hopes are gone before: from all things here
They have departed; thou shouldst now depart!
  A light is past from the revolving year,
  And man and woman; and what still is dear
Attracts to crush, repels to make thee wither.
  The soft sky smiles, the low wind whispers near:
'Tis Adonais calls! Oh! hasten thither!
No more let Life divide what Death can join together.

LIV.

That light whose smile kindles the Universe,
  That Beauty in which all things work and move,
That Benediction which the eclipsing curse
  Of birth can quench not, that sustaining Love
  Which, through the web of being blindly wove
By man and beast and earth and air and sea,
  Burns bright or dim, as each are mirrors of
The fire for which all thirst, now beams on me,
Consuming the last clouds of cold mortality.

LV.

The breath whose might I have invoked in song
    Descends on me; my spirit's bark is driven
Far from the shore, far from the trembling throng
    Whose sails were never to the tempest given;
    The massy earth and sphered skies are riven!
I am borne darkly, fearfully afar!
    Whilst, burning through the inmost veil of Heaven,
The soul of Adonais, like a star,
Beacons from the abode where the Eternal are.

CHORUSES FROM HELLAS.

Chorus.

In the great morning of the world,
The Spirit of God with might unfurled
The flag of Freedom over chaos,
  And all its banded anarchs fled,
Like vultures frighted from Imaus
     Before an earthquake's tread.—
So from Time's tempestuous dawn
Freedom's splendour burst and shone:—
Thermopylæ and Marathon
Caught, like mountains beacon-lighted,
  The springing Fire.—The winged glory
On Philippi half alighted,
  Like an eagle on a promontory.
Its unwearied wings could fan
The quenchless ashes of Milan.
From age to age, from man to man,
It lived; and lit from land to land
Florence, Albion, Switzerland.
Then night fell; and, as from night,
Re-assuming fiery flight,
From the West swift Freedom came,
  Against the course of heaven and doom,
A second sun arrayed in flame,
  To burn, to kindle, to illume.
From far Atlantis its young beams
Chased the shadows and the dreams.

France, with all her sanguine steams,
Hid, but quenched it not; again
Through clouds its shafts of glory rain
From utmost Germany to Spain.
As an eagle fed with morning
Scorns the embattled tempest's warning
When she seeks her aerie hanging
  In the mountain-cedar's hair,
And her brood expect the clanging
  Of her wings through the wild air,
Sick with famine;—Freedom, so
To what of Greece remaineth now
Returns; her hoary ruins glow
Like orient mountains lost in day;
  Beneath the safety of her wings
Her renovated nurslings play,
  And in the naked lightenings
Of truth they purge their dazzled eyes.
Let Freedom leave, where'er she flies,
A Desert, or a Paradise;
Let the beautiful and the brave
Share her glory, or a grave!

SEMICHORUS I.
With the gifts of gladness
Greece did thy cradle strew;

SEMICHORUS II.
With the tears of sadness
Greece did thy shroud bedew;

SEMICHORUS I.
With an orphan's affection
She followed thy bier through time!

SEMICHORUS II.
And at thy resurrection
Re-appeareth, like thou, sublime!

Semichorus I.
If Heaven should resume thee,
To Heaven shall her spirit ascend

Semichorus II.
If Hell should entomb thee,
To Hell shall her high hearts bend.

Semichorus I.
If Annihilation—

Semichorus II.
Dust let her glories be;
And a name and a nation
Be forgotten, Freedom, with thee

Chorus.
Worlds on worlds are rolling ever
  From creation to decay,
Like the bubbles on a river,
  Sparkling, bursting, borne away.
    But they are still immortal
    Who, through birth's orient portal
And death's dark chasm hurrying to and fro,
    Clothe their unceasing flight
    In the brief dust and light
Gathered around their chariots as they go:
    New shapes they still may weave,
    New gods, new laws, receive:
Bright or dim are they, as the robes they last
    On Death's bare ribs had cast.

A Power from the unknown God,
  A Promethean Conqueror, came;
Like a triumphal path he trod
  The thorns of death and shame.
    A mortal shape to him
    Was like the vapour dim
Which the orient planet animates with light.

Hell, sin, and slavery, came,
Like bloodhounds mild and tame,
Nor preyed until their lord had taken flight.
    The moon of Mahomet
    Arose, and it shall set:
While, blazoned as on heaven's immortal noon,
    The cross leads generations on.

    Swift as the radiant shapes of sleep
      From one whose dreams are paradise
    Fly, when the fond wretch wakes to weep,
      And Day peers forth with her blank eyes;
      So fleet, so faint, so fair,
      The Powers of Earth and Air
Fled from the folding-star of Bethlehem:
      Apollo, Pan, and Love,
      And even Olympian Jove,
Grew weak, for killing Truth had glared on them.
      Our hills and seas and streams,
      Dispeopled of their dreams,
Their waters turned to blood, their dew to tears,
      Wailed for the golden years.

Chorus.

The world's great age begins anew,
    The golden years return,
The earth doth like a snake renew
    Her winter weeds outworn:
Heaven smiles, and faiths and empires gleam
Like wrecks of a dissolving dream.

A brighter Hellas rears its mountains
    From waves serener far;
A new Peneus rolls his fountains
    Against the morning star;
Where fairer Tempes bloom, there sleep
Young Cyclads on a sunnier deep.

A loftier Argo cleaves the main,
    Fraught with a later prize;
Another Orpheus sings again,
    And loves, and weeps, and dies;
A new Ulysses leaves once more
Calypso for his native shore.

Oh! write no more the tale of Troy,
    If earth death's scroll must be—
Nor mix with Laian rage the joy
    Which dawns upon the free,
Although a subtler Sphinx renew
Riddles of death Thebes never knew.

Another Athens shall arise,
    And to remoter time
Bequeath, like sunset to the skies,
    The splendour of its prime;
And leave, if nought so bright may live,
All earth can take or heaven can give.

Saturn and Love their long repose
    Shall burst, more bright and good
Than all who fell, than One who rose,
    Than many unsubdued:
Not gold, not blood, their altar dowers,
But votive tears and symbol flowers.

Oh cease! must hate and death return?
    Cease! must men kill and die?
Cease! drain not to its dregs the urn
    Of bitter prophecy!
The world is weary of the past,—
Oh might it die or rest at last!

THE END.

www.ingramcontent.com/pod-product-compliance
Lightning Source LLC
Chambersburg PA
CBHW020305240426
43673CB00039B/705